S0-BGN-398

Illustrated Edition

OLD VIRGINIA AND HER NEIGHBOURS

By JOHN FISKE

IN TWO VOLUMES

VOLUME II

W Byrd.

OLD VIRGINIA AND HER NEIGHBOURS

BY JOHN FISKE

ILLUSTRATED WITH
PORTRAITS MAPS FACSIMILES
CONTEMPORARY VIEWS PRINTS AND
OTHER HISTORIC MATERIALS
IN TWO VOLUMES
VOLUME II

Οὐ λίθοι, οὐδὲ ξύλα, οὐδὲ
Τέχνη τεκτόνων αἱ πόλεις εἶσιν
᾿Αλλ᾿ ὅπου ποτ᾿ ἂν ὦσιν ἌΝΔΡΕΣ
Αὑτοὺς σώζειν εἰδότες,
᾿Ενταῦθα τείχη καὶ πόλεις.

Alcæus

BOSTON AND NEW YORK
HOUGHTON, MIFFLIN AND COMPANY
The Riverside Press, Cambridge
MDCCCC

CONTENTS

CHAPTER X

THE COMING OF THE CAVALIERS

CHAPTER XI

BACON'S REBELLION

CHAPTER XII

WILLIAM AND MARY

CHAPTER XIII

MARYLAND'S VICISSITUDES

CHAPTER XIV

SOCIETY IN THE OLD DOMINION

CHAPTER XV

THE CAROLINA FRONTIER

CHAPTER XVI

THE GOLDEN AGE OF PIRATES

CHAPTER XVII

FROM TIDEWATER TO THE MOUNTAINS

NOTES ON THE ILLUSTRATIONS

OLD VIRGINIA AND HER NEIGHBOURS

CHAPTER X

THE COMING OF THE CAVALIERS

"THESE things that follow in this ensuing relation are certified by divers letters from Virginia, by men of worth and credit there, written to a friend in England, that for his own and others' satisfaction was desirous to know these particulars and the present estate of that country. And let no man doubt of the truth of it. There be many in England, land and seamen, that can bear witness of it. And if this plantation be not worth encouragement, let every true Englishman judge."

Virginia depicted

Such is the beginning of an enthusiastic little pamphlet, of unknown authorship, published in London in 1649,[1] the year in which Charles I. perished on the scaffold. It is entitled "A Perfect Description of Virginia," and one of its effects, if not its purpose, must have been to attract immigrants to that colony from the mother country. In Virginia "there is nothing wanting" to make people happy; there are "plenty, health, and wealth." Of English about 15,000 are settled there, with 300 negro servants. Of kine, oxen, bulls, and calves, there are 20,000, and there is plenty of good butter and cheese. There are 200 horses, 50 asses, 3000 sheep with good wool, 5000 goats,

Animals

[1] It is reprinted in Force's *Tracts*, vol. ii.; and in Maxwell's *Virginia Historical Register*, ii. 61–78. The original, of which there is one in the library of Harvard University, was priced by Rich, in 1832, at £1 10s., and by Quaritch, in 1879, at £20. See Winsor, *Narr. and Crit. Hist.* iii. 157.

and swine and poultry innumerable. Besides these European animals, there are many deer, with "rackoons, as good meat as lamb," and "passonnes" [opossums], otters and beavers, foxes and dogs that "bark not." In the waters are "above thirty sorts" of fish "very excellent good in their kinds." The wild turkey sometimes weighs sixty pounds, and besides partridges, ducks, geese, and pigeons, the woods abound in sweet songsters and "most rare coloured parraketoes, and [we have] one bird we call the mock-bird; for he will imitate all other birds' notes and cries, both day and night birds, yea, the owls and nightingales."

The farmers have under cultivation many hundred acres of excellent wheat; their maize, or "Virginia corn," yields an increase of 500 for 1, and makes "good bread and furmity" [porridge]; they have barley in plenty, and six brew-houses which brew strong and well-flavoured beer. There are fifteen kinds of fruit that for delicacy rival the fruits of Italy; in the gardens grow potatoes, turnips, carrots, parsnips, onions, artichokes, asparagus, beans, and better peas than those of England, with all manner of herbs and "physick flowers." The tobacco is everywhere "much vented and esteemed," but such immense crops are raised that the price is but three pence a pound. There is also a hope that indigo, hemp and flax, vines and silk-worms, can be cultivated with profit, since it is chiefly hands that are wanted. It surely would be better to grow silk here, where mulberry trees are so plenty, than to fetch it as we do from Persia and China "with great charge and expense and hazard," thereby enriching "heathen and Mahumetans."

Agriculture

At the same time they are hoping soon to discover a way to China, "for Sir Francis Drake was on the back side of Virginia in his voyage about the world in 37 degrees . . . and now all the question is only how broad the land may be to that place [*i. e.* California] from the head of James River above the falls." By prosecuting discovery in this direction "the planters in Virginia shall gain the rich trade of the East India, and so cause it to be driven

Northwest passage

A Perfect Description of

VIRGINIA:

BEING,

A full and true Relation of the present State of the Plantation, their Health, Peace, and Plenty: the number of people, with their abundance of Cattell, Fowl, Fish, &c. with severall sorts of rich and good Commodities, which may there be had, either Naturally, or by Art and Labour. Which we are fain to procure from *Spain, France, Denmark, Swedeland, Germany, Poland*, yea, from the *East-Indies*. There having been nothing related of the true estate of this Plantation these 25 years.

Being sent from Virginia, *at the request of a Gentleman of worthy note, who desired to know the true State of* Virginia *as it now stands.*

ALSO,

A Narration of the Countrey, within a few dayes journey of *Virginia, West and by South*, where people come to trade: being related to the Governour, Sir *William Berckley*, who is to go himselfe to discover it with 30 horse, and 50 foot, and other things needfull for his enterprize.

With the manner how the Emperor Nichotawance came to Sir *William Berckley*, attended with five petty Kings, to doe Homage, and bring Tribute to King CHARLES. With his solemne Protestation, that the Sun and Moon should lose their Lights, before he (or his people in that Country) should prove disloyall, but ever to keepe Faith and Allegiance to King CHARLES.

Lond[illegible]rind for *Richard Wodenoth*, at the Star und[illegible] *Peters* Church in *Cornhill*. 1649.

TITLE OF "A PERFECT DESCRIPTION OF VIRGINIA"

through the continent of Virginia, part by land and part by water, and in a most gainful way and safe, and far less expenseful and dangerous, than now it is."

It behooves the English, says our pamphlet, to be more vigilant, and to pay more heed to their colonies ; for behold, "the Swedes have come and crept into a river called Delawar, that is within the limits of Virginia," and they are driving "a great and secret trade of furs." Moreover, "the Hollanders have stolen into a river called Hudson's River, in the limits also of Virginia, . . . they have built a strong fort . . . and drive a trade of fur there with the natives for above £10,000 a year. These two plantations are . . . on our side of Cape Cod which parts us and New England. Thus are the English nosed in all places, and out-traded by the Dutch. They would not suffer the English to use them so; but they have vigilant statesmen, and advance all they can for a common good, and will not spare any encouragements to their people to discover."

Commercial rivals

"Concerning New England," which is but four days' sail from Virginia, a trade goes to and fro ; but except for the fishing, "there is not much in that land," which in respect of frost and snow is as Scotland compared with England, and so barren withal that, "except a herring be put into the hole that you set the corn or maize in, it will not come up." What a pity that the New England people, "being now about 20,000, did not seat themselves at first to the south of Virginia, in a warm and rich country, where their industry would have produced sugar, indigo, ginger, cotton, and the like commodities !" But here in Virginia the land "produceth, with very great increase, whatsoever is committed into the bowels of it ; . . . a fat rich soil everywhere watered with many fine springs, small rivulets, and wholesome waters." As to healthiness, fewer people die in a year proportionately than in England ; "since that men are provided with all necessaries, have plenty of victual, bread, and good beer, . . . all which the Englishman loves full dearly." Nor is their

New England

Health of body and soul

spiritual welfare neglected, for there are twenty churches, with "doctrine and orders after the church of England;" and "the ministers' livings are esteemed worth at least £100 per annum; they are paid by each planter so much tobacco per poll, and so many bushels of corn; they live all in peace and love."

"I may not forget to tell you we have a free school, with 200 acres of land, a fine house upon it, 40 milch kine, and other accommodations; the benefactor deserves perpetual memory; his name, Mr. Benjamin Symes, worthy to be chronicled; other petty schools also we have." Various details of orchards and vineyards, of Mr. Kinsman's pure perry and Mr. Pelton's strong metheglin, entertain us; and a pleasant tribute is paid to "worthy Captain Mathews," the same who fourteen years before had assisted at the thrusting out of Sir John Harvey. "He hath a fine house, and all things answerable to it; he sows yearly store of hemp and flax, and causes it to be spun; he keeps weavers, and hath a tan house, causes leather to be dressed, hath eight shoemakers employed in their trade, hath forty negro servants, brings them up to trades in his house; he yearly sows abundance of wheat, barley, &c., the wheat he selleth at four shillings the bushel, kills store of beeves, and sells them to victual the ships when they come thither; hath abundance of kine, a brave dairy, swine great store, and poultry; he married the daughter of Sir Thomas Hinton, and, in a word, keeps a good house, lives bravely, and a true lover of Virginia; he is worthy of much honour."

Schools

Captain Mathews and his household

It will be observed that Captain Mathews possessed, in his forty black servants, nearly one seventh part of the negro population. Of the conditions under which wholesale negro slavery grew up, I shall treat hereafter. In the third quarter of the seventeenth century it was still in its beginnings. Between 1650 and 1670, along with an extraordinary growth in the total population, we observe a marked increase in the number of black slaves. In

Rapid growth of population

the latter year Berkeley estimated the population at 32,000 free whites, 6000 indentured white servants, and 2000 negroes. Large estates, cultivated by wholesale slave labour, were coming into existence, and a peculiar type of aristocratic or in some respects patriarchal society was growing up in Virginia. It was still for the most part confined to the peninsula between the James and York rivers and the territory to the south of the former, from Nansemond as far as the Appomattox, although in Gloucester likewise there was a considerable population, and there were settlements in Middlesex and Lancaster counties, on opposite banks of the Rappahannock, and even as far as Northumberland and Westmoreland on the Potomac. In the course of the disputes over Kent Island, settlements began upon those shores and increased apace.

Some significant history is fossilized in the names of Virginia counties. When they are not the old shire names imported from England, like those just mentioned, they are apt to be personal names indicating the times when the counties were first settled, or when they acquired a distinct existence as counties. For a long time such personal names were chiefly taken from the royal household. Thus, while Charles City County bears the name of Charles I., bestowed upon the region before that king ascended the throne, the portion of it south of James River, set off in 1702 as Prince George County, was named for George of Denmark, consort of Queen Anne. So King William County on the south bank of the Mattapony, and King and Queen County on its north bank, carry us straight to the times of William and Mary, and indicate the position of the frontier in the days of Charles II.; while to the west of them the names of Hanover and the two Hanoverian princesses, Caroline and Louisa, carry us on to the days of the first two Georges.[1] At the time with which our narra-

Names of Virginia counties

[1] The following list of Virginia counties bearing royal names, founded between 1689 and 1765, is interesting: —

King and Queen, 1691, after William and Mary.

tive is now concerned, all that region to the south of Spottsylvania was unbroken wilderness. In 1670 a careful estimate was made of the number of Indians comprised within the immediate neighbourhood of the colony, and there were counted up 725 warriors, of whom more than 400 were on the Appomattox and Pamunkey frontiers, and nearly 200 between the Potomac and Rappahannock.

The map of Virginia, in the light in which I have here considered it, shows one remarkable point of contrast with the map of New England. On the coast of the latter one finds a very few names commemorative of royalty, such as Charles River, named by Captain John Smith, Cape Ann, named by Charles I. when Prince of Wales, and the Elizabeth Islands, named by Captain Gosnold still earlier and in the lifetime of the great Queen. But when it comes to names given by the settlers themselves, one cannot find in all New England a county name taken from any English sovereign or prince, except Dukes for the island of Martha's Vineyard, and that simply recalls the fact that the island once formed a part of the proprietary domain of James, Duke of York, and sent a delegate to the

Scarcity of royalist names on the map of New England

Princess Anne,	1691,	after the princess who was afterwards Queen Anne.
King William,	1701,	William III.
Prince George,	1702,	the Prince Consort.
King George,	1720,	George I.
Hanover,	1720,	one of the king's foreign dominions.
Brunswick,	1720,	do. do.
Caroline,	1727,	the queen of George II.
Prince William,	1730,	William, Duke of Cumberland.
Orange,	1734,	the Prince of Orange, who in that year married Anne, daughter of George II.
Amelia,	1734,	a daughter of George II.
Frederick,	1738,	Frederick, Prince of Wales.
Augusta,	1738,	the Princess of Wales.
Louisa,	1742,	a daughter of George II.
Lunenburg,	1746,	one of the king's foreign dominions.
Prince Edward,	1753,	a son of Frederick, Prince of Wales.
Charlotte,	1764,	the queen of George III.
Mecklenburg,	1764,	her father, Duke of Mecklenburg.

first legislature that assembled at Manhattan. Except for this one instance, we should never know from the county names of New England that such a thing as kingship had ever existed. As for names of towns, there is in Massachusetts a Lunenburg, which is said to have received its name at the suggestion of a party of travellers from England in the year 1726;[1] it was afterward copied in Vermont; and by diligently searching the map of New England we may find half a dozen Hanovers and Brunswicks, counting originals and copies. Between this showing and that of Virginia, where the sequence of royal names is full enough to preserve a rude record of the country's expansion, the contrast is surely striking. The difference between the Puritan temper and that of the Cavaliers seems to be written ineffaceably upon the map.

The Cavaliers in Virginia: some popular misconceptions

We are thus brought to the question as to how far the Cavalier element predominated in the composition of Old Virginia. It is a subject concerning which current general statements are apt to be loose and misleading. It has given rise to much discussion, and, like a good deal of what passes for historical discussion, it has too often been conducted under the influence of personal or sectional prejudices. Half a century ago, in the days when the people of the slave states and those of the free states found it difficult to think justly or to speak kindly of one another, one used often to hear sweeping generalizations. On the one hand, it was said that Southerners were the descendants of Cavaliers, and therefore presumably of gentle blood, while Northerners were descendants of Roundheads, and therefore presumably of ignoble origin. Some such notion may have prompted the famous remark of Robert Toombs, in 1860: "We [*i. e.* the Southerners] are the gentlemen of this country." On the other hand, it was retorted that the people of the South were in great part descended from indentured white servants sent from the jails

[1] Jewett's *History of Worcester County, Massachusetts*, ii. 30. Charlestown was named from the river at the mouth of which it stands.

and slums of England.[1] This point will receive due attention in a future chapter. At present we may note that descent from Cavaliers has not always been a matter of pride with Southern speakers and writers. There was a time when the fierce spirit of democracy was inclined to regard such a connection as a stigma. The father of President Tyler "used to say that he cared naught for any other ancestor than Wat Tyler the blacksmith, who had asserted the rights of oppressed humanity, and that he would have no other device on his shield than a sledge hammer raised in the act of striking." [2] On the subject of Cavaliers a well known Virginian writer, Hugh Blair Grigsby, once grew very warm. "The Cavalier," said he, "was essentially a slave, a compound slave, a slave to the King and a slave to the Church. I look with contempt on the miserable figment which seeks to trace the distinguishing points of the Virginia character to the influence of those butterflies of the British aristocracy." [3] Historical questions are often treated in this way. We grow up with a vague conception of something in the past which we feel in duty bound to condemn, and then if we are told that our own forefathers were part and parcel of the hated thing we lose our tempers. Mr. Grigsby's remarks are an expression of American feeling in what may be called its Elijah Pogram period, when the knowledge of history was too slender and the historic sense too dull to be shocked at the incongruity of classing such men as Strafford and Falkland with "butterflies." The study of history in such a mood is not likely to be fruitful of much beside rhetoric.

Some democratic protests

Before we proceed, a few further words are desirable concerning the fallacies and misconceptions which abound in

[1] W. H. Whitmore, *The Cavalier Dismounted*, Salem, 1864.

[2] *William and Mary College Quarterly*, i. 53. In the same connection we are told that Beverley Tucker apologized for putting on record a brief account of his family, saying, "at this day it is deemed arrogant to remember one's ancestors. But the fashion may change," etc.

[3] See Cooke's *Virginia*, p. 161.

the opinions cited in the foregoing paragraph. It is impossible to make any generalization concerning the origin of the white people of the South as a whole, or of the North as a whole, further than to say that their ancestors came from Europe and a large majority of them from the British islands. The facts are too complicated to be embraced in any generalization more definitely limited than this. When sweeping statements are made about "the North" and "the South," it is often apparent that the speaker has in mind only Massachusetts and tidewater Virginia, making these parts do duty for the whole. The present book will make it clear that it is only in connection with tidewater Virginia that the migration of Cavaliers from England to America has any historical significance.

Sweeping statements are inadmissible

It is a mistake to suppose that the contrast between Cavaliers and Roundheads was in any wise parallel with the contrast between high-born people and low-born. A majority of the landed gentry, titled and untitled, supported Charles I., while the chief strength of the Parliament lay in the smaller landholders and in the merchants of the cities. But the Roundheads also included a large and powerful minority of the landed aristocracy, headed by the Earls of Bedford, Warwick, Manchester, Northumberland, Stamford, and Essex, the Lords Fairfax and Brooke, and many others. The leaders of the party, Pym and Hampden, Vane and Cromwell, were of gentle blood; and among the officers of the New Model were such as Montagues, Pickerings, Fortescues, Sheffields, and Sidneys. In short, the distinction between Cavalier and Roundhead was no more a difference in respect of lineage or social rank than the analogous distinction between Tory and Whig. The mere fact of a man's having belonged to the one party or the other raises no presumption as to his "gentility."

Difference between Cavaliers and Roundheads was political, not social

It is worth while here to correct another error which is quite commonly entertained in the United States. It is the error of supposing that in Great Britain there are distinct orders of society, or that there exists anything like a sharp and well defined line between the nobility and the commonalty. The American reader is apt to imagine a "peerage," the members of which have from time immemorial constituted a kind of caste clearly marked off from the great body of the people, and into which it has always been very difficult for plain people to rise. In this crude conception the social differences between England and America are greatly exaggerated. In point of fact the British islands are the one part of Europe where the existence of a peerage has not resulted in creating a distinct upper class of society. The difference will be most clearly explained by contrasting England with France. In the latter country, before the Revolution of 1789, there was a peerage consisting of great landholders, local rulers and magistrates, and dignitaries of the church, just as in England. But in France all the sons and brothers of a peer were nobles distinguished by a title and reckoned among the peerage, and all were exempt from sundry important political duties, including the payment of taxes. Thus they constituted a real *noblesse*, or caste apart from the people, until the Revolution at a single blow destroyed all their privileges. At the present day French titles of nobility are merely courtesy titles, and through excessive multiplication have become cheap. On the other hand, in England, the families of peers have never been exempt from their share of the public burdens. The "peerage," or hereditary right to sit in the House of Lords, belongs only to the head of the family; all the other members of the family are commoners, though some may be addressed by courtesy titles. During the formative period of modern political society, from the fourteenth century onward, the sons of peers habitually competed for seats in the House of Commons, side by side with merchants and yeomen. This has prevented anything like a severance between the interests of the higher and of the lower classes in England, and has had much to do with the peaceful and healthy political development which has so eminently characterized our mother

England has never had a *noblesse*, or upper caste

Contrast with France

country. England has never had a *noblesse*. As the upper class has never been sharply distinguished politically, so it has not held itself separate socially. Families with titles have intermarried with families that have none, the younger branches of a peer's family become untitled gentry, ancient peerages lapse while new ones are created, so that there is a "circulation of gentle blood" that has thus far proved eminently wholesome. More than two thirds of the present House of Lords are the grandsons or great-grandsons of commoners. Of the 450 or more hereditary peerages now existing, three date from the thirteenth century and four from the fourteenth; of those existing in the days of Thomas Becket not one now remains in the same family. It has always been easy in England for ability and character to raise their possessor in the social scale; and hence the middle class has long been recognized as the abiding element in England's strength. Voltaire once compared the English people to their ale, — froth at the top and dregs at the bottom, but sound and bright and strong in the middle. As to the last he was surely right.

Importance of the middle class

One further point calls for mention. In mediæval and early modern England, great respect was paid to incorporated crafts and trades. The influence and authority wielded by county magnates over the rural population was paralleled by the power exercised in the cities by the livery companies or guilds. Since the twelfth century, the municipal franchise in the principal towns and cities of Great Britain has been for the most part controlled by the various trade and craft guilds. In the seventeenth century, when the migrations to America were beginning, it was customary for members of noble families to enter these guilds as apprentices in the crafts of the draper, the tailor, the vintner, or the mason, etc. Many important consequences have flowed from this. Let it suffice here to note that this fact of the rural aristocracy keeping in touch with the tradesmen and artisans has been one of the safeguards of English liberty; it has been one source of the

Respect paid to industry in England

power of the Commons, one check upon the undue aspirations of the Crown. It indicates a kind of public sentiment very different from that which afterward grew up in our southern states under the malignant influence of slavery, which proclaimed an antagonism between industry and gentility that is contrary to the whole spirit of English civilization.

With these points clear in our minds, we may understand the true significance of the arrival of the Cavaliers in Virginia. The date to be remembered in connection with that event is 1649, and it is instructive to compare it with the exodus of Puritans to New England. The little settlement of the Mayflower Pilgrims was merely a herald of the great Puritan exodus, which really began in 1629, when Charles I. entered upon his period of eleven years of rule without a parliament, and continued until about 1642, when the Civil War broke out. During those thirteen years more than 20,000 Puritans came to New England. The great Cavalier exodus began with the king's execution in 1649, and probably slackened after 1660. It must have been a chief cause of the remarkable increase of the white population of Virginia from 15,000 in 1649 to 38,000 in 1670.

The Cavalier exodus

The period of the Commonwealth in England thus marks an important epoch in Virginia, and we must be on our guard against confusing what came after with what preceded it. As to the political complexion of Virginia in the earliest time, it would be difficult to make a general statement, except that there was a widespread feeling in favour of the Company as managed by Sandys and Southampton. This meant that the settlers knew when they were well governed. They did not approve of a party that sent an Argall to fleece them, even though it were the court party. So, too, in the thrusting out of Sir John Harvey in 1635 we see the temper of the councillors and burgesses flatly opposed to the king's unpopular representative. But such instances do not tell us much concerning the attitude of the colonists upon questions of

Political complexion of Virginia before 1649

English politics. The fortunes of the Puritan settlers in Virginia afford a surer indication. At first, as we have seen, when the Puritans as a body had not yet separated from the Church, there were a good many in Virginia; and by 1640 they probably formed about seven per cent. of the population. The legislation against them beginning in 1631 seems to indicate that public sentiment in Virginia favoured the policy of Laud; while the slackness with which such legislation was enforced raises a suspicion that such sentiment was at first not very strong. It seems probable that as the country party in England came more and more completely under the control of Puritanism, and as Puritanism grew more and more radical in temper, the reaction toward the royalist side grew more and more pronounced in Virginia. If there ever was a typical Cavalier of the more narrow-minded sort, it was Sir William Berkeley, who at the same time was by no means the sort of person that one might properly call a "butterfly." If the eloquent Mr. Grigsby had once got into those iron clutches, he would have sought some other term of comparison. When Berkeley arrived in Virginia, and for a long time afterward, he was extremely popular. We have seen him acting with so much energy against the Puritans that in the course of the year 1649 not less than 1000 of them left the colony. Upon the news of the king's death, Berkeley sent a message to England inviting royalists to come to Virginia, and within a twelvemonth perhaps as many as 1000 had arrived, picked men and women of excellent sort. Thus it curiously happened that the same moment which saw Virginia lose most of her Puritan population, also saw it replaced by an equal number of devoted Cavaliers.

The great exchange of 1649

From this moment we may date the beginnings of Cavalier ascendency in Virginia. But for the next ten years that growing ascendency was qualified by the necessity of submitting to the Puritan government in England. In 1652 Berkeley was obliged to retire from the governorship, and the king's men in Virginia found it

Moderation shown in Virginia

prudent to put some restraint upon the expression of their feelings. But in this change, as we have seen, there was no violence. It is probable that there was a considerable body of colonists "comparatively indifferent to the struggle of parties in England, anxious only to save Virginia from spoliation and bloodshed, and for that end willing to throw in

COLONEL RICHARD LEE

their lot with the side whose success held out the speediest hopes of peace. There is another consideration which helps to explain the moderation of the combatants. In England each party was exasperated by grievous wrongs, and hence its hour of triumph was also its hour of revenge. The struggle in Virginia was embittered by no such recollections."[1]

A name inseparably associated with Berkeley is that of

[1] Doyle's *Virginia*, etc. p. 283.

Colonel Richard Lee, who is described as "a man of good stature, comely visage, an enterprising genius, a sound head, vigorous spirit, and generous nature,"[1] qualities that may be recognized in many of his famous descendants. This Richard Lee belonged to an ancient family, the Lees of Coton Hall, in Shropshire, whom we find from the beginning of the thirteenth century in positions of honour and trust. He came to Virginia about 1642, and obtained that year an estate which he called Paradise, near the head of Poropotank Creek, on the York River. He was from the first a man of much importance in the colony, serving as justice, burgess, councillor, and secretary of state. In 1654 we find him described as "faithful and useful to the interests of the Commonwealth," but, as Dr. Edmund Lee says, "it is only fair to observe that this claim was made for him by a friend in his absence;"[2] or perhaps it only means that he was not one of the tribe of fanatics who love to kick against the pricks.[3] Certain it is that Colonel Lee was no Puritan, though doubtless he submitted loyally to the arrangement of 1652, as so many others did. There was nothing for the king's men to do but possess their souls in quiet until 1659, when news came of the resignation of Richard Cromwell. "Worthy Captain Mathews," whom the assembly had chosen governor, died about the same time. Accordingly, in March, 1660, the assembly resolved that, since there was then in England no resident sovereign generally recognized, the supreme power in Virginia must be regarded as lodged in the assembly, and that all writs should issue in the name of the Grand Assembly of Virginia until such a command should come from England as the assembly should judge to be law-

Colonel Richard Lee

Election of Berkeley by the assembly

[1] Written in 1771 by his great-grandson William Lee, alderman of London, and quoted in Edmund Lee's *Lee of Virginia*, Philadelphia, 1895, p. 49.

[2] "The petition of John Jeffreys, of London," in Sainsbury's *Calendar of State Papers*, 1574–1660, p. 430; *Lee of Virginia*, p. 61.

[3] Compare L. G. Tyler's remarks in *William and Mary College Quarterly*, i. 155.

ful. Having passed this resolution, the assembly showed its political complexion by electing Sir William Berkeley for governor: and in the same breath it revealed its independent spirit by providing that he must call an assembly at

CHARLES II

least once in two years, and oftener if need be; and that he must not dissolve it without the consent of a majority of the members. On these terms Berkeley accepted office at the hands of the assembly.

Before this transaction, perhaps in 1658, Colonel Lee seems to have visited Charles II. at Brussels, where he handed over to the still exiled prince the old commission of

Berkeley, and may have obtained from him a new one for future use, reinstating him as governor.[1] There is a vague tradition that on this occasion he asked how soon Charles would be likely to be able to protect the colony in case it should declare its allegiance to him; and from this source may have arisen the wild statement, recorded by Beverley and promulgated by the eminent historian Robertson, that Virginia proclaimed Charles II. as sovereign a year or two before he was proclaimed in England.[2] The absurdity of this story was long ago pointed out;[3] but since error has as many lives as a cat, one may still hear it repeated. Charles II. was proclaimed king in England on the 8th of May, 1660, and in Virginia on the 20th of September following.[4] In October the royal commission for Berkeley arrived, and the governor may thus have felt that the conditions on which he accepted his office from the assembly were no longer binding. Our next chapter will show how lightly he held them.

Lee's visit to Brussels

Charles II. proclaimed king

If one may judge from the public accounts of York County in 1660, expressed in the arithmetic of a tobacco currency, the 20th of September must have been a joyful occasion: —

Att the proclaiming of his sacred Maisty:

To ye Ho^{ble} Govn^{r} p a barrell powd^{r}, 112 lb.	.00996
To Capt ffox six cases of drams	.00900
To Capt ffox for his great gunnes	.00500
To Mr Philip Malory	.00500
To ye trumpeters	.00800
To Mr Hansford 176 Gallons Syd^{r} at 15 & 35 gall at 20, caske 264	.03604

[1] See the testimony of John Gibbon, in *Lee of Virginia*, p. 60.

[2] Beverley, *History and Present State of Virginia*, London, 1705, p. 56; Robertson, *History of America*, iv. 230.

[3] Hening's *Statutes*, i. 526.

[4] The document is given in *William and Mary College Quarterly*, i. 158, where the bill of items quoted in the next paragraph may also be found. Mr. Philip Malory was an officiating clergyman.

There can be no doubt that it was an occasion prolific in legend. The historian Robert Beverley, who was born about fifteen years afterward, tells us that Governor Berkeley's proclamation named Charles II. as "King of England, Scotland, France, Ireland, and Virginia." The document itself, however, calls him "our most gratious soveraigne, Charles the Second, King of England, Scotland, ffrance, & Ireland," and makes no mention of Virginia.

The seal of Virginia

William Lee tells us that it was "in consequence of this step" that the motto *En dat Virginia quintam* was placed upon the seal of the colony.[1] Since "this step" was never taken, the statement needs some qualification. The idea of designating Virginia as an additional kingdom to those over which the English sovereign ruled in Europe was already entertained in 1590 by Edmund Spenser, who dedicated his "Faëry Queene" to Elizabeth as queen of "England, France,[2] and Ireland, and of Virginia."[3] As early as 1619 the London Company adopted a coat-of-arms, upon which was the motto *En dat Virginia quintum,* in which the unexpressed noun is *regnum:* "Behold, Virginia gives the fifth [kingdom]." After the restoration of Charles II. a new seal for Virginia, adopted about 1663, has the same motto, the effect of which was to rank Virginia by the side of his Majesty's other four

SEAL OF VIRGINIA AFTER THE RESTORATION

[1] Meade's *Old Churches*, ii. 137.

[2] The claim to the French crown set up by Edward III. in 1328 led to the so-called Hundred Years' War, in the course of which Henry VI. was crowned King of France in the church of Notre Dame at Paris in 1431. His sway there was practically ended in 1436, but the English sovereigns continued absurdly to call themselves Kings of France until 1801.

[3] See above, vol. i. p. 238.

dominions, England, Scotland, "France," and Ireland. We are told by the younger Richard Henry Lee that in these circumstances originated the famous epithet "Old Dominion." In 1702, among several alterations in the seal, the word *quintum* was changed to *quintam*, to agree with the unexpressed noun *coronam*: "Behold, Virginia gives the fifth [crown]." After the legislative union of England with Scotland in 1707, another seal, adopted in 1714, substituted *quartam* for *quintam*.[1]

Just how many members of the royalist party came to Virginia while their young king was off upon his travels, it would be difficult to say. But there were unquestionably a great many. We have already remarked upon the very rapid increase of white population, from about 15,000 in 1649 to 38,000 in 1670. Along with this there was a marked increase in the size of the land grants, both the average size and the maximum; and in this coupling of facts there is great significance, for they show that the increase of population was predominantly an increase in the numbers of the upper class, of the people who could afford to have large estates. In these respects the year 1650 marks an abrupt change,[2] which may best be shown by a tabular view of the figures:—

Increase in the size of land grants

Years.	Largest number of acres in a single grant.	Average number of acres in a grant.
1632	350	
1634	5,350	719
1635	2,000	380
1636	2,000	351
1637	5,350	445
1638	3,000	423
1640	1,300	405
1641	872	343
1642	3,000	559
1643	4,000	595

[1] See the able paper by Dr. L. G. Tyler on "The Seal of Virginia," *William and Mary College Quarterly*, iii. 81–96.

[2] For my data regarding land grants I am much indebted to the very learned and scholarly work of Mr. Philip Bruce, *Economic History of Virginia in the Seventeenth Century*, i. 487–571.

1644	670	370
1645	1,090	333
1646	1,200	360
1647	650	361
1648	1,800	412
1649	3,500	522
1650	5,350	677
1651–55	10,000	591
1656–66	10,000	671
1667–79	20,000	890
1680–89	20,000	607

Another way of showing the facts is still more striking: —

Years.	Number of grants exceeding 5,000 acres.
1632–50	3
1651–55	3
1656–66	20
1667–70	37
1680–89	19

The increase in the number of slaves after 1650 is a fact of similar import with the greater size of the estates. All the circumstances agree in showing that there was a large influx of eminently well-to-do people. It is well known, moreover, who these people were. It is in the reign of Charles II. that the student of Virginian history begins to meet frequently with the familiar names, such as Randolph, Pendleton, Madison, Mason, Monroe, Cary, Ludwell, Parke, Robinson, Marshall, Washington, and so many others that have become eminent. All these were Cavalier families that came to Virginia after the downfall of Charles I. Whether President Tyler was right in claiming descent from the Kentish rebel of 1381 is not clear, but there is no doubt that his first American ancestor, who came to Virginia after the battle of Worcester, was a gentleman and a royalist.[1] Until recently there was some uncertainty as to the pedigree of George Washington, but the researches of Mr. Fitz Gilbert Waters of Salem have conclusively proved that he was descended from the Washingtons of Sulgrave, in Northamptonshire, a

Cavalier families

Ancestry of George Washington

[1] *Letters and Times of the Tylers*, i. 41.

family that had for generations worthily occupied positions of honour and trust. In the Civil War the Washingtons were distinguished royalists. The commander who surrendered Worcester in 1646 to the famous Edward Whalley was Colonel Henry Washington;[1] and his cousin John, who came to Virginia in 1657, was great-grandfather of George Washington. After the fashion that prevailed a hundred years ago, the most illustrious of Americans felt little interest in his ancestry; but with the keener historic sense and broader scientific outlook of the present day, the importance of such matters is better appreciated. The pedigrees of horses, dogs, and fancy pigeons have a value that is quotable in terms of hard cash. Far more important, for the student of human affairs, are the pedigrees of men. By no possible ingenuity of constitution-making or of legislation can a society made up of ruffians and boors be raised to the intellectual and moral level of a society made up of well-bred merchants and yeomen, parsons and lawyers. One might as well expect to see a dray horse win the Derby. It is, moreover, only when we habitually bear in mind the threads of individual relationship that connect one country with another, that we get a really firm and concrete grasp of history. Without genealogy the study of history is comparatively lifeless. No excuse is needed, therefore, for giving in this connection a tabulated abridgment of the discoveries of Mr. Waters concerning the forefathers of George Washington.[2] Beside the personal interest attaching to everything associated with that immortal name, this pedigree has interest and value as being in large measure typical. It is a fair sample of good English middle-class pedigrees, and it is typical as regards the ancestry of leading Cavalier families

Value of genealogy

[1] He is mentioned by Pepys in his *Diary*, Oct. 12, 1660: "Office day all the morning, and from thence with Sir W. Batten and the rest of the officers to a venison party of his at the Dolphin, where dined withal Colonel Washington, Sir Edward Brett, and Major Norwood, very noble company."

[2] Waters, *An Examination of the English Ancestry of George Washington*, Boston, 1889.

WASHINGTON OF NORTHAMPTON AND VIRGINIA

ARMS. — *Argent, two bars and in chief three mullets Gules*

John Washington,
of Whitfield, Lancashire, time of Henry VI.

Robert Washington,
of Warton, Lancashire, 2d son.

John Washington,
of Warton, m. Margaret Kitson, sister of Sir Thomas Kitson, alderman of London.

Lawrence Washington,
of Gray's Inn, mayor of Northampton, obtained grant of Sulgrave Manor, 1539, d. 1584; m. Anne Pargiter, of Gretworth.

Robert Washington,
of Sulgrave, b. 1544; m. Elizabeth Light.

Lawrence Washington,
of Gray's Inn, register of High Court of Chancery, d. 1619.

Lawrence Washington,
of Sulgrave and Brington, d. 1616; m. Margaret Butler.

Sir Lawrence Washington,
register of High Court of Chancery, d. 1643.

Sir William Washington, d. 1643; m. Anne Villiers, half-sister of George Villiers, Duke of Buckingham.

Sir John Washington, d. 1678.

Rev. Lawrence Washington, M. A., Fellow of Brasenose College, Oxford, Rector of Purleigh, d. before 1665.

Lawrence Washington, d. 1652; m. Eleanor Gyse.

Henry Washington, colonel in the royalist army, governor of Worcester, d. 1664.

John Washington, b. 1631, d. 1677; came to Virginia, 1657; m. Anne Pope.

Lawrence Washington, b. 1635, came to Virginia, 1657.

Elizabeth Washington, heiress, d. 1693; m. Earl Ferrers.

Lawrence Washington,
d. 1697; m. Mildred, dau. of Augustine Warner.

Augustine Washington,
b. 1694, d. 1749; m. Mary Ball.

GEORGE WASHINGTON,
b. 1732, d. 1799.
First President of the United States.

in Virginia; an inspection of many genealogies of those who came between 1649 and 1670 yields about the same general impression. Moreover, this pedigree is equally typical as regards the ancestry of leading Puritan families in New England. The genealogies, for example, of Winthrop, Dudley, Saltonstall, Chauncey, or Baldwin give the same general impression as those of Randolph, or Cary, or Cabell, or Lee. The settlers of Virginia and of New England were opposed to each other in politics, but they belonged to one and the same stratum of society, and in their personal characteristics they were of the same excellent quality. To quote the lines of Sir William Jones, written as a paraphrase of the Greek epigram of Alcæus, inscribed upon my title-page: —

> "What constitutes a State?
> Not high-raised battlement or laboured mound,
> Thick wall or moated gate;
> Not cities proud with spires and turrets crowned;
> Not bays and broad-armed ports,
> Where, laughing at the storm, rich navies ride;
> Not starred and spangled courts,
> Where low-browed baseness wafts perfume to pride.
> No: — MEN, high-minded MEN,
> . . . .
> Men who their duties know,
> But know their rights, and, knowing, dare maintain,
> Prevent the long-aimed blow,
> And crush the tyrant while they rend the chain:
> These constitute a State."[1]

Such men were the Cavaliers of Virginia and the Puritans of New England.

Importance of the Cavalier element in Virginia

There can be little doubt that these Cavaliers were the men who made the greatness of Virginia. To them it is due that her history represents ideas and enshrines events which mankind will always find interesting. It is apt to be the case that men who leave their country for reasons connected with conscience and principle, men who have once consecrated themselves to a

[1] Sir William Jones's *Works*, ed. Lord Teignmouth, London, 1807, x. 389.

cause, are picked men for ability and character. Such men are likely to exert upon any community which they may enter an influence immeasurably greater than an equal number of men taken at random. It matters little what side they may

Falkland

have espoused. Very few of the causes for which brave men have fought one another have been wholly right or wholly wrong. Our politics may be those of Samuel Adams, but we must admit that the Thomas Hutchinson type of mind and character is one which society could ill afford to lose. Of the gallant Cavaliers who drew the sword for King Charles, there were many who no more approved of his crooked methods and despotic aims than Hutchinson approved of the Stamp Act. No better illustration could be found than Lord Falkland, some of whose kinsmen emigrated to Virginia and played a conspicuous part there. A proper combination of circumstances was all that was required to bring the children of these royalists into active political alliance with the children of the Cromwellians.

Both in Virginia and in New England, then, the principal element of the migration consisted of picked men and women of the same station in life, and differing only in their views of civil and ecclesiastical polity. The differences that grew up between the relatively aristocratic type of society in Virginia and the relatively democratic type in New England were due not at all to differences in the social quality of the settlers, but in some degree to their differences in church politics, and in a far greater degree to the different economic circumstances of Virginia and New England. It is worth our while to point out some of these contrasts and to indicate their effect upon the local government, the nature of which, perhaps more than anything else, determines the character of the community as aristocratic or democratic.

Differences between New England and Virginia

That extreme Puritan theory of ecclesiastical polity, according to which each congregation was to be a little self-governing republic, had much to do with the way in which New England was colonized. The settlers came in congregations, led by their favourite ministers, — such men, for example, as Higginson and Cotton, Hooker and Davenport. When such men, famous in England for their bold preaching and imperilled thereby, decided to move to America, a considerable number of their parishioners would decide to accompany them, and similarly minded members of neighbouring churches would leave their own pastor and join in the migration. Such a group of people, arriving on the coast of Massachusetts, would naturally select some convenient locality, where they might build their houses near together and all go to the same church.

Settlement of New England by congregations

This migration, therefore, was a movement, not of individuals or of separate families, but of church-congregations, and it continued to be so as the settlers made their way inland and westward. The first river towns of Connecticut were thus founded by congregations coming from Dorchester, Cambridge, and Watertown. This kind of settlement was favoured by the government of Massachusetts, which made grants of land, not to individuals but to companies of people who wished to live together and attend the same church.

Land grants in Massachusetts

It was also favoured by economic circumstances. The soil of New England was not favourable to the cultivation of great quantities of staple articles, such as rice or tobacco, so that there was nothing to tempt people to undertake extensive plantations. Most of the people lived on small farms, each family raising but little more than enough food for its own support; and the small size of the farms made it possible to have a good many in a compact neighbourhood. It appeared also that towns could be more easily defended against the Indians than scattered plantations; and this doubtless helped to keep people together, although if there had been any strong inducement for solitary pioneers to plunge into the great woods, as in later years so often happened at the West, it is not likely that any dread of the savages would have hindered them.

Small farms

Thus the early settlers of New England came to live in townships. A township would consist of about as many farms as could be disposed within convenient distance from the meeting-house, where all the inhabitants, young and old, gathered every Sunday, coming on horseback or afoot. The meeting-house was thus centrally situated, and near it was the town pasture or "common," with the school-house and the block-house, or rude fortress for defence against the Indians. For the latter building some commanding position was apt to be selected, and hence we so often find the old village streets of New England running along elevated ridges or climbing over beetling hilltops. Around the meeting-house and common the dwellings grad-

Township and village

ually clustered into a village, and after a while the tavern, store, and town-house made their appearance.

Among the people who thus tilled the farms and built up the villages of New England, the differences in what we should call social position, though noticeable, were not extreme. While in England some had been esquires or country magistrates, or "lords of the manor," — a phrase which does not mean a member of the peerage, but a landed proprietor with dependent tenants, — some had been yeomen, or persons holding farms by some free kind of tenure; some had been artisans or tradesmen in cities. All had for many generations been more or less accustomed to self-government and to public meetings for discussing local affairs. That self-government, especially as far as church matters were concerned, they were stoutly bent upon maintaining and extending. Indeed, that was what they had crossed the ocean for. Under these circumstances they developed a kind of government which has remained practically unchanged down to the present day. In the town meeting the government is the entire adult male population. Its merits, from a genuine democratic point of view, have long been recognized, but in these days of rampant political quackery they are worth recalling to mind, even at the cost of a brief digression.

Social position of settlers in New England

Within its proper sphere, government by town meeting is the form of government most effectively under watch and control. Everything is done in the full daylight of publicity. The specific objects for which public money is to be appropriated are discussed in the presence of everybody, and any one who disapproves of any of these objects, or of the way in which it is proposed to obtain it, has an opportunity to declare his opinions. Under this form of government people are not so liable to bewildering delusions as under other forms. I refer especially to the delusion that "the Government" is a sort of mysterious power, possessed of a magic inexhaustible fund of wealth, and able to do all manner of

Some merits of the town meeting

The "magic fund" delusion

things for the benefit of "the People." Some such notion as this, more often implied than expressed, is very common, and it is inexpressibly dear to demagogues. It is the prolific root from which springs that luxuriant crop of humbug upon which political tricksters thrive as pigs fatten upon corn. In point of fact no such government, armed with a magic fund of its own, has ever existed upon the earth. No government has ever yet used any money for public purposes which it did not first take from its own people, — unless when it may have plundered it from some other people in victorious warfare.

MRS. RICHARD LEE

The inhabitant of a New England town is perpetually reminded that "the Government" is "the People." Although he may think loosely about the government of his state or the still more remote government at Washington, he is kept pretty close to the facts where local affairs are concerned, and in this there is a political training of no small value.

Educational value of the town meeting

In the kind of discussion which it provokes, in the necessity of facing argument with argument and of keeping one's temper under control, the town meeting is the best political training school in existence. Its educational value is far higher than that of the newspaper, which, in spite of its many merits as a diffuser of information, is very apt to do its best to bemuddle and sophisticate plain facts. The period when town meetings were most important from the wide scope of their transactions was the period of earnest and sometimes stormy discussion that ushered in our Revolutionary War. In those days great principles of government were discussed with a wealth of knowledge and stated with masterly skill in town meeting.

In Virginia the economic circumstances were very different from those of New England, and the effects were seen in a different kind of local institutions. In New England the system of small holdings facilitated the change from primogeniture to the Kentish custom of gavelkind, with which many of the settlers were already familiar, in which the property of an intestate is equally divided among the children.[1] In Virginia, on the other hand, the large estates, cultivated by servile labour, were kept together by the combined customs of primogeniture and entail, which lasted until they were overthrown by Thomas Jefferson in 1776. In this circumstance, more than in anything else, originated the more aristocratic features in the local institutions of Virginia. To this should be added the facts that before the eighteenth century there was a large servile class of whites, to which there was nothing even remotely analogous in New England; and that the introduction of negro slavery, which was beginning to assume noticeable dimensions about 1670, served to affix a stigma upon manual labour.

Primogeniture and entail in Virginia

In view of this group of circumstances we need not wonder that in Old Virginia there were no town meetings. The distances between plantations coöperated with the distinction between classes to prevent the growth of such an institution. The English parish, with its churchwardens and vestry and clerk, was reproduced in Virginia under the same name, but with some noteworthy peculiarities.

Virginia parishes

[1] The change was somewhat gradual, *e. g.* in Massachusetts at first the eldest son received a double portion. See *The Colonial Laws of Massachusetts, reprinted from the edition of 1660*, ed. W H. Whitmore, Boston, 1889, pp. 51, 201.

If the whole body of ratepayers had assembled in vestry meeting, to enact by-laws and assess taxes, the course of development would have been like that of the New England town meeting. But instead of this the vestry, which exercised the chief authority in the parish, was composed of twelve chosen men. This was not government by a primary assembly, it was representative government. At first the twelve vestrymen were elected by the people of the parish, and thus resembled the selectmen of New England; but in 1662 "they obtained the power of filling vacancies in their own number," so that they became what is called a "close corporation," and the people had nothing to do with choosing them. Strictly speaking, that was not representative government; it was a step on the road that leads towards oligarchical or despotic government. It was, as we shall see, one of the steps ineffectually opposed in Bacon's rebellion.

The vestry a close corporation

It was the vestry, thus constituted, that apportioned the parish taxes, appointed the churchwardens, presented the minister for induction into office, and acted as overseers of the poor. The minister presided in all vestry meetings. His salary was paid in tobacco, and in 1696 it was fixed by law at 16,000 pounds of tobacco yearly. In many parishes the churchwardens were the collectors of the parish taxes. The other officers, such as the sexton and the parish clerk, were appointed either by the minister or by the vestry.

Powers of the vestry

With the local government thus administered, we see that the larger part of the people had little directly to do. Nevertheless, in those small neighbourhoods government could be kept in full sight of the people, and so long as its proceedings went on in broad daylight and were sustained by public sentiment, all was well. As Jefferson said, "The vestrymen are usually the most discreet farmers, so distributed through the parish that every part of it may be under the immediate eye of some one of them. They are well acquainted with the details and economy of private life, and they find sufficient inducements to execute their charge well, in their philanthropy, in the approbation of their neighbours, and the distinction which that gives them."[1]

The difference, however, between the New England township and the Virginia parish, in respect of self-government, was striking enough. We have now to note a further difference. In New England, the township was the unit of representation in the colonial legislature; but in Virginia the parish was not the unit of representation. The county was that unit. In the colonial legislature of Virginia the representatives sat, not for parishes but for counties. The difference is very significant. As the political life of New England was in a manner built up out of the political life of the towns, so the political life of Virginia was built up out of the political life of the counties. This was partly because the vast plantations were not grouped about a compact village nucleus like the small farms at the North, and partly because there was not in Virginia that Puritan theory of the church according to which each congregation is a self-governing democracy. The conditions which made the New England town meeting were absent. The only alternative was some kind of representative government, and for this the county was a small enough area. The county in Virginia was much smaller than in Massachusetts or Connecticut. In a few instances the county consisted of only a single parish; in some cases it was divided into two parishes, but oftener into three or more.

The county was the unit of representation

In Virginia, as in England and in New England, the county was an area for the administration of justice. There were usually in each county eight justices of the peace, and their court was the counterpart of the quarter session in England. They were appointed by the governor, but it was customary for them to nominate candidates for the governor to appoint, so that

The county court was virtually a close corporation

[1] See Howard, *Local Constitutional History of the United States*, i. 122.

practically the court filled its own vacancies and was a close corporation, like the parish vestry. Such an arrangement tended to keep the general supervision and control of things in the hands of a few families.

This county court usually met as often as once a month in some convenient spot answering to the shire town of England or New England. More often than not, the place originally consisted of the court-house and very little else, and was named accordingly from the name of the county, as Hanover Court House or Fairfax Court House; and the small shire towns that have grown up in such spots often retain these names to the present day. Such names occur commonly in Virginia, West Virginia, and South Carolina, and occasionally elsewhere. Their number has diminished from the tendency to omit the phrase "Court House," leaving the name of the county for that of the shire town, as for example in Culpeper, Va. In New England the process of naming has been just the reverse; as in Hartford County, Conn., or Worcester County, Mass., which have taken their names from the shire towns. Here, as in so many cases, whole chapters of history are wrapped up in geographical names.[1]

The county seat or Court House

The county court in Virginia had jurisdiction in criminal actions not involving peril of life or limb, and in civil suits where the sum at stake exceeded twenty-five shillings. Smaller suits could be tried by a single justice. The court also had charge of the probate and administration of wills. The court appointed its own clerk, who kept the county records. It superintended the construction and repair of bridges and highways, and for this purpose divided the county into "precincts," and appointed annually for each precinct a highway surveyor. The court also seems to have

Powers of the court

[1] A few of the oldest Virginia counties, organized as such in 1634, had arisen from the spreading and thinning of single settlements originally intended to be cities and named accordingly. Hence the curious names (at first sight unintelligible) of "James City County" and "Charles City County."

appointed constables, one for each precinct. The justices could themselves act as coroners, but annually two or more coroners for each parish were appointed by the governor. As we have seen that the parish taxes — so much for salaries of minister and clerk, so much for care of church buildings, so much for the relief of the poor, etc. — were computed and assessed by the vestry; so the county taxes, for care of court-house and jail, roads and bridges, coroner's fees, and allowances to the representatives sent to the colonial legislature, were computed and assessed by the county court. The general taxes for the colony were estimated by a committee of the legislature, as well as the county's share of the colony tax. The taxes for the county, and sometimes the taxes for the parish also, were collected by the sheriff. They were usually paid, not in money, but in tobacco; and the sheriff was the custodian of this tobacco, responsible for its proper disposal. The sheriff was thus not only the officer for executing the judgments of the court, but he was also county treasurer and collector, and thus exercised powers almost as great as those of the sheriff in England in the twelfth century. He also presided over elections for representatives to the legislature. It is interesting to observe how this very important officer was chosen. "Each year the court presented the names of three of its members to the governor, who appointed one, generally the senior justice, to be the sheriff of the county for the ensuing year."[1] Here again we see this close corporation, the county court, keeping the control of things within its own hands.

The sheriff

One other important county officer needs to be mentioned. In early New England each town had its train-band or company of militia, and the companies in each county united to form the county regiment. In Virginia it was just the other way. Each county raised a certain number of troops, and because it was not convenient for the men to go many miles

[1] Edward Channing, "Town and County Government in the English Colonies of North America," *Johns Hopkins Univ. Studies*, vol. ii.

This 1. Aug. 1622. 20 Jac. remayneth theis as servants in Virginia.

dead. — Thomas [illegible], governor.

Thomas Bantye

Richard Milton,

John Gybbs

Thomas Shipway

Alexander Bradway

Willm Clement

Richard Sheriffe,

Thomas Molton

George Hale drummer.

Frances the daughter of Willm Finch and Eliz his wife. wch her mother is now married to—

Eliz was maried to [illegible]

Eliz [illegible] daughter of Thomas

And theis 4. yt went over in the Furtherance in June. 1622. 20. Jac. before the newes of the massacre was heard of. viz.

George Polton,

dead — Richard Willis,

Clement Molton

Richard Buttry.

And John Bradley, who bore his owne charges, And went in August. 1622. in ye Margaret and John, wth [illegible]

9 of Peter Dun.

LIST OF SERVANTS IN VIRGINIA, AUGUST 1, 1622

from home in assembling for purposes of drill, the county was subdivided into military districts, each with its company, according to rules laid down by the governor. The military command in each county was vested in the county lieutenant, an officer answering in many respects to the lord lieutenant of the English shire at that period. Usually he was a member of the governor's council, and as such exercised sundry judicial functions. He bore the honorary title of "colonel," and was to some extent regarded as the governor's deputy; but in later times his duties were confined entirely to military matters.[1]

The county lieutenant

If now we sum up the contrasts between local government in Virginia and that in New England, we observe:—

1. That in New England the management of local affairs was mostly in the hands of town officers, the county being superadded for certain purposes, chiefly judicial; while in Virginia the management was chiefly in the hands of county officers, though certain functions, chiefly ecclesiastical, were reserved to the parish.

2. That in New England the local magistrates were almost always, with the exception of justices, chosen by the people; while in Virginia, though some of them were nominally appointed by the governor, yet in practice they generally contrived to appoint themselves,—in other words, the local boards practically filled their own vacancies and were self-perpetuating.

These differences are striking and profound. There can be no doubt that, as Thomas Jefferson clearly saw, in the long run the interests of political liberty are much safer

[1] For an excellent account of local government in Virginia before the Revolution, see Howard, *Local Const. Hist. of the U. S.* i. 388–407; also Edward Ingle in *Johns Hopkins Univ. Studies*, iii. 103–229. With regard to the county lieutenant's honorary title, Mr. Ingle suggests that it may help to explain the superabundance of military titles in the South, and he quotes from a writer in the *London Magazine* in 1745: "Wherever you travel in Maryland (as also in Virginia and Carolina) your ears are astonished at the number of colonels, majors, and captains that you hear mentioned."

under the New England system than under the Virginia system. Jefferson said: "Those wards, called townships in New England, are the vital principle of their governments, and have proved themselves the wisest invention ever devised by the wit of man for the perfect exercise of self-government, and for its preservation.[1] . . . As Cato, then, concluded every speech with the words *Carthago delenda est*, so do I every opinion with the injunction: 'Divide the counties into wards!'"[2]

Jefferson's opinion of township government

We must, however, avoid the mistake of making too much of this contrast. As already hinted, in those rural societies where people generally knew one another, its effects were not so far-reaching as they would be in the more complicated society of to-day. Even though Virginia had not the town meeting, "it had its familiar court-day," which "was a holiday for all the countryside, especially in the fall and spring. From all directions came in the people on horseback, in wagons, and afoot. On the court-house green assembled, in indiscriminate confusion, people of all classes, — the hunter from the backwoods, the owner of a few acres, the grand proprietor, and the grinning, heedless negro. Old debts were settled, and new ones made; there were auctions, transfers of property, and, if election times were near, stump-speaking."[3]

"Court-day"

For seventy years or more before the Declaration of Independence the matters of general public concern, about which stump speeches were made on Virginia court-days, were very similar to those that were discussed in Massachusetts town meetings when representatives were to be chosen for the legislature. Such questions generally related to some real or alleged encroachment upon popular liberties by the royal governor, who, being appointed and sent from beyond sea, was apt to have ideas and purposes of his own that conflicted with those of the people. This perpetual antagonism to the governor, who represented British impe-

[1] Jefferson's *Works*, vii. 13.
[2] Id. vi. 544.
[3] Ingle, in *J. H. U. Studies*, iii. 90.

rial interference with American local self-government, was an excellent schooling in political liberty, alike for Virginia and for Massachusetts. When the stress of the Revolution came, these two leading colonies cordially supported each other, and their political characteristics were reflected in the kind of achievements for which each was especially distinguished. The Virginia system, concentrating the administration of local affairs in the hands of a few county families, was eminently favourable for developing skilful and vigorous leadership. And while in the history of Massachusetts during the Revolution we are chiefly impressed with the remarkable degree in which the mass of the people exhibited the kind of political training that nothing in the world except the habit of parliamentary discussion can impart; on the other hand, Virginia at that time gave us — in Washington, Jefferson, Henry, Mason, Madison, and Marshall, to mention no others — such a group of leaders as has seldom been equalled.

Virginia prolific in great leaders

CHAPTER XI

BACON'S REBELLION

THE rapid development of maritime commerce in the seventeenth century soon furnished a new occasion for human folly and greed to assert themselves in acts of legislation. Crude mediæval methods of robbery began to give place to the ingenious modern methods in which men's pockets are picked under the specious guise of public policy. Your mediæval baron would allow no ship or boat to pass his Rhenish castle without paying what he saw fit to extort for the privilege, and at the end of his evil career he was apt to compound with conscience and buy a ticket to heaven by building a chapel to the Virgin. Your modern manufacturer obtains legislative aid in fleecing his fellow-countrymen, while he seeks popularity by bestowing upon the public a part of his ill-gotten gains in the shape of a new college or a town library. This change from the more brutal to the more subtle devices for living upon the fruits of other men's labour was conspicuous during the seventeenth century, and one of the most glaring instances of it was the Navigation Act of 1651, which forbade the importation of goods into England except in English ships, or ships of the nation that produced the goods. This foolish act was intended to cripple the Dutch carrying-trade, and speedily led to a lamentable and disgraceful war between England and Holland. In its application to America it meant that English colonies could trade only with England in English ships, and it was generally greeted with indignation. Cromwell, however, did little or nothing to enforce it in America. Charles II.'s government was more active in

The Navigation Act of 1651

the matter and soon became detested. One of the earliest causes of the American Revolution was thus set in operation. The policy begun in the Navigation Act was one of the grievances that kept Massachusetts in a chronic quarrel with Charles II. during the whole of his reign, and it was a source of no less irritation in Virginia.

A second Navigation Act, passed at the beginning of the reign of Charles II., prescribed that "no goods or commodities whatsoever shall be imported into or exported from any of the king's lands, islands, plantations, or territories in Asia, Africa, or America, in any other than English, Irish, or plantation built ships, and whereof the master and at least three-fourths of the mariners shall be Englishmen, under forfeiture of ships and goods." It was further provided that "no sugar, tobacco, cotton, wool, indigo, ginger, fustic and other dyeing woods, of the growth or manufacture of our Asian, African, or American colonies, shall be shipped from the said colonies to any place but to England, Ireland, or to some other of his Majesty's said plantations, there to be landed, under forfeiture of goods and ships."

The second Navigation Act

The motive in these restrictions is obvious enough. Their effects were ably set forth in 1677, in a memorial by John Bland, a sagacious London merchant, whose grasp of the principles of political economy was very remarkable for that age.[1] In order that merchants in England might buy Virginia tobacco very cheap, the demand for it was restricted by cutting off the export to foreign markets. In order that they might sell their goods to Virginia at exorbitant prices, the Virginians were prohibited from buying anything elsewhere. The shameless rapacity of these merchants was such as might have been expected under such fostering circumstances. If the planter shipped his own tobacco to England, the charges for freight would be put so high as to leave him scarcely any margin of profit.

Bland's remonstrance

[1] "The humble Remonstrance of John Bland, of London, Merchant, on the behalf of the Inhabitants and Planters in Virginia and Mariland," reprinted in *Virginia Historical Magazine*, i. 142–155.

THE

RELATION OF

the Right Honourable the Lord *De-La-Warre*, Lord Gouernour and *Captaine Generall of the Colonie, planted in* VIRGINEA.

LONDON

¶ *Printed by* William Hall, for *William Welbie*, dwelling in Pauls Church-yeard at the Signe of the Swan.

1611.

TITLE OF LORD DELAWARE'S "RELATION"

Such restrictions were apt to have other effects than those contemplated. The "protected" merchants chuckled over their sagacity in keeping Dutchmen away from Virginia, for thus it would become possible to make the Dutchmen pay three or four shillings in England for tobacco that cost a ha'penny in the colony. But the worthy burghers of the Netherlands took a different view of the matter. They began planting tobacco for themselves in the East Indies, so that it became less necessary to buy it of the English. Another somewhat curious consequence may be stated in Bland's own words: "Again, if the Hollanders must not trade to Virginia, how shall the planters dispose of their tobacco? The English will not buy it [all], for what the Hollander carried thence was a sort of tobacco not . . . used by us in England, but merely to transport for Holland. Will it not then perish on the planters' hands? which undoubtedly is not only an apparent loss of so much stock and commoditie to the plantations who suffer thereby, but for want of its employment an infinite prejudice to the commerce in general."

Some direct consequences

There was yet another aspect of the matter. "I demand then, in the next place, which way shall the charge of the governments be maintained, if the Hollanders be debarred trade in Virginia and Maryland, or anything raised to defray the constant and yearly levies for the securing the inhabitants from invasions of the Indians? How shall the forts and public places be built and repaired, with many other incident charges daily arising, which must be taken care for, else all will come to destruction? for when the Hollanders traded thither, they paid upon every anchor of brandy (which is about 25 gallons) 5 shillings import brought in by them, and upon every hogshead of tobacco carried thence 10 shillings; and since they were debarred trade, our English, as they did not, whilst the Hollander traded there, pay anything, neither would they when they traded not . . . ; so that all these charges being taxed on the poor planters, it hath so impoverished them that they

Some indirect consequences

scarce can recover wherewith to cover their nakedness. As foreign trade makes rich and prosperous any country that hath within it any staple commodities to invite them thither, so it makes men industrious, striving with others to gather together into societies, and building of towns, and nothing doth it sooner than the concourse of shipping, as we may see before our eyes, Dover and Deal what they are grown into, the one by the Flanders trade, the other by ships riding in the Downs."

But if in spite of all these arguments the Navigation Act must stand, then, says this acute writer, "let me on the behalf of the said colonies of Virginia and Maryland make these following proposals, which I hope will appear but equitable : —

Exposure of the humbug

"*First*, that the traders to Virginia and Maryland from England shall furnish and supply the planters and inhabitants of those colonies with all sorts of commodities and necessaries which they may want or desire, at as cheap rates and prices as the Hollanders used to have when the Hollander was admitted to trade thither.

"*Secondly*, that the said traders out of England to those colonies shall not only buy of the planters such tobacco . . . as is fit for England, but take off all that shall be yearly made by them, at as good rates and prices as the Hollanders used to give for the same, by bills of exchange or other wise. . . .

"*Thirdly*, that if any of the inhabitants or planters of the said colonies shall desire to ship his tobacco or goods for England, that the traders from England to Virginia and Maryland shall let them have freight in their ships at as low and cheap rates as they used to have when the Hollanders and other nations traded thither.

"*Fourthly*, that for maintenance of the governments, raising of forces to withstand the invasions of the Indians, building of forts and other public works needful in such new discovered countries, the traders from England to pay there in Virginia and Maryland as much yearly as was received of the Hollanders and strangers as did trade thither, whereby the country may not have the whole burden to lie on their hard and painful labour and industry, which ought to be encouraged but not discouraged.

"Thus having proposed in my judgment what is both just and equal, to all such as would not have the Hollanders permitted to trade into Virginia and Maryland, I hope if they will not agree hereunto, it will easily appear it is their own profits and interest they seek, not those colonies's nor your Majesty's service, but in contrary the utter ruin of all the inhabitants and planters there; and if they perish, that vast territory must be left desolate, to the exceeding disadvantage of this nation and your Majesty's honour and revenue."

After this keen exposure of the protectionist humbug the author concludes by offering his own proposal. "Let all Hollanders and other nations whatsoever freely trade into Virginia and Maryland, and bring thither and carry thence whatever they please," with only one qualification. It had been urged that, without legislative aid, English shipping could not compete successfully with that of other countries. Insatiableness of commercial greed begets a fidgetty, unreasoning dread of anything like free competition. Just as the Frenchman puts tariff duties upon German goods because he knows he cannot compete with Germans in a free market, while at the same moment the German puts tariff duties upon French goods because he knows he cannot compete with Frenchmen in a free market, so it was with men's arguments two centuries ago. It was urged that French and Dutch ships could be built and navigated at smaller expense than English ships; and this point our author meets by suggesting a differential tonnage-duty "to counterpoise the cheapness," only great care must be taken not to make it prohibitory.

Bland's own proposal

The principal effect of the Navigation Act upon Virginia and Maryland was to lower the price of tobacco while it increased the cost of all articles imported from England. As tobacco was the circulating medium in these colonies, the effect was practically a depreciation of the currency with the usual disastrous consequences. There was an inflation of prices, and all commodities became harder to get. Efforts were made from time to time to contract the currency by curtailing the tobacco crop. It was proposed, for example, in 1662, that no tobacco should be planted in Maryland or Virginia for the following year. Such proposals recurred from time to time, but it proved impossible to secure concerted action between the two colonies. In 1664 the whole tobacco crop of Virginia was worth less than £3 15s. for each person in the colony. In 1666 so much tobacco was left on the hands of the planters that a determined effort was made to enforce the cessation of planting, and after much discussion an agreement was reached between Maryland, Virginia, and the new settlements in Carolina, but the plan was defeated by disapproval in Maryland which led to a veto from Lord Baltimore. In 1667 the price of tobacco fell to a ha'penny a pound, and Thomas Ludwell, writing to Lord Berkeley in London, "declared that there were but three influences restraining the smaller landowners of Virginia from rising in rebellion, namely, faith in the mercy of God, loyalty to the king, and affection for the government." [1]

Distress caused by low price of tobacco

The discontent sometimes took the form of a disposition to resist the collection of taxes, as in Surry, in December, 1673, when "a company of seditious and rude people to y[e] number of ffourteene did unlawfully Assemble at y[e] pish church of Lawnes Creeke, wth Intent to declare they would not pay theire publiq taxes, & y[t] they Expected diverse oth[rs] to meete them, who faileing they did not put theire wicked design in Execution." Nevertheless these persons assembled again, some three weeks later, in an old field "called y[e] Divell's field," where they passed divers lawless resolutions interspersed with heated harangues. In particular one Roger Delke did say, "we will

The Surry protest, 1673

[1] Bruce, *Economic History of Virginia in the Seventeenth Century*, i. 394.

burne all before one shall Suffer," and when brought before the magistrates, "ye s^{d} Delke Acknowledged he said ye same words, & being asked why they meet at ye church he said by reason theire taxes were soe unjust, & they would not pay it."[1] The ringleaders in this affair were fined, but Governor Berkeley remitted the fines, provided "they acknowledged their faults and pay the court charges."

Another cause of trouble was the king's recklessness in rewarding public services or gratifying favourites by extensive grants of wild land in America. It was an easy way to pay debts, for it cost the king nothing, and all the labour and expense of making the grant valuable fell upon the grantee. To many of these grants there could, of course, be no objection. Those that founded the Carolinas and Pennsylvania and the Hudson Bay Company were all proper enough. The trouble began when territory already granted and occupied by Englishmen was given away again. There were some complicated and obscure instances of this in New England, but a flagrant and exasperating case occurred in Virginia in 1673, when Charles made a grant of the whole country to the Earl of Arlington and Lord Culpeper, to hold for thirty-one years at a yearly rent of 40 shillings to be paid at Michaelmas.

The Arlington-Culpeper grant, 1673

The practical effect of this grant was to convert Virginia into something like a proprietary government, with Arlington and Culpeper for proprietors. It was, of course, not the intention to disturb individuals in the possession of lands already acquired by a valid title; but escheated lands were to go to these proprietors instead of the crown, and there was an opportunity for grievous injustice, for many escheated lands were occupied by persons who had purchased them in good faith. The lord proprietors were to receive the revenues of the colony, to appoint all public officers, and to present pastors for installation. In short, the entire control of the internal administration of the colony

Some of its effects

[1] Papers from the Records of Surry County, *William and Mary College Quarterly*, iii. 123–125.

was to be placed in their hands, and against such favourites of the king an appeal at any time was likely to be of little avail. It is needless to add that the grant was made without consulting the Virginians. For people who had lavished so

much loyalty upon a worthless sovereign, this was a scurvy requital. To find its match for ingratitude one must go to the story of Inkle and Yarico. No sooner did the House of Burgesses hear of it than they sent commissioners to England to make an energetic protest. They found the king rather surprised to hear that the Virginians cared anything about such a trifle; he promised to satisfy everybody, and that naturally took some time, so that the matter was still under discussion when things came to a blaze in Virginia.

Character of Sir William Berkeley

The unprincipled government of Charles II. in England was matched in some respects by the oppressive administration of Sir William Berkeley in Virginia. We have already met this gentleman on several occasions; it is now time to notice him more particularly. He was son of Sir Maurice Berkeley, who was one of the members of the London Company when it was first organized in 1606. Several members of the family were interested in American affairs. Sir William's elder brother, Lord Berkeley of Stratton, was a favourite of Charles II., and one of the group of proprietors to whom that king granted Carolina in 1663. Sir William was an aristocrat to the ends of his fingers, a man of velvet and gold lace, a brave soldier, a devoted husband, a chivalrous friend, and withal as narrow and bigoted and stubborn a creature as one could find anywhere. He had no sympathy with common people, nor any very clear sense of duty toward them. When he first arrived in Virginia in 1642, at the age of thirty-four, he was considered very gracious and affable in manners, and during the ten years of his first governorship he seems to have been generally popular. From 1652 to 1660 he lived in retirement on his rural estate of Greenspring near Jamestown, where he had an orchard of more than 2000 fruit trees — apples, pears, quinces, peaches, and apricots — and a stable of seventy fine horses. There he entertained Cavalier guests and drank healths to King Charles until he was once more called to Jamestown to be governor. In 1661 he went to London and stayed for a year, and it was afterwards thought that his visit with his froward and hot-tempered brother[1] worked a change in him for the worse. Berkeley's errand in London was to oppose an attempt which the old London Company was making to have its charter restored; the people of Vir-

[1] Pepys, *Diary*, Nov. 29, Dec. 3, 1664.

LOWER BRANDON: NORTH FRONT

ginia had long ago passed the stage at which they regretted the overthrow of the Company. During his stay in London, Berkeley saw one of his own plays performed at the theatre, for this courtier and Cavalier dabbled in literature. Of this tragi-comedy, "The Lost Lady," Pepys tells us in his Diary that at first he did not care much for it, but liked it better the next time he saw it.[1]

After Berkeley's return to Virginia the evils of Charles's misgovernment soon began to show themselves. A swarm of place-hunters beset the king, who carelessly gave them appointments in Virginia, or recommended them to Berkeley for places. Judges and sheriffs, revenue collectors and parsons, were thus appointed without reference to fitness, with the natural results; the law was ill-administered, the public money embezzled, and the church scandalized. The custom-house charges on exported tobacco afforded chances for extortion and blackmailing, of which abundant advantage was taken, and Berkeley was not the sort of man who was quick to punish the rogues of his own party. Enemies accused him of profiting by the maladministration of his officials, and he himself confessed in a rather cynical letter to Lord Arlington that, while advancing years had taken away his ambition, they had left him covetous. A little group of wealthy planters, friends of Berkeley, obtained places on the council, and contrived to have everything their own way for several years. With their aid the governor tried to do away with the popular election of representatives. Amid the blaze of royalist exultation over the restoration of monarchy, the House of Burgesses elected in 1661 contained a large majority of members who believed in high prerogative and divine right; and Berkeley, having thus secured a legislature that was quite to his mind, kept it alive for fifteen years, until 1676, simply by the ingenious expedient of *adjourning* it from year to year, and refusing to issue writs for a new election. The effect of such things was to carry more than one staunch Cavalier over into what was by no means a Puritan but none

Corruption and extortion

The Long Assembly, 1661–1676

[1] *Diary*, Jan. 19 and 28, 1661.

the less a strong opposition party. As this opposition could not find adequate voice in the legislature, it became ready for an explosion. As Berkeley's old popularity ebbed away he grew arrogant and cross, and now and then some instance of mean vindictiveness swelled the rising tide of hatred against him. He became subject to fits of violent passion. The famous Quaker preacher, William Edmundson, who visited Virginia in 1672, called on the governor and sought to intercede with him for the Society of Friends, the members of which were shamefully treated in that colony. "He was very peevish and brittle," says Edmundson, "and I could fasten nothing on him, with all the soft arguments I could use. . . . The next day was the men's meeting at William Wright's house [where I met] Major-General Bennett. . . . He asked me 'How I was treated by the governor?' I told him 'he was brittle and peevish.' . . . He asked me 'if the governor called me dog, rogue, etc.' I said 'No.' 'Then,' said he, 'you took him in his best humour, those being his usual terms when he is angry, for he is an enemy to every appearance of good.'"[1]

Berkeley's violent temper

Such was the governor of Virginia and such the state of things there, when to the many troubles that were goading the people to rebellion the horrors of the tomahawk and scalping-knife were suddenly added. In 1672, after a fearful struggle of twenty years' duration, the Five Nations of New York had completely overthrown and nearly annihilated their kinsmen the Susquehannocks. The defeated barbarians, slowly retreating southward, roamed on both sides of the Potomac, while parties of the victors, mostly from the Seneca tribe, pursued and harassed them. Early in the summer of 1675 some Algonquins of the Doeg tribe, dwelling in Stafford County, not far from the site of Fredericksburg, got into a dispute with one of the settlers and stole some of his pigs. The thieves were pursued, and in the chase one or two of them were shot. A few days afterward a herdsman was found mortally wounded at the door of his cabin, and said with his dying breath that it

Beginning of the Indian war, 1675

[1] Neill, *Virginia Carolorum*, p. 341.

was Doegs who had done it. Then the county lieutenant of Stafford turned out with his militia to punish the offenders. This officer was Colonel George Mason, whose cavalry troop had gone down before Cromwell's resistless blows in the crowning mercy at Worcester. He was great-grandfather of the George Mason who sat in the Federal Convention of 1787. One party of Colonel Mason's men overtook and slew eleven of the Algonquins, and another party at some distance in the forest had already shot fourteen red men, when a chief came running up to Colonel Mason and told him that these latter were friendly Susquehannocks, and that the murderers of the herdsman were neither Algonquins nor Susquehannocks, but Senecas. The firing was instantly stopped, but the unfortunate affair had evil consequences. Murders by Indians along the Potomac became frequent. The Susquehannocks occupied an old blockhouse on the Maryland side of the river, and a force of Marylanders, commanded by Major Thomas Truman, marched out to dislodge them.

At the request of the Maryland government, Virginia sent a party to coöperate in this task. Its commander bore a name which his great-grandson was to make forever illustrious. Colonel John Washington had come over from England in 1657, with his younger brother Lawrence, and settled in Westmoreland County. He was now forty-four years old, a man of wealth and influence, a leading judge, and member of the House of Burgesses.

John Washington

When the Virginia troops crossed the Potomac they found their Maryland allies assembled before the blockhouse, with five Susquehannocks in custody. These Indians were envoys who had come out for a parley, but had apparently taken alarm and sought to escape, whereupon Major Truman seized and detained them until the Virginians should arrive. Then Colonel Washington, with his next in command, Major Isaac Allerton, proceeded to interrogate the Indians, while Major Truman listened in silence. Washington demanded satisfaction for the murders and other outrages committed in Virginia, but the Indians denied

The five Susquehannock envoys

everything and declared that their deadly enemies the Senecas were the sole offenders. Washington then asked how it happened that several canoe-loads of beef and pork, stolen from the plantations, had been carried into the Susquehannock fort; was it their foes the Senecas who were thus supplying them with food? And how did it happen that a party of Susquehannocks just captured in Virginia were dressed in the clothes of Englishmen lately murdered? The falsehood was too palpable. The guilt of the Susquehannocks was plain, and they must either make amends or taste the rigours of war.

There can be little doubt that Colonel Washington was right. Then, as always until after 1763, the Long House was from end to end the steadfast ally of the English, and nothing could be more unlikely than that one of its tribes should have been guilty of these murders. It is quite clear that the Susquehannocks lied, with the double purpose of saving themselves and bringing down vengeance upon the Senecas. The first murders had been committed by Algonquins, and evidently the Susquehannocks had joined in the work in retaliation for the unfortunate mistake committed by Colonel Mason's men.

At the close of the conference Major Truman called to Colonel Washington, asking if these were not impudent rogues to deny the murders they had done, when at that very moment the corpses of nine of their own tribe were lying unburied at Hurston's plantation, where in a fight the defenders of the place had just slain them. As the envoys persisted in denying that these dead Indians were Susquehannocks, Washington suggested that they should be taken to Hurston's and confronted with the bodies. So Truman's men marched away with the five envoys, and presently put them to death, "wch was occation," says one of the Virginian witnesses, "y^t^ much amaized & startled us & ou^r^ Comanders, being a thing y^t^ was never imagined or expected." [1]

The killing of the envoys

[1] In describing this affair I have relied chiefly upon the affidavits

The killing of these envoys was in violation of a rule that holds in all warfare, whether savage or civilized, and Truman was impeached for it in the Maryland assembly; but owing to an obstinate disagreement between the two houses as to the penalty to be inflicted, he escaped without further punishment than the loss of his seat in the council.

Colonel Washington's force proved too small to hold in check the infuriated Susquehannocks, who seem to have entered into alliance with the Algonquins of the country. Soon the whole border, from the Potomac to the falls of the James, was swarming with painted barbarians, and day after day renewed the tale of burning homes and slaughtered wives and children. This sort of thing went on through the fall and winter, driving people into frenzy, but Berkeley would not call out a military force for the occasion. He insisted that it was enough to instruct the county lieutenants, each in his county, to keep his militia in readiness. It was charged against him that fear of losing his share in a very lucrative fur trade made him unwilling to engage in war with the Indians. However this may have been, the spirit of the people had become so mutinous that he was probably afraid to entrust himself to the protection of a popular militia. Whatever the motive of his conduct, its consequences were highly disastrous. On a single day in January, 1676, within a circle of ten miles' radius, thirty-six people were murdered; and when the governor was notified, he coolly answered that "nothing could be done until the assembly's regular meeting in

Berkeley's perverseness

Indian atrocities

from the records of Westmoreland County, reprinted by Dr. L. G. Tyler, in his admirable *William and Mary College Quarterly*, ii. 39-43. The affidavits were taken by Nicholas Spencer and Richard Lee, son of the Richard Lee mentioned in the preceding chapter. In Browne's *Maryland*, p. 131, an attempt is made to throw the blame for killing the envoys upon the Virginians, but the affidavits seem to me trustworthy and conclusive. It is not likely that there was or is any discernible difference between human nature in Virginia and in Maryland, and public opinion in both colonies condemned Truman's conduct.

March"![1] Meanwhile the work of firebrand and tomaha went on. In Essex County (then known as Rappahannoc sixty plantations were destroyed within seventeen days. was thought by some persons that the Indians were stimulated by reports of the fearful havoc which their brethren were making in New England, where King Philip's war was raging. Surely the wrath of the planters must have been redoubled when they heard of the stalwart troop led by Josiah Winslow into the Narragansett country, and noted the stern vengeance it wrought there on a December day of 1675, and contrasted these things with what they saw before them. As the Charles City people afterward declared with bitterness, "we do acknowledge we were so unadvised then . . . as to believe it our duty incumbent on us both by the laws of God and nature, and our duty to his sacred Majesty, notwithstanding . . . Sir William Berkeley's prohibition, . . . to take up arms . . . for the just defence of ourselves, wives, and children, and this his Majesty's country."[2] At length, in March, the Long Assembly, as people called it, which had been elected in 1661, was convened for the last time; a force of 500 men was gathered, and all things were in readiness for a campaign, when Berkeley by proclamation disbanded the little army, declaring that the frontier forts, if duly prepared and equipped, afforded all the protection the country needed. To many people this seemed to be adding insult to injury; for while no fortress could prevent the skulking approach of the enemy through the tangled wilderness, it was widely believed that the repairing of forts was simply a device for enabling the governor's friends to embezzle the money granted for the purpose.

Nathaniel Bacon

At this time there was a young man of eight-and-twenty living on his plantation on James River, hard by Curl's Wharf. His name was Nathaniel Bacon, son of Thomas Bacon, of Friston Hall, Suffolk, a kinsman

[1] "Cittenborne Parish Grievances, reprinted from Winder Papers, Virginia State Library," in *Virginia Magazine*, iii. 35.

[2] "Charles City County Grievances," *Virginia Magazine*, iii. 137.

of the great Lord Bacon.[1] His mother was daughther of a Suffolk knight, Sir Robert Brooke. He had studied law at Gray's Inn, and after extensive travel on the continent of Europe had come to Virginia with his young wife shortly before the beginning of these Indian troubles. His father's cousin, Nathaniel Bacon, of King's Creek, who had dwelt in the colony since about 1650, was a man of large wealth and influence. The abilities and character of the young Nathaniel were rated so high that he already had a seat in the council. He was clearly an impetuous youth, brave and cordial, fiery at times, and gifted with a persuasive tongue. He was in person tall and lithe, with swarthy complexion and melancholy eyes, and a somewhat lofty demeanour. One writer says that his discourse was "pestilent and prevalent logical," and that it "tended to atheism," which doubtless means that he criticised things freely. Two other prominent men were much of his way of thinking. One was a hard-headed and canny Scotchman, William Drummond, who had been governor of the Albemarle colony in Carolina.[2] The other was Richard Lawrence, an Oxford graduate of scholarly tastes, whom an old chronicler has labelled for posterity as "thoughtful Mr.

Drummond and Lawrence

[1] The following abridged table shows the relationship (see *Virginia Magazine*, ii. 125): —

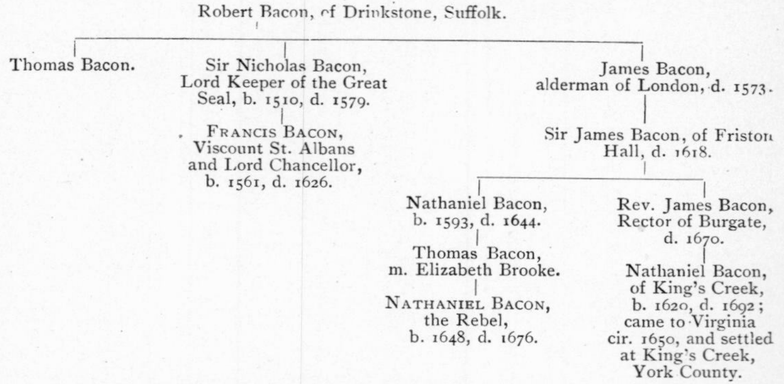

[2] Drummond Lake, in the Dismal Swamp, was named for him.

Lawrence." Both Drummond and Lawrence were wealthy men, and lived, it is said, in the two best built and best furnished houses in Jamestown, which, it should be remembered, had scarcely more than a score of houses all told.

Beside the estate where Bacon lived, he had another one farther up, on the site still marked by the name "Bacon Quarter Branch" in the suburbs of Richmond. "If the redskins meddle with me," quoth the fiery young man, "damn my blood but I 'll harry them, commission or no commission!" One May morning in 1676 news came to Curl's Wharf that the Indians had attacked the upper estate, and killed Bacon's overseer and one of his servants. A crowd of armed planters on horseback assembled, and offered to march under Bacon's lead. He made an eloquent speech, accepted the command, and sent a courier to the governor to ask for a commission. Berkeley returned an evasive answer, whereupon Bacon sent him a polite note, thanking him for the promised commission, and forthwith started on his campaign. He had not gone many miles when a proclamation from the governor overtook him, commanding the party to disperse. A few obeyed; the rest kept on their way and inflicted a severe defeat upon the Indians. Then Bacon and his volunteers marched homeward.[1]

Bacon's plantation attacked, May, 1676

He defeats the Indians

[1] For the picturesque details of this narrative I have followed the well-known document found by Rufus King when minister to Great Britain in 1803, and published by President Jefferson in the *Richmond Enquirer* in 1804; since reprinted in Force's *Tracts*, vol. i., Washington, 1836, and in Maxwell's *Virginia Historical Register*, vol. iii., Richmond, 1850. The original manuscript was written in 1705, and addressed to Robert Harley, Queen Anne's secretary of state, afterward Earl of Oxford. The writer signs himself "T. M.," and speaks of himself as dwelling in Northumberland County and possessing a plantation also in Stafford County, which he represented in the House of Burgesses. From these indications it is pretty certain that he was Thomas Mathews, son of Governor Samuel Mathews heretofore mentioned. His account of the scenes of which he was an eye-witness is quite vivid.

Meanwhile the indignant Berkeley had gathered a troop of horse and taken the field in person to arrest this refractory young man. But suddenly came the news that the whole York peninsula was in revolt. The governor must needs hasten back to Jamestown, where he soon realized that if he would avoid civil war he must dissolve his moss-grown House of Burgesses and issue writs for a new election. This was done. In anticipation of such an emergency, an act had been passed in 1670 restricting the suffrage by a property qualification, which had called forth much indignation, since previously universal suffrage had prevailed. In this excited election of 1676 the restriction was openly disregarded in many places, and unqualified persons voted illegally. Bacon offered himself as a candidate for Henrico County and was elected by a large majority. As he drew near to Jamestown in his sloop with thirty followers, a warship lay at anchor awaiting him, and the high sheriff arrested him with his whole party. He was taken into the brick State House and confronted with the governor, who simply said, "Mr. Bacon, have you forgot to be a gentleman?" "No, may it please your honour," said Bacon. "Very well," said Berkeley, "then I 'll take your parole." This was discreet in the governor, since the election had gone so heavily against him. Bacon was released and went to lodge in the house of Richard Lawrence.

Election of a new House of Burgesses

Arrest of Bacon

This "thoughtful" gentleman, the Oxford scholar, "for wit, learning, and sobriety equalled by few," is said to have "kept an ordinary," while his house was one of the best in Jamestown. It should be remembered that the permanent residents in the town numbered less than a hundred,[1] while the sessions of the assembly brought a great influx of temporary sojourners, so that any or every house would be made to serve as a tavern. Some years before, Mr. Lawrence had been "partially treated at law, for a considerable estate on behalf of a corrupt favour-

"Thoughtful" Mr. Lawrence

[1] Bruce, *Economic History*, ii. 455.

ite" of Sir William Berkeley; a fact well certified by the testimony of the governor's friend, Colonel Lee. For this reason Lawrence bore the governor a grudge and spoke of him as a treacherous old villain. It was believed by some

SITE OF HOUSE OF BURGESSES, JAMESTOWN

people that in the conduct of the rebellion Lawrence was the Mephistopheles and Bacon simply the Faust whom he prompted.

Bacon's submission

There seems to have been an understanding that, if Bacon were to acknowledge his offence in marching without a commission, he should be received back to his seat in the council, and the governor would give him a commission to go and finish the Indian war. The old Nathaniel Bacon, of King's Creek, being "a very rich politic man and childless," and intending to leave his estates to young Nathaniel, succeeded in persuading him, "not without much pains," to accept the compromise. The old gentleman wrote out a formal recantation, which his young kinsman consented to read in public, and a scene was made of it. The State

House was a two-story building in which the burgesses had lately begun sitting apart on the second floor, while the governor and council (in point of dignity the "upper house") held their session on the first floor. On the 5th of June, 1676, the burgesses were summoned to attend in the council chamber while Berkeley opened parliament. In his opening speech the governor referred to the Indian troubles, and expressed himself with strong emphasis on the slaying of the five envoys: "If they had killed my grandfather and grandmother, my father and mother and all my friends, yet if they had come to treat of peace they ought to have gone in peace!"[1] Then, changing the subject, the governor announced: "If there be joy in the presence of the angels over one sinner that repenteth, there is joy now, for we have a penitent sinner come before us. Call Mr. Bacon." The young man knelt at the bar of the assembly and read aloud the prepared paper in which he confessed that he had acted illegally, and offered sureties for future good behaviour. Then said the governor impressively, and thrice repeating the words, "God forgive you! I forgive you." "And all that were with him," interposed a member of the council. "Yea," continued Berkeley, "and all those that were with you." The sheriff at once released Bacon's followers, and he took his old seat in the council, while the burgesses filed off upstairs. Our informant, the member for Stafford, tells us that while he was on his way up to the burgesses that afternoon, and through the open door of the council chamber descried "Mr. Bacon on his quondam seat," it seemed "a

[1] T. M. goes on to remark that "the two chief commanders . . . who slew the four Indian great men" were present among the burgesses. This may seem to implicate Colonel Washington and Major Allerton in the killing of the envoys; but T. M.'s recollection, thirty years after the event, is of not much weight when contradicted by the sworn affidavits above cited. The facts that, while Truman was impeached in Maryland, no such action seems to have been undertaken in Virginia against Washington and Allerton, and that, after the governor's strong words regarding the slaying, the friendly relations between him and these gentlemen continued, would indicate that their skirts were clear.

marvellous indulgence" to one who had so lately been proscribed as a rebel.

The governor's chief dread was the free discussion of affairs in general by a hostile assembly. Now that the Indian imbroglio had brought these new burgesses together, he wanted them to confine their talk to Indian affairs and then go home, but this was not their way of thinking. They aimed, though feebly, at greater independence than heretofore, and the governor's intent was to frustrate this aim. It was moved by one of his partisans in the House of Burgesses "to entreat the governor would please to assign two of his council to sit with and assist us in our debates, as had been usual." At this the friends of Bacon scowled, and the member for Stafford ventured to suggest that such aid might not be necessary, whereat there was an uproar. The Berkeleyans urged that "it had been customary and ought not to be omitted," but a shrewd old assemblyman named Presley replied, "'T is true it has been customary, but if we have any bad customs amongst us, we are come here to mend 'em."[1] This happy retort was greeted with laughter, but the Cavalier feeling of loyalty to the king's representative was still strong, and Berkeley's friends had their way, apparently in a tumultuous fashion. As the member for Stafford says, the affair "was huddled off without coming to a vote," so that the burgesses must "submit to be overawed and have every carped at expression carried straight to the governor." Nevertheless,

Governor *vs.* Burgesses

[1] Beverley *H(istory and Present State of Virginia*, London, 1705, bk. iv. p. 3) tells us that before 1680 the council and burgesses sat together, like the Scotch parliament, and that the separation occurred under Lord Culpeper's administration; and his statement is generally repeated by historians without qualification. Yet here in 1676 we find the two houses sitting separately, and the discussion cited shows that it had often been so before; otherwise the sending of two councillors to sit with the burgesses could not have been customary. Beverley's date of 1680 was evidently intended as the final date of separation; not as the date before which the two houses never sat separately, but as the date after which they never sat together.

they went sturdily on to their work of reform, and the acts which they passed most clearly reveal the nature of the evils from which the people had been suffering. They restored universal suffrage; they enacted that vestrymen should be elected by popular vote, and limited their term of office to three years; they reduced the sheriff's term to a single year; they declared that no person should hold at one and the same time any two of the offices of sheriff, surveyor, escheator, and clerk of court; and they imposed penalties upon the delay of public business and the taking of excessive fees. Councillors with their families, and the families of clergymen, had been exempted from taxation; this odious privilege was now abolished. Sundry trade monopolies were overthrown; two magistrates, Edward Hill and John Stith, were disfranchised for alleged misconduct; and provision was made for a general inspection of public expenses and the proper auditing of accounts.[1]

Reform of abuses

The Indian troubles were not neglected. Arrangements were made for raising and maintaining an army of 1000 men, and the aid of friendly Indians was solicited. There was a picturesque scene when the "Queen of Pamunkey" was brought before the House of Burgesses. That interesting squaw sachem appears to have been a descendant of the fierce Opekankano. Her tribe was the same that John Smith had visited on the winter day when he held his pistol to the old warrior's head, with the terse mandate, "Corn or your life!" That remnant of the Powhatan confederacy was still flourishing in Bacon's time, and indeed it has survived to the present day, a mongrel compound of Indian and negro, on two small reservations in King William County.[2] The "Queen of Pamunkey" in Bacon's time

An Indian "princess"

[1] The acts of this assembly, known as "Bacon's Laws," are given in Hening's *Statutes*, ii. 341–365.

[2] "It is still their boast that they are the descendants of Powhatan's warriors. A good evidence of their present laudable ambition is an application recently made by them for a share in the privileges of the Hampton schools. These bands of Indians are known by two names:

commanded about 150 warriors, and what the assembly wanted was to secure their aid in suppressing the hostile Indians. The dusky princess "entered the chamber with a comportment graceful to admiration, bringing on her right hand an Englishman interpreter, and on the left her son, a stripling twenty years of age, she having round her head a plat of black and white wampum peag three inches broad in imitation of a crown, and was clothed in a mantle of dressed deerskins with the hair outwards and the edge cut round six inches deep, which made strings resembling twisted fringe from the shoulders to the feet; thus with grave courtlike gestures and a majestic air in her face she walked up our long room to the lower end of the table, where after a few entreaties she sat down; the interpreter and her son standing by her on either side as they had walked up. Our chairman asked her what men she would lend us for guides in the wilderness and to assist us against our enemy Indians. She spake to the interpreter to inform her what the chairman said (though we believed she understood him). He told us she bid him ask [her] son to whom the English tongue was familiar (and who was reputed the son of an English colonel), yet neither would he speak to or seem to understand the chairman, but, the interpreter told us, he referred all to his mother, who being again urged, she, after a little musing, with an earnest passionate countenance as if tears were ready to gush out, and a fervent sort of expression, made a harangue about a quarter of an hour, often interlacing (with a high shrill voice and vehement passion) these words, *Totapotamoy chepiack!* i. e. *Totapotamoy dead!* Colonel Hill, being next me, shook his head. I asked him what was the matter. He told me all she said was too true, to our shame, and that his father was general in that battle where divers

the larger band is called the Pamunkeys (120 souls); the smaller goes by the name of the Mattaponies (50). They are both governed by chiefs and councillors, together with a board of white trustees chosen by themselves." Hendren, "Government and Religion of the Virginia Indians," *Johns Hopkins Univ. Studies*, xiii. 591.

years before[1] Totapotamoy her husband had led a hundred of his Indians in help to the English against our former enemy Indians, and was there slain with most of his men; for which no compensation at all had been to that day rendered to her, wherewith she now upbraided us."

The candid member for Stafford calls the chairman of the committee morose and rude for not so much as "advancing one cold word towards assuaging the anger and grief" of the squaw sachem. Having once obtained a favour and so ill requited it, the white men in an emergency were now suppliants for further good offices of the same sort. But disregarding all this, the chairman imperiously demanded to be informed how many Indians she would now contribute. A look of angry disdain passed over the cinnamon face; she turned her head away and "sat mute till that same question being pressed a third time, she, not returning her face to the board, answered with a low slighting voice in our own language, *Six!* but, being further importuned, she, sitting a little while sullen, without uttering a word between, said, *Twelve!* . . . and so rose up and walked gravely away, as not pleased with her treatment."

The chairman's rudeness

Small wisdom was shown in this mean and discourteous treatment of a useful ally, but men's thoughts were at once abruptly turned from such matters. "One morning early a bruit ran about the town, Bacon is fled! Bacon is fled!" and for the moment Indian alliances and legislative reforms were alike forgotten. Mr. Lawrence's house was searched at daybreak, but his lodger had gone. Not only had the governor withheld the expected commission, but the air was heavy with suspicion of treachery. The elder Bacon, of King's Creek, who was fond of "this uneasy

Bacon's flight

[1] In 1656 a tribe called Ricahecrians, about 700 in number, from beyond the Blue Ridge, had advanced eastward as far as the falls of the James River, where they encountered and defeated Hill and Totapotamoy. After this the Ricahecrians may have retraced their steps westward; we hear no more of them on the Atlantic seaboard.

cousin" without approving his conduct, secretly informed him that his life was in danger at Jamestown. So the young man slipped away to his estate at Curl's, and within a few days marched back upon Jamestown at the head of 600 men. Berkeley's utmost efforts could scarcely muster 100 men, of whom we are told that not half could be relied on. Early in the warm June afternoon Bacon halted his troops upon the green before the State House, and walked up toward the building with a little guard of fusileers. The upper windows were filled with peering burgesses, and crowds of expectant people stood about the green. Out from the door came the old white-haired governor, trembling with fury, and, plucking open the rich lace upon his bosom, shouted to Bacon, "Here I am! Shoot me! 'Fore God, a fair mark, a fair mark — shoot!" Bacon answered mildly, "No, may it please your honour, we have not come to hurt a hair of your head or of any man's. We are come for a commission to save our lives from the Indians, which you have so often promised, and now we will have it before we go."

His return

But we are told that after the old man had gone in to talk with his council, Bacon fell into a rage and swore that he would kill them all if the commission were not granted. The fusileers presented their pieces at the windows and yelled, "We will have it! we will have it!" till shortly one of the burgesses shook "a pacifick handkercher" and called down, "You shall have it." All was soon quiet again. The assembly drew up a memorial to the king, setting forth the grievances of the colony and Bacon's valuable services; and it made out a commission for him as general of an army to be sent against the Indians. Next day the governor was browbeaten into signing both these papers; but the same ship that carried the memorial to Charles II. carried also a private letter wherein Berkeley told his own story in his own way. The assembly was then dissolved.

The governor intimidated, June, 1676

Bacon was a commander who could move swiftly and strike

hard. Within four weeks the remnant of the Susquehannocks had been pretty nearly wiped out of existence, when he heard that the governor had proclaimed him and his followers rebels. It was like a cry of despair from the old man, who felt his power and dignity gone while this young Cromwell rode over him rough-shod. He tried to raise the people in Gloucester, reputed the most loyal of the counties, but his efforts were vain. Ominous groans and calls of "a Bacon! a Bacon!" greeted him, until in anticipation of still worse difficulties he fled across Chesapeake Bay to the Accomac peninsula, launching the proclamation behind him like a Parthian arrow. This was on July 29, and Richard Lawrence carried the news up-stream to Bacon, who was probably somewhere about the North Anna River. The young leader was stung by what he felt to be cruel injustice. "It vexed him to the heart for to think that while he was hunting Indian wolves, tigers, and foxes, which daily destroyed our harmless sheep and lambs, that he and those with him should be pursued with a full cry, as a more savage or a no less ravenous beast." He quickly marched back at the head of his troops to Middle Plantation, half way between Jamestown and York River, the site where Williamsburg was afterward built. What had best be done was matter of discussion between Bacon and his friends, and the affair began to assume a more questionable and dangerous aspect than before. The Scotch adviser, William Drummond, was a gentleman who did not believe in half measures. When some friend warned him of the danger of rebellion he was heard to reply, "I am in over shoes; I will be over boots!" His wife was equally bold. It was suggested one day that King Charles might by and by have something to say about these proceedings, whereupon Sarah Drummond picked up a stick and broke it in two, exclaiming, "I care no more for the power of England than for this broken straw!" Bacon was advised by Drummond to have Berkeley deposed and the more pla-

Bacon crushes the Susquehannocks

Berkeley flies to Accomac, and proclaims Bacon a rebel

Bacon's march to Middle Plantation

cable Sir Henry Chicheley put in his place; and as a precedent he cited the thrusting out of Sir John Harvey, forty-one years before. But Bacon preferred a different course of action. First, he issued a manifesto in rejoinder to Berkeley's proclamation. A few ringing sentences from it will serve as a sample of his peculiar eloquence.

His manifesto

"If virtue be a sin, if piety be guilt, all the principles of morality, goodness and justice be perverted, we must confess that those who are now called Rebels may be in danger of those high imputations. Those loud and several bulls would affright innocents, and render the defence of our brethren and the inquiry into our sad and heavy oppressions Treason. But if there be (as sure there is) a just God to appeal to, if religion and justice be a sanctuary here, if to plead the cause of the oppressed, if sincerely to aim at his Majesty's honour and the public good without any reservation or by-interest, if to stand in the gap after so much blood of our dear brethren bought and sold, if after the loss of a great part of his Majesty's colony deserted and dispeopled freely with our lives and estates to endeavour to save the remainders, be treason — God Almighty judge and let guilty die. But since we cannot in our hearts find one single spot of rebellion or treason, or that we have in any manner aimed at subverting the settled government or attempting of the person of any either magistrate or private man, notwithstanding the several reproaches and threats of some who for sinister ends were disaffected to us and censured our innocent and honest designs, and since all people in all places where we have yet been can attest our civil, quiet, peaceable behaviour, far different from that of rebellion [rebellious ?] and tumultuous persons, let Truth be bold and all the world know the real foundations of pretended guilt. We appeal to the country itself, what and of what nature their oppressions have been, or by what cabal and mystery the designs of many of those whom we call great men have been transacted and carried on. But let us trace these men in authority and favour to whose hands the dispensation of the country's wealth has been committed." [1]

This is the prose of the seventeenth century, which had not learned how to smite the reader's mind with the short incisive sentences to which we are at the present day accustomed; but there is no mistaking the writer's passionate earnestness, his straightforward honesty and dauntless courage. As we read, we seem to see the gleam of lightning in those melancholy eyes, and we quite understand how the impetuous youth was a born leader of men. With strong words tumbling from a full heart the manifesto goes on to "trace these men in authority," these "juggling parasites whose tottering fortunes have been repaired at the public charge." He points out at some length the character of the public grievances, and appeals to the king with a formal indictment of Sir William Berkeley:—

His arraignment of Berkeley

"For having upon specious pretences of public works raised unjust taxes upon the commonalty for the advancement of private favourites and other sinister ends, but no visible effects in any measure adequate.

"For not having, during the long time of his government, in any measure advanced this hopeful colony either by fortification, towns, or trade.

"For having abused and rendered contemptible the majesty of justice, of advancing to places of judicature scandalous and ignorant favourites.

"For having wronged his Majesty's prerogative and interest by assuming the monopoly of the beaver trade.

"[For] having in that unjust gain bartered and sold his Majesty's country and the lives of his loyal subjects to the barbarous heathen.

"For having protected, favoured, and emboldened the Indians against his Majesty's most loyal subjects, never contriving, requiring or appointing any due or proper means of

[1] The original MS. of the manifesto is in the British State Paper Office. It is printed in full in the *Virginia Magazine*, i. 55–61.

Richd. Lee

satisfaction for their many invasions, murders, and robberies committed upon us."

And so on through several further counts. At the close of the indictment nineteen persons are mentioned by name as the governor's "wicked and pernicious counsellors, aiders and assisters against the commonalty in these our cruel commotions." Among these names we read those of Sir Henry Chicheley, Richard Lee, Robert Beverley, Nicholas Spencer, and the son of our old friend William Claiborne, who had once been such a thorn in the side of Maryland. The manifesto ends by demanding that Berkeley and all the persons on this list be promptly arrested and confined at Middle Plantation until further orders. Let no man dare aid or harbour any one of them, under penalty of being declared a traitor and losing his estates.

"Wicked counsellors"

When he had launched this manifesto Bacon called for a meeting of notables at Middle Plantation, to concert measures for making it effective. There on August 3, accordingly, were assembled "most of the prime gentlemen of those parts," including four members of the council. The discussion lasted all day, and was kept up by the light of torches until midnight. There were many who were not willing to go all lengths with Bacon. All were willing to subscribe an agreement not to aid Berkeley in molesting Bacon and his men, but all were not prepared to promise military aid to Bacon in resisting Berkeley. Bacon insisted upon this and even more. It was not unlikely that the king, influenced by calumnies and misrepresentations, might send troops to Virginia to suppress the so-called "rebellion." In that case all must unite in opposing the royal forces until his Majesty should be brought to see these matters in their true light. Many demurred at this. It was equivalent to armed rebellion. They would sign the first part of the agreement, but not this. Bacon replied that the governor had already proclaimed them rebels, and would hang them for signing any part of the agreement; one might as well be hanged for a sheep as for a lamb, and as for himself he was not going to be satisfied with half support. They must choose between Berkeley and himself. It is said that they might have argued all that summer night but for a sudden Indian scare which emphasized the need for prompt action. Then the

The oath at Middle Plantation

hesitating gentlemen came forward and signed the entire paper, while the whole company, and no one more emphatically than Bacon himself, asseverated that these proceedings in no way impaired their allegiance. In other words, they were ready if need be to make war on the king for his own good. It was "We, the inhabitants of Virginia," that drew up this remarkable agreement, which Charles II. was presently to read. Writs were then made out in the king's name for a new election of burgesses and signed by the four councilmen. Then Bacon crossed the James River and defeated the Appomattox Indians near the spot where Petersburg now stands. After this he moved about the country, capturing and dispersing the barbarians, until early in September it might be said that every homestead in the colony was safe.

Defeat of the Indians

In the proceedings which attended the taking of the oath at Middle Plantation it may be plainly seen that Bacon was in danger of alienating his followers by pursuing too radical a policy. This is strikingly confirmed by a document which has only lately attracted attention, a letter from John Goode to Sir William Berkeley, dated January 30, 1677. This John Goode was a veteran frontiersman of sixty years, a man of importance in the colony. He seems to have been a faithful adherent of Bacon from his first march against the Indians in May until the beginning of September, when there occurred the conversation which, after all was over, he reported to the governor as follows. The affair is so important and so little known that I quote the dialogue entire, with the original spelling and punctuation:[1] —

Startling conversation between Bacon and Goode

HON'D SR. — In obedient submission to your honours command directed to me by Capt. Wm. Bird[2] I have written the full

[1] The original is in the *Colonial Entry Book*, lxxi. 232–240. It is printed in G. B. Goode's *Virginia Cousins; a Study of the Ancestry and Posterity of John Goode, of Whitby*, Richmond, 1887, pp. 30A–30D. A brief summary is given in Doyle's *Virginia*, p. 251.

[2] Bacon's neighbour and adherent, William Byrd, purchaser of the Westover estate, and father of William Byrd the historian.

substance of a discourse Nath : Bacon, deceased, propos'd to me on or about the 2d day of September last, both in order and words as followeth : —

BACON. — There is a report Sir Wm. Berkeley hath sent to the king for 2,000 Red Coates, and I doe believe it may be true, tell me your opinion, may not 500 Virginians beat them, wee having the same advantages against them the Indians have against us.

GOODE. — I rather conceive 500 Red Coats may either Subject or ruine Virginia.

B. — You talk strangely, are not wee acquainted with the Country, can lay Ambussadoes, and take Trees and putt them by, the use of their discipline, and are doubtlesse as good or better shott than they.

G. — But they can accomplish what I have sayd without hazard or coming into such disadvantages, by taking Opportunities of landing where there shall bee noe opposition, firing out [our ?] houses and Fences, destroying our Stocks and preventing all Trade and supplyes to the Country.

B. — There may bee such prevention that they shall not bee able to make any great Progresse in Mischeifes, and the Country or Clime not agreeing with their Constitutions, great mortality will happen amongst them, in their Seasoning which will weare and weary them out.

G. — You see Sir that in a manner all the principall Men in the Countrey dislike your manner of proceedings, they, you may bee sure will joine with the Red Coates.

B. — But there shall none of them bee [permitted ?].

G. — Sir, you speake as though you design'd a totall defection from Majestie, and our native Country.

B. — Why (smiling) have not many Princes lost their Dominions soe.

G. — They have been such people as have been able to subsist without their Prince. The poverty of Virginia is such, that the Major part of the Inhabitants can scarce supply their wants from hand to mouth, and many there are besides can hardly shift, without Supply one yeare, and you may bee sure that this people which soe fondly follow you, when they come to feele the miserable wants of food and rayment, will bee in greater heate to leave you, then [than] they were to come after you, besides here are many people in Virginia that receive considerable benefitts, comforts, and advantages by Parents, Friends and Correspondents in England, and many which expect patrimonyes and Inheritances which they will by no meanes decline.

B. — For supply I know nothing: the Country will be able to provide it selfe withall, in a little time, save Amunition and Iron, and I believe the King of France or States of Holland would either of them entertaine a Trade with us.

G. — Sir, our King is a great Prince, and his Amity is infinitely more valuable to them, then [than] any advantage they can reape by Virginia, they will not therefore provoke his displeasure by supporting his Rebells here; besides I conceive that your followers do not think themselves inagaged against the King's Authority, but against the Indians.

B. — But I think otherwise, and am confident of it, that it is the mind of this country, and of Mary Land, and Carolina also, to cast off their Governor and the Governors of Carolina have taken no notice of the People, nor the People of them, a long time;[1] and the people are resolv'd to own their Governour further; And if wee cannot prevaile by Armes to make our Conditions for Peace, or obtaine the Priviledge to elect our own Governour, we may retire to Roanoke.

And here hee fell into a discourse of seating a Plantation in a great Island in the River, as a fitt place to retire to for Refuge.

G. — Sir the prosecuting what you have discoursed will unavoidably produce utter ruine and destruction to the people and Countrey, & I dread the thoughts of putting my hand to the promoting a designe of such miserable consequence, therefore hope you will not expect from me.

B. — I am glad I know your mind, but this proceeds from meer Cowardlynesse.

G. — And I desire you should know my mind, for I desire to harbour noe such thoughts, which I should fear to impart to any man.

B. — Then what should a Gentleman engaged as I am, doe, you doe as good as tell me, I must fly or hang for it.

G. — I conceive a seasonable Submission to the Authority you

[1] Bacon's allusion is to the troubles in North Carolina which broke out during the governorship of George Carteret and were chiefly due to the Navigation Act. See below, p. 260; and as to Maryland, see p. 140.

have your Commission from, acknowledging such Errors and Excesse, as are yett past, there may bee hope of remission.

I perceived his cogitations were much on this discourse, hee nominated, Carolina, for the watch word.

Three days after I asked his leave to goe home, hee sullenly Answered, you may goe, and since that time, I thank God, I never saw or heard from him.

This interesting dialogue reveals the nature of the situation into which Bacon had drifted. As the days went by, he could hardly fail to see that the king was more likely to take Berkeley's view of the case than his. According to that view the deliverer of Virginia from the Indians was a proscribed rebel who must "fly or hang for it." There was little hope for Bacon in "seasonable submission." He would, therefore, consider it safer and better for Virginia to hold out until the king could be induced to take Bacon's view of the case; or failing this, it might still be possible to wear out the king's troops and achieve independence for Virginia, with the aid of the discontented people in the neighbouring colonies. These were the speculations of a man whom circumstances were making desperate, and the effect which they wrought upon John Goode was likely to be repeated with many who had hitherto loyally followed his fortunes.

Bacon's perilous situation

Thus far Bacon's fighting had been against Indians. His quarrel with the governor had been confined to fulminations. Now the two men were to come into armed collision and give Virginia a brief taste of civil war. Bacon sent Giles Bland, "a gentleman of an active and stirring disposition," with four armed vessels, to arrest Berkeley in Accomac, but Colonel Philip Ludwell, aided by treachery, succeeded in capturing Bland with his flotilla. Bland was put in irons, and one ship's captain was hanged for an example. Meanwhile Berkeley was enlisting troops by promising as rewards the estates of all the gentlemen who had taken the oath at Middle Plantation. He also sought to win over the indentured servants of gentlemen fighting

Berkeley takes the offensive

LOWER BRANDON: SOUTH FRONT

under Bacon by promising to give them the estates of their masters. Many longshoremen also were enrolled. Having in these ways scraped together about 1000 men, the governor sailed up the river to Jamestown and took possession of the place, from which Lawrence and Drummond fled in the nick of time.

When this news reached Bacon it found him at West Point, with the work of subduing the red men practically finished. Not four months had yet elapsed since the first attack on his plantation. It was clearly no ordinary young man that had done that summer's arduous work. Now he advanced upon Jamestown, and made his headquarters in his adversary's comfortable mansion at Green Spring. Sir William had thrown an earthwork across the neck of the promontory, and Bacon began building a parallel. It is said that he compelled a number of ladies in white aprons — wives of leading Berkeleyans — to stand upon the works, and sent a message to the governor not to fire upon these guardian angels. "The poor gentlewomen were mightily astonished," says the chronicle, "and neither were their husbands void of amazement at this subtle invention."[1] The incident is an ugly spot in that brief career. One would gladly disbelieve the story, but our contemporary authority for it seems unimpeachable, and is friendly withal to Bacon.

The white aprons

The speech made by the young commander to his men at Green Spring before the final assault is a good specimen of his eloquence: "Gentlemen and Fellow Soldiers, how I am transported with gladness to find you thus unanimous, bold and daring, brave and gallant. You have the victory before the fight, the conquest before the battle. . . . Your hardiness will invite all the country along as we march to come in and second you. . . . The ignoring of their actions cannot but so much reflect upon their spirit, as they will have no courage left to fight you. I know you have the prayers and well wishes of all the people in Vir-

Bacon's speech

[1] One of these ladies is said to have been the wife of the elder Nathaniel Bacon!

ginia, while the others are loaded with their curses. Come on, my hearts of gold ; he that dies in the field lies in the bed of honour ! "[1]

The governor's motley force was indeed no match for these determined men. In the desultory fighting that ensued about Jamestown he was badly defeated and at last fled again to Accomac. Jamestown remained at Bacon's mercy, and he burned it to the ground, that it might no longer "harbour the rogues." We are told that Lawrence and Drummond took the lead in this work by applying the torch to their own houses with their own hands. At Green Spring an "oath of fidelity" was drawn up, which was taken voluntarily by many people and forced upon others. Bacon seems now to have shown more severity than formerly in sending men to prison and seizing their property. One deserter he shot, but from bloodthirstiness he was notably free. Among the gentlemen who suffered most at his hands were Richard Lee and Sir Henry Chichely, who were kept several weeks in prison, Philip and Thomas Ludwell, Nicholas Spencer and Daniel Parke, Robert Beverley and Philip Lightfoot, whose estates were at various times plundered. John Washington and others who were denounced as "delinquents" saw their corn and tobacco, cattle and horses, impressed and carried away. Colonel Augustine Warner, another great-grandfather of George Washington, "was plundered as much as any, and yet speaks little of his losses, though they were very great."[2] Among the sufferers appears "the good Queen of Pamunkey," who was "driven out into the wild woods and there almost famished,

Burning of Jamestown

Sufferers at Bacon's hands

[1] "A True Narrative of the Rise, Progresse, and Cessation of the Late Rebellion in Virginia, most humbly and impartially reported by his Majestyes Commissioners appointed to enquire into the Affairs of the said Colony," [Winder Papers, Virginia State Library], reprinted in *Virginia Magazine*, iv. 117–154.

[2] "Persons who suffered by Bacon's Rebellion; Commissioners' Report," [Winder Papers], reprinted in *Virginia Magazine*, v. 64–70. See, also, the extracts from the Westmoreland County records, in *William and Mary College Quarterly*, ii. 43.

plundered of all she had, her people taken prisoners and sold; the queen was also robbed of her rich watchcoat for which she had great value, and offered to redeem at any rate." The next paragraph in the commissioners' report is delightful: "We could not but present her case to his Majesty, who, though he may not at present so well or readily provide remedies or rewards for the other worthy sufferers, yet since a present of small price may highly oblige and gratify this poor Indian Queen, we humbly supplicate his Majesty to bestow it on her."

One of the accusations against Bacon was that to him a good Indian meant a dead Indian, so that he did not take the trouble to discriminate between friends and foes. But what shall we say when we find him plundering his own kinsman, the affectionate cousin whose timely warning had once perhaps saved his life? The commissioners report the losses of Nathaniel Bacon the elder, at the hands of his "unnatural kinsman," as at least £1000 sterling. The old gentleman was "said to have been a person soe desirous and Industrious to divert the evil consequences of his Rebell kinsman's proceedings, that at the beginning hee freely proposed and promised to invest him in a considerable part of his Estate in present, and to leave him the Remainder in Reversion after his and his wife's death, offering him other advantages upon condicion hee would lay downe his Armes, and become a good subject to his Majestie, that that colony might not be disturbed or destroyed, nor his owne ffamily stained with soe foule a Blott."

Bacon and his cousin

At the burning of Jamestown the end of Bacon and of his rebellion was not far off. "This Prosperous Rebell, concluding now the day his owne, marcheth with his army into Gloster County, intending to visit all the northern part of Virginia . . . and to settle affairs after his own measures . . . But before he could arrive to the Perfection of his designes (wch none but the eye of omniscience could Penetrate) Providence did that which noe other hand durst (or at least did) doe and cut him off." Malarious Jamestown wreaked its own vengeance upon its destroyer. When Bacon marched away from it he was already ill with fever, and on the first day of October, at the house of a friend in Gloucester, he "surrendered up that fort he was no longer able to keep, into the hands of the grim and all-conquering Captain, Death." Accusations of poison were raised, but it is not likely that any other poison was concerned than impure water and marsh gases. The funeral was conducted with extraordinary secrecy. If a sudden turn of fortune should put Berkeley in possession of the body, he would surely hang it on a gibbet; so thoughtful Mr. Lawrence took measures to prevent any such indignity. One chronicler darkly hints that Bacon's remains were buried in some very secret place in the woods, but another mentions stones laid in the coffin, which suggests that it was sunk beneath the waves of York River, as Soto was buried in the Mississippi and mighty Alaric in the Busento.

Death of Bacon, Oct. 1, 1676

A strange meteoric career was that of young Bacon, begun and ended as it was in the space of about twenty weeks. On the news of his death the rebellion collapsed with surprising suddenness. His followers soon began giving in their submissions to the governor; the few that held out were dispersed or captured. Although it was not until January that the work of suppression was regarded as complete, yet that work consisted chiefly in catching fugitives. In January an English fleet arrived, with a regiment of troops, and a commission for investigating the affairs of Virginia. The commissioners were Sir John Berry, Sir Herbert Jeffries, and Colonel Francis Morison, three worthy and fair-minded gentlemen. They found nothing left for soldiers to do. They had authority for trying rebels, but in that business Berkeley had been beforehand. Soon after Bacon's death one of his best officers, Colonel Thomas Hansford, was captured by Robert Beverley, and carried over to Accomac. He asked no favour save that he might be "shot like a soldier and not hanged like a dog," but this was not granted.

Collapse of the rebellion

Arrival of royal commissioners, January, 1677

Hansford has been called "the first native martyr to American liberty." [1] Soon afterward two captains were hanged, and the affair of Major Edward Cheesman seems to have occurred while Berkeley was still at Accomac. It is the foulest incident recorded in Berkeley's career. When Cheesman was brought before him, the governor fiercely demanded, "Why did you engage in Bacon's designs?" Before the prisoner could answer, his young wife stepped forward and said, "It was my provocations that made my husband join the cause; but for me he had never done what he has done." Then falling on her knees before the governor, she implored him that she might be hanged as the guilty one instead of her husband.[2] The old wretch's answer was an insult so atrocious that the royalist chronicler can hardly abide it. "His Honour" must have been beside himself with anger and could not have meant what he said; for no woman could have "so small an affection for her husband as to dishonour him by her dishonesty, and yet retain such a degree of love, that rather than he should be hanged she will be content to submit her own life to the sentence." Perhaps the governor's thirst for vengeance was satisfied by his ruffian speech, for Major Cheesman was not put to death, but remanded to jail, where he died of illness.

Outrageous conduct of Berkeley

After Berkeley had occupied the York peninsula little work remained for him but that of the hangman. Not all the leaders were easy to find. Richard Lawrence, thoughtful as always, escaped from the scene. "The last account of him," says T. M., "was from an uppermost plantation, whence he and four other desperadoes, with horses, pistols, etc., marched away in a snow ankle-deep." Here the schol-

[1] See F. P. Brent, "Some unpublished facts relating to Bacon's Rebellion on the Eastern Shore of Virginia," and Mrs. Tyler, "Thomas Hansford, the First Native Martyr to American Liberty," in *Virginia Historical Society's Collections*, vol. xi.

[2] Some interesting information about the Cheesmans may be found in *William and Mary College Quarterly*, vol. i.

STRANGE NEWS

FROM

VIRGINIA;

Being a full and true

ACCOUNT

OF THE

LIFE and DEATH

OF

Nathanael Bacon Eſquire,

Who was the only Cauſe and Original of all the late Troubles in that COUNTRY.

With a full Relation of all the Accidents which have happened in the late War there between the Chriſtians and Indians.

LONDON,
Printed for *William Harris*, next door to the Turn-Stile without *Moor-gate*. 1677.

TITLE OF "STRANGE NEWS FROM VIRGINIA"

arly rebel vanishes from our sight, and whether he perished in the wilderness or made his way to some safer country, we do not know. On a cold day in January his friend Drummond, hiding in White Oak Swamp, was found and taken to the governor. "Aha!" cried the old man, with a low bow, "you are very welcome. I would rather see you just now than any other man in Virginia. Mr. Drummond, you shall be hanged in half an hour!" "What your honour pleases," said the undaunted Scotchman. He was strung up that afternoon, but not until his wife's ring had been pulled from his finger, for rapacity vied with ferocity in the governor's breast. Before the end of January some twenty more had been hanged. An election was then going on, and the newly-elected assembly called upon Berkeley to desist from this carnival of blood. "If we had let him alone," said Presley, the venerable member for Northampton, to T. M., the member for Stafford, "he would have hanged half the country!"

Execution of Drummond

The governor's rage had carried him too far. His conduct did not meet with the approval of the commissioners, whose report on the disturbances is written in a fair and impartial spirit. He treated the commissioners with crazy rudeness. It is said that when they had called on him at Green Spring and were about to return to their boat on the river, he offered them his state-coach with the hangman for driver! whereupon they preferred to walk to the landing-place. Fresh seeds of contention were sown, to bear fruit in the future. The complaints of Drummond's widow and others found their way to the throne. "As I live," quoth the king, "the old fool has put to death more people in that naked country than I did here for the murder of my father." In the spring the royal order for Berkeley's removal arrived, and on April 27 he sailed for England, apparently expecting to return, for he left his wife at Green Spring. Sir Herbert Jeffries, one of the commissioners, succeeded him with a special commission as lieutenant-governor. Berkeley's departure was joyfully celebrated with bonfires and salutes of cannon. He cherished hopes of justifying himself in a personal interview with the king, but the interview was delayed until, about the middle of July, the old man fell sick and died. It was believed that his death was caused by vexation and chagrin. A few weeks afterward the other two commissioners, Sir John Berry and Colonel Morison, returned to England; and we are told that one day the late governor's brother, Lord Berkeley, meeting Sir John Berry in the council chamber, told him, "with an angry voice and a Berkeleyan look," that he and Morison had murdered his brother.[1] In October a royal order for the relief of Sarah Drummond declared that her husband "had been sentenced and put to death contrary to the laws of the kingdom."

Death of Berkeley

Thus ended the first serious and ominous tragedy in the history of the United States, a story preserved for us in many of its details with striking vividness, yet concerning the innermost significance of which we would fain know more than we do. It may fairly be pronounced the most interesting episode in our early history, surpassing in this regard the Leisler affair at New York, which alone can be compared with it for intensity of human interest. As ordinarily told, however, the story of Bacon presents some features that are unintelligible. It is customary to liken the little rebellion of 1676 to the great rebellion of 1776, and we are thus led to contemplate Bacon and Virginia as arrayed against Berkeley and England. In such a view the facts are unduly simplified and strangely distorted. If it were possible thus fully to identify Bacon's cause with the cause of Virginia, it would become impossible to explain the ease with which his followers were suppressed by Virginians, without any aid from England. But when all the facts are considered, we can see at once that such a result was inevitable.

Significance of the rebellion

Careful inspection of the relevant facts will show us that Bacon was contending against four things: —

[1] Neill's *Virginia Carolorum*, p. 379.

1. The Indian depredations.
2. The misrule of Sir William Berkeley.
3. The English navigation laws.
4. The tendency toward oligarchical government which had been rapidly growing since the beginning of the great influx of Cavaliers in 1649.

How far Bacon represented public sentiment in Virginia

Under the first three heads little need be said. The facts have been generally recognized. It was by Bacon's zeal and success in suppressing the Indian power that he acquired public favour. As for the peculation and extortion practised or permitted by Berkeley, it cannot for a moment be supposed that such men as John Washington, Richard Lee, etc., were inclined to tolerate or connive at it. As for the navigation laws, it was a common remark, after the oath at Middle Plantation, that now Virginians might look forward hopefully to trading with all countries. It is therefore altogether probable that on all these grounds the public sentiment of Virginia was overwhelmingly on the side of Bacon.

The leading families were in general opposed to him

Under the fourth head some explanation is needed, for historians have generally overlooked or disregarded it. One of the most conspicuous facts in the story of Bacon's rebellion is the fact that a great majority of the wealthiest and most important men in the colony were opposed to him from first to last. The list of those who were pillaged by his followers is largely a list of the names most honoured in Virginia, the great-grandfathers of the illustrious men who were among the foremost in winning independence for the United States and in building up our federal government. It is also largely a list of the names of Cavaliers who had come from England to Virginia since 1649. The political ideas of these men were

LOWER BRANDON: DINING-ROOM

surely not democratic. If they were devout disbelievers in popular government, the fact is in nowise to their discredit. Popular government is still on its trial in the world, and the last word on the subject has not yet been said. In our day the men who do the most to throw discredit upon it are often those who prate most loudly in its favour; political blatherskites, like the famous "Colonel Yell of Yellville," whose accounts were sadly delinquent though his heart beat with fervour for his native land. The Cavaliers who came to Virginia were staunch and honourable men who believed — with John Winthrop and Edmund Burke and Alexander Hamilton — that society is most prosperous when a select portion of the community governs the whole. Such a doctrine seems to me less defensible than the democratic views of Samuel Adams and Thomas Jefferson and Herbert Spencer, but it is still entitled to all the courtesies of debate. Two centuries ago it was of course the prevailing doctrine.

In the preceding chapter I pointed out that the period of Cavalier immigration, between 1650 and 1670, was characterized by a rapid increase in the dimensions of landed estates and in the employment of servile labour. The same period witnessed a change of an eminently symptomatic kind in local government. In any state the local institutions are the most vitally important part of the whole political structure. Now, as I have already mentioned,[1] the English parish was at an early time reproduced in Virginia, and its authority was exercised by a few chosen men, usually twelve, who constituted a vestry. At first, and until after 1645,[2] the vestrymen were elected by the people of the parish, so that they were analogous to the selectmen of New England. A vestry thus elected is called an open vestry. Now soon after the Long Assembly had begun its sessions in 1661, in the full tide of royalist reaction, we find on its records a statute which transformed the open vestry into a close vestry. In March, 1662, it was enacted that "in case of the death of any vestryman,

Political changes since 1660; the close vestry

[1] See above, p. 30.

[2] Hening's *Statutes*, i. 290.

or his departure out of the parish, . . . the minister and vestry make choice of another to supply his room."[1] The speedy effect of this was to dispense with the popular election and to convert the vestry into a self-perpetuating close corporation. When we consider the great powers wielded by the vestry, we realize the importance of this step. The vestry made up the parish budget, apportioned the taxes, and elected the churchwardens, who were in many places the tax-collectors. By its "processioning of the bounds of every person's land," the vestry exercised control over the record of land-titles. Its supervision of the counting of tobacco was also a function of no mean importance. The vestry also presented the minister for induction. All the local government not in the hands of the vestry was administered by the county court, which consisted of eight justices appointed by the governor. So that when the people lost the power of electing vestrymen they parted with the only share they had in the local government.[2] Nothing was left them except the right to vote for burgesses, and not only was this curtailed in 1670 by a property qualification, but it was of no avail while the Long Assembly lasted, since during those fifteen years there were no elections. That political power should thus rapidly become concentrated in the hands of the leading families was under the circumstances but natural. That the deprivation of suffrage was by many people felt to be a grievance is unquestionable.[3] No testimony can outweigh that of the statute book,

Restriction of the suffrage

[1] Hening's *Statutes*, ii. 45. In the same statute it was further enacted "that none shall be admitted to be of the vestry that doth not take the oath of allegiance and supremacy to his Majesty and subscribe to be conformable to the doctrine and discipline of the Church of England." This effectually excluded Dissenters from taking a part in local government.

[2] See Channing, "Town and County Government in the English Colonies of North America," *J. H. U. Studies*, ii. 484; Howard, *Local Constitutional History of the United States*, i. 388–404.

[3] "We have not had liberty to choose vestrymen wee humbly desire that the wholle parish may have a free election." "Surry County Grievances," *Virginia Magazine*, ii. 172.

and two of the notable acts of Bacon's assembly in June, 1676, were those which restored universal suffrage and the popular election of vestrymen, and limited the terms of service of vestrymen to three years. The first assembly after the rebellion, which met at Green Spring in February, 1677, with Augustine Warner as speaker, declared all the acts of Bacon's assembly null and void. Then in the course of that year and the three years following several of those wholesome acts were reënacted, especially those which related to exorbitant fees and the misuse of public money. Great pains were taken to guard against extortion and corruption,[1] but the provisions concerning vestrymen were not reënacted. A law was passed allowing the freeholders and housekeepers in each parish to elect six "sober and discrete" representatives to sit with the vestry and have equal votes with the vestrymen in assessing the parish taxes; in case the parish should neglect to choose such representatives, or in case they should fail to appear at the time appointed, the vestry was to proceed without them.[2] This act seems to have had little effect, and the law of 1662, which created the close vestry, still remained law after more than a century had passed.[3] As for the right to vote for burgesses, the royal instructions received from Charles II. in January, 1677, restricted it to "ffreeholders, as being more agreeable to the custome of England, to which you are as nigh as you conveniently can to conforme yourselves."[4] According to the same instructions the assembly was to be called together only once in two years, "unlesse some emergent occasion shall make it necessary;" and it was to sit "ffourteene days . . . and noe longer, unlesse you find goode cause to continue it beyond that tyme;" qualifications which could easily be made to defeat the restriction.

The legislation of Bacon's assembly concerning the suf-

[1] See *e.g.* Hening's *Statutes*, ii. 402, 411, 412, 419, 421, 443, 445, 478, 486.

[2] Hening's *Statutes*, ii. 396.

[3] *Laws in Force in 1769*, p. 2.

[4] Id. ii. 425.

frage and the vestries proves that the people whom he represented were not in sympathy with the political and social changes which had been growing up since the middle of the century. These enactments were a protest against the increasing tendency toward a more aristocratic type of society. It was, therefore, natural that a large majority of the aristocrats should have been opposed to Bacon. Doubtless they sympathized with his protests against legislative oppression and official corruption, but they did not approve of his levelling schemes. Their language concerning Bacon's followers shows how they felt about them and toward them.

How the aristocrats regarded Bacon's followers

William Sherwood calls them "ye scum of the Country." [1] According to Philip Ludwell, deputy secretary and member of the council, Bacon "gathers about him a Rabble of the basest sort of People, whose Condicion was such, as by a chaunge could not admitt of worse, wth these he begins to stand at Defyance ag't the Governm't." [2] Again, "Mr. Bacon had Gotten at severall places about 500 men, whose fortune and Inclinations being equally desperate, were ffit for y^e purpose there being not 20 in y^e whole Route, but what were

[1] Sherwood to Sir Joseph Williamson, June 28, 1676, *Virginia Magazine*, i. 171. Sherwood was a gentleman, probably educated as a lawyer, who had been convicted of robbery in England and pardoned through the intercession of Sir Joseph Williamson, secretary of state. (As to gentlemen robbers, compare the reference to Sir John Popham, above, vol. i. p. 84 of the present work.) Sherwood became attorney-general of Virginia in 1677, and was for thirty years an esteemed member of society.

[2] Ludwell to Sir Joseph Williamson, June 28, 1676, *Virginia Magazine*, i. 179.

Idle & will not worke, or such whose Debaucherie or Ill Husbandry has brought in Debt beyond hopes or thought of payment these are the men that are sett up ffor the Good of ye Countrey; who for ye ease of the poore will have noe taxes paied, though for ye most p[t] of them, they pay none themselves, would have all magistracie & Governm'nt taken away & sett up one themselves, & to make their Good Intentions more manifest *stick not to talk openly of shareing mens Estates among themselves,*[1] with these (being Drawne together) Mr. Bacon marches speedly toward the towne, etc." [2] Governor Berkeley's testimony should not be omitted; he wrote to the king in June, "I have above thirty-five years governed the most flourishing country the sun ever shone over, but am now encompassed with rebellion like waters in every respect like to that of Masaniello except their leader." [3] In other words, the rebels were a mere rabble, except their leader, who was not a humble fisherman like the Italian, but a gentleman of high birth and breeding. According to the careful and fair-minded commissioners, Bacon "seduced the Vulgar and most ignorant People (two-thirds of each county being of that Sort) Soe that theire whole hearts and hopes were set now upon" him.[4]

The real state of the case

Allowance for prejudice must of course be made in considering the general statements of hostile witnesses, such as Berkeley and Sherwood and Philip Ludwell. It is quite clear that Bacon's followers were by no means all of the baser sort. This is distinctly recognized in a letter to the king by Thomas Ludwell and Robert Smith, containing proposals for reducing the rebels. In a certain event, they say, "there will be a speedy separation of the

[1] In other words, they entertained communistic ideas. I have italicised the statement, to mark its importance.

[2] The same letter, *Virginia Magazine*, i. 183.

[3] T. M.'s Narrative, *Virginia Historical Register*, iii. 126. It will be remembered that Masaniello's insurrection occurred in 1647, and was thus fresh in men's memories. Masaniello was twenty-four years of age, and was murdered in his hour of apparent triumph.

[4] "A True Narrative," etc., *Virginia Magazine*, iv. 125.

sound parts from the rabble." [1] Here we have an explicit admission that there was a "sound part." It will be remembered that Drummond had been a colonial governor, and that his house and Lawrence's were the best in Jamestown. The officers we have met in the story, Hansford and Bland and Cheesman, were men of good family; and among the foremost men in the colony we are told that Colonel George Mason was inclined to sympathize with the insurgents.[2] In this he was clearly by no means alone. On the whole, however, there can be no doubt that Bacon's cause was to a considerable extent the cause of the poor against the rich, of the humble folk against the grandees.

When we take into account this aspect of the case, which has never received the attention it deserves, the whole story becomes consistent and intelligible. The years preceding the rebellion were such as are commonly called "hard times." People felt poor and saw fortunes made by corrupt officials; the fault was with the Navigation Act and with the debauched civil service of Charles II. and Berkeley. Besides these troubles, which were common to all, the poorer people felt oppressed by taxation in regard to which they were not consulted and for which they seemed to get no service in return.[3] The distribution of taxation by polls, equal amounts for rich and for poor, was

Effect of hard times

[1] *Virginia Magazine*, i. 433.

[2] See Miss Rowland's admirable *Life of George Mason*, 1725-1792, New York, 1892, i. 17.

[3] From the list of Surry grievances we may cite "6. That the 2 s per hhd Imposed by ye 128th act for the payment of his majestyes officers & other publique debts thereby to ease his majestyes poore subjects of their great taxes : wee humblely desire that an account may be given thereof. . . . 10. That it has been the custome of County Courts att the laying of the levy to withdraw into a private Roome by wch meanes the poore people not knowing for what they paid their levy did allways admire how their taxes could be so high. Wee most humbly pray that for the future the County levy may be laid publickly in the Court house." From the Isle of Wight grievances, "21. Wee doe also desire to know for what purpose or use the late publique leavies of 50 pounds of tobacco and cask per poll and the 12 pound per polle is for

resented as a cruel injustice.[1] The subject of taxation was closely connected with the Indian troubles, for people paid large sums for military defence and nevertheless saw their houses burned and their families massacred. Under these circumstances the sudden appearance of the brave and eloquent Bacon seemed to open the way of salvation. The indomitable queller of Indians could also curb the tyrant. Naturally, along with a more respectable element, the rabble gathered under his standard; it is always the case in revolutions with the men who have little or nothing to lose. It is likewise usual for men with much property at stake to be conservative on such occasions. Philip Ludwell's statement, that some of the rebels entertained communistic notions, is just what one might have expected. There is always more or less socialist tomfoolery at such times. In some of its aspects there is a resemblance between Bacon's rebellion and that of Daniel Shays in Massachusetts one hundred and ten years later. But the Massachusetts leader was a weak and silly creature, and his resistance to government had nothing to justify it, though there were palliating circumstances. The course of Bacon, on the other hand, was in the main a justifiable protest against misgovernment, and until after the oath at Middle Plantation a great deal of the sound sentiment in Virginia must have sympathized with him. In the unwillingness of some of the gentlemen present to take the oath, we seem to see the first ebbing of the tide. Evidently there began to be, as Thomas Ludwell had predicted, "a separation of the sound parts from the rabble;" and this appears very distinctly in the defection of Goode about four weeks later.

Populist aspects of the rebellion

Its sound aspects

In the intention of resisting the king's troops, which thus

and what benefit wee are to have for it." *Virginia Magazine*, ii. 171, 172, 389.

[1] Isle of Wright grievances, "16. Also wee desire that evrie man may be taxed according to the tracks [tracts] of Land they hold." *Virginia Magazine*, ii. 388.

weakened Bacon's position, he certainly showed more zeal than judgment. It has the look of the courage that comes from desperation. Had he lived to persist in this course, the policy most likely to strengthen him would have been to make his foremost demand the repeal of the Navigation Act which all Virginians detested and even Berkeley disapproved. But it is not likely that anything could have saved him from defeat and the scaffold. Death seems to have intervened in kindness to him and to Virginia.[1]

In the early history of our country Bacon must ever remain one of the bright and attractive figures. Our heart is always with the man who boldly stands out against corruption and oppression. To many persons the name of rebel seems fraught with blame and reproach; but the career of mankind so abounds in examples of heroic resistance to intolerable wrongs that to any one familiar with history the name of rebel is often a title of honour. Bacon's brief career was an episode in the perennial fight against taxation without representation, the ancient abuse of living on other men's labour. We cannot fail to admire his quick incisiveness, his cool head, his determined courage; and the spectacle of this young Cavalier taking the lead, like Tiberius Gracchus, in a movement for justice and liberty will always make a pleasing picture.

[1] "One proclamation commanded all men in the land on pain of death to joine him, and retire into the wildernesse upon arrival of the forces expected from England, and oppose them untill they should propose or accept to treat of an accomodation, which we who lived comfortably could not have undergone, so as the whole land must have become an Aceldama if god's exceeding mercy had not timely removed him." So says T. M., whose narrative is by no means unfriendly to Bacon.

CHAPTER XII

WILLIAM AND MARY

BETWEEN the breaking out of Bacon's rebellion in the summer of 1676 and the Declaration of Independence, the interval was exactly a hundred years. It was for Virginia a century of political education. It prepared her for the great work to come, and it brought her into sympathy more or less effective with other colonies that were struggling with similar political questions, especially with Massachusetts. It was in that same year, 1676, that Charles II. sent Edward Randolph to Boston, to enforce the Navigation Act and to report upon New England affairs in general. This mission of Randolph led to quarrels which resulted in the overthrow of the charter and the sending of royal governors to Massachusetts. From that time forth the legislatures of Massachusetts and Virginia had to contend with similar questions concerning the powers and prerogatives of the royal governors, so that the two colonies kept a close watch upon each other's proceedings, while both received a thorough training in constitutional politics. Amid such circumstances came into existence the necessary conditions for the establishment of political independence and the formation of our Federal Union.

Political education

The suppression of Bacon's rebellion was far from equivalent to a surrender to Charles II. or his representatives. Questions of privilege soon arose, and it was not long before Berkeley's most efficient officer came himself to be regarded almost in the light of a rebel. Major Robert Beverley, of Beverley in Yorkshire, an ardent royalist, had come to Virginia in 1663. He was elected clerk of the

Robert Beverley

House of Burgesses in 1670, and held that office for many years. No one was more active in stamping out rebellion in the autumn of 1676, but after the arrival of the royal commissioners he was soon at feud with them. As the disturbances had been quieted without the aid of their troops, there was a disposition to resent their coming as an interference, especially as they seemed to lend too ready an ear to the complaints of the malcontents. In the list of grievances of Gloucester County we find "a complaint against Major Robert Beverley that when the country had (according to Order) raised 60 armed men to be an Outguard for the Governor — who not finding the Governor nor their appointed Comander they were by Beverly comanded to goe to work, fall trees and maule and toate railes, which many of them refusing to doe, he presently disbanded them & sent them home at a tyme when the countrey were infested by the Indians, who had a little before cut off six persons in one family, and attempted others." Upon this the commissioners remarked, "Wee conceive this dealing of Beverly's to be a notorious abuse and Grievance, to take away the peoples armes while ther famlies were cutt off by the Indians, and they deserve just reparation here." But Berkeley declared that what Beverley had done was by his orders, and the newly elected House of Burgesses stood by its clerk. After Berkeley had sailed for England, in April, 1677, the commissioners called upon the House of Burgesses to give up its journals for their inspection, and Beverley refused to comply with the demand. No king in England, said the burgesses, would venture to make such a demand of the House of Commons. Then the commissioners seized the journals, and the burgesses indignantly voted that such an act was a violation of privilege. This enraged the king, and in February, 1679, the privy council ordered that Beverley should be removed from office.

His refusal to give up the journals

A change of governors, however, altered the situation. After Jeffries and Chichely, who served but a year each, came Lord Culpeper, whom Charles II. had undertaken to make co-proprietor of Virginia, along with the Earl of Arlington. Culpeper was an average specimen of the public officials of the time, fairly agreeable and easy-going, but rapacious and utterly unprincipled. In one respect he might be contrasted unfavourably with all the governors since Harvey. Such men as Bennett and Mathews and Berkeley looked upon Virginia as home. After his own fashion the tyrannical Berkeley had the interest of Virginia at heart. But Culpeper regarded the Virginians simply as people to be fleeced. Through four years of chronic brawl he kept coming and going, coming to manage the assembly and returning to consult with the king. Charles wished to have the power of initiating legislation taken away from the burgesses. All laws were to be drafted by the governor and council, and then sent to England for the royal approval, before being submitted to the burgesses. With such an arduous task before him, it was wise for Culpeper to avoid giving needless offence; and seeing the high regard in which Beverley was held, he caused the order for his removal to be revoked.

Lord Culpeper

The evil effects of the Navigation Act still continued. In 1679 the tobacco crop was so large that a considerable surplus was left over till the next year unsold. In 1680 the surplus was still greater, so that there was evidently more than enough to supply the English market for two years. The assembly therefore proposed to order a cessation of planting for the year 1681, but on account of the customs revenue it was necessary to obtain the king's assent to such an order. By the same token the assent was refused, and great was the indignation in Virginia. The price of tobacco had fallen so low that, according to Nicholas Spencer, a whole year's crop would not so much as buy the clothes which people needed.[1] The distress was like that which was caused in the War of Independence by the Continental currency and the rag money issued by the several states. It was the kind of sickness that has always

The Plant-cutters' Riot, 1682

[1] Bruce, *Economic History of Virginia*, i. 402.

come and always will come with "cheap money." Culpeper insisted that the only chance of relief was in exporting beef, pork, and grain to the West Indies. A more effective measure would have been the repeal of the Navigation Act. In

LORD CULPEPER

the spring of 1682, on the petition of several counties, the assembly was convened for the purpose of ordering a cessation of planting. Amid great popular excitement the assembly adjourned without taking any decisive action. Then a fury for destroying the young plants seized upon the people. "The growing tobacco of one plantation was no sooner destroyed than the owner, having been deprived either with or without his consent of his crop, was seized with the same frenzy and ran with the crowd as it marched to destroy the crop of his neighbour."[1] The contagion spread until ten

[1] Bruce, *Economic History of Virginia*, i. 405; Hening's *Statutes*, ii. 562.

thousand hogsheads of tobacco had been destroyed. In Gloucester, where the most damage was done, two hundred plantations were laid waste. The riot was suppressed by the militia, three ringleaders were hung, and the rest pardoned. One, we are told, received pardon on condition that he should build a bridge.[1]

This was contracting the currency with a vengeance, but it produced the desired effect. In 1683 the purchasing power of tobacco was greatly increased, and a feeling of contentment returned. But the destruction of the plants served to heighten the king's indignation at Culpeper's ill success in curtailing the power of the burgesses. Culpeper tried to play a double part and appear complaisant to the assembly without offending the king. Consequently he pleased nobody, and early in 1684 he was removed. Shortly afterward the king confirmed him in the possession of the territory known as the Northern Neck, and he relinquished all proprietary claims upon the rest of Virginia in exchange for a pension of £600 yearly for twenty years.

Culpeper's removal

Culpeper's successor was Lord Howard of Effingham, an unworthy descendant of Elizabeth's gallant admiral. He was as greedy and dishonest as Culpeper, without his conciliatory temper. The difference between the two has been aptly compared to the difference between Charles II. and his brother. Howard was indeed as domineering and wrong-headed as James II., and rapacious besides. He treated public opinion with contempt. His administration was noted for corruption and tyranny. No accounts were rendered of the use of public funds, and men were arbitrarily sent to jail. Howard went so far as to claim the right to repeal the acts of the assembly, and over this point there was hot contention. The subject of "plant-cutting," or the destruction of growing tobacco, came up again, and the crown was enabled in one and the same act to wreak its vengeance upon an eminent victim and to aim a blow at the independence of the House of Burgesses.

Lord Howard of Effingham

[1] Doyle's *Virginia*, p. 261.

Robert Beverley, as we have seen, had incurred the royal displeasure by refusing to hand over to the commissioners the journals of the House of Burgesses. In 1682 he was strongly in favour of a cessation of planting, and accordingly it suited the purposes of his enemies to point to him as the prime instigator of the plant-cutting riots. On this accusation he was turned out of office and several times imprisoned. At last, just after Lord Howard's arrival, he was set free after asking pardon on his

More trouble for Beverley

LORD HOWARD OF EFFINGHAM

bended knees and giving security for future good behaviour. A statute passed about this time made plant-cutting high treason, punishable with death and confiscation.[1]

As soon as Beverley was set free the House of Burgesses again chose him for its clerk. But presently Lord Howard tried to get the burgesses to allow him to levy a tax, and

[1] Hening's *Statutes*, iii. 10.

in the course of the quarrel sundry trumped-up charges were brought against Beverley, so that in 1686 James II. instructed Howard to declare him incapable of holding any office of public trust. The same letter ordered that henceforth the clerk of the House of Burgesses should be appointed by the governor.[1]

It is worthy of note that the most despicable and lawless of modern English kings did not venture to deny the right of Virginians to tax themselves by their own representatives. Howard's instructions merely authorized him to "recommend" certain measures to the assembly. His attempt to get permission to levy a tax independently of the burgesses was such a recommendation. However arrogant and illegal in spirit, it still conceded to the colonists the constitutional principle over which the fatuous George III. and his rotten-borough parliaments were to try to ride rough-shod.

For stupid audacity James II. was outdone by George III.

By 1688 Howard concluded that it would be pleasant and comfortable for him to live on his governor's salary in England and send out a deputy-governor to deal with refractory burgesses. When he arrived in England he found William and Mary on the throne, but they showed no disposition to interfere with his plans. Just the right sort of man for deputy-governor appeared at the right moment. Francis Nicholson had held that position in New York under the viceroy of united New York and New England, Sir Edmund Andros. When that unpopular viceroy was deposed and cast into jail in Boston, Nicholson was deposed in New York by Jacob Leisler, and went to England with the tale of his woes, which King William sought to assuage by sending him to Virginia as deputy-governor.

Francis Nicholson

Nicholson was a man of integrity and fair ability, though highly eccentric and cantankerous. "Laws of Virginia," he cried one day, seizing the attorney-general by the lapel of his

[1] Doyle's *Virginia*, pp. 259-265; Stanard, "Robert Beverley and his Descendants," *Virginia Magazine*, ii. 405-413; Hening's *Statutes*, iii. 41, 451-571.

JAMES II

silk robe, "I know no laws of Virginia! I know my commands are going to be obeyed here!" At another time he told the council that they were "mere brutes who understood not manners, . . . that he would beat them into better manners and make them feel that he was governor of Virginia."[1]

His manners

In spite of his queer peppery ways, the rule of Nicholson

[1] *William and Mary College Quarterly*, i. 66.

was a decided relief after such worthless creatures as Culpeper and Howard. It is chiefly memorable for the founding of the second American college, a work which encountered such obstacles on both sides of the ocean as only an iron will could vanquish. Such was found in the person of James Blair, a Scotch clergyman, who in 1689 was appointed commissioner of the Church in Virginia. The need for a bishop was felt, and a little later there was some talk of sending out the famous Jonathan Swift in that capacity, but no Episcopal bishopric was created in America until after the War of Independence. Dr. Blair had a seat in the colonial council, presided at ecclesiastical trials, and exercised many of the powers of a bishop. Since the old scheme of Nicholas Ferrar and his friends for a college in Virginia had been extinguished amid lurid scenes of Indian massacre, nearly seventy years had elapsed[1] when Blair in 1691 revived it. He began by collecting some £2500 by subscription, and then went to England to get more money and obtain a charter. He was aided by two famous divines, Tillotson, Archbishop of Canterbury, and Stillingfleet, Bishop of Worcester, but from the treasury commissioner, Sir Edward Seymour, he received a coarse rebuff, which shows the frankly materialistic view at that time entertained by the British official mind regarding England's colonies. When Blair urged that a college was needed for training up clergymen, Seymour thought it was no time to be sending money to America for such purposes; every penny was wanted in Europe for carrying on the necessary and righteous war against Louis XIV. Blair could not deny that it was an eminently righteous war, but he was not thus to be turned from his purpose. "You must not forget," said he, "that people in Virginia have souls to save, as well as people in England." "Souls!" cried Seymour, "damn your souls! Grow tobacco!" In spite of this discouraging view of the case, the good doctor persevered until

James Blair, founder of William and Mary College

[1] From time to time there had been futile attempts to take up the matter afresh; see, for example, Hening's *Statutes*, ii. 30.

James Blair

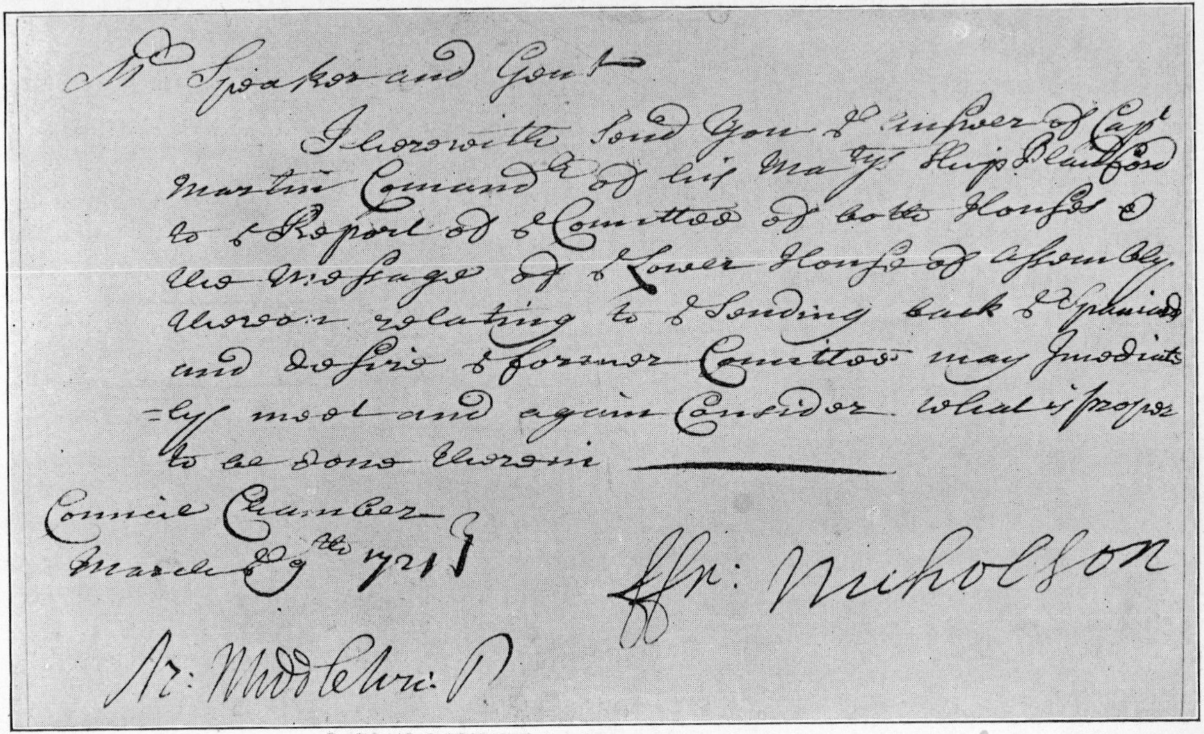

Mr Speaker and Gent

I herewith send You ye answer of Capt Martin Comandr of his Matys Ship Blanford to ye Report of ye Comittee of both Houses & the Message of ye Lower House of Assembly thereon relating to ye sending back ye Spaniards and desire ye former Comittee may Imediate=ly meet and again Consider what is proper to be done therein

Council Chamber
March ye 9th 1721

Fr: Nicholson

Ar: Middleton P

AUTOGRAPH OF FRANCIS NICHOLSON

he obtained from William and Mary the charter that founded the college ever since known by their names.

The college was established in 1693, with Blair for its president.[1] Governor Nicholson, with seventeen other persons appointed by the assembly, formed the board of trustees. From the outset Nicholson was warmly in sympathy with the enterprise, but now this friend was called away for a time. In the anti-Catholic fervour which attended the accession of King William and Queen Mary, the palatinate government in Maryland had been overturned, and the new royal governor, Sir Lionel Copley, died in 1693. Nicholson was then promoted from deputy-governor of Virginia to be

EARLY VIEW OF WILLIAM AND MARY COLLEGE

governor of Maryland. About the same time Lord Howard of Effingham resigned or was removed, and Sir Edmund Andros was sent out to Virginia as governor. It may seem a strange appointment in view of the obloquy which Andros had incurred at the north. But in all these appointments William III. seems

Nicholson succeeded by Sir Edmund Andros

[1] Dr. Blair held the presidency for fifty years, until his death in 1743.

A List of Debtors to the Estate of Collon^ll Frances Lovelace In the books of Isar Bedlow deceased Inhabiting In Gravesend upon Long Island /

Catalina Barents	f 77 : —
Micha: Spicer	208 : 8
George: Cumens	127 : —
Richard: Hardey	113 : 4
Charles: Morgan	80 : 12
Capt. Wilkins	141 : 10
Samuell: Spicer	320 : —

By the Governour

You are hereby desired and required to give notice to ye above persons of yor Towne, That they appeare and pay to Mr Philip Wells in ye fort ye summes herein menconed, being ye ballance of their Accts in Mr Isaak Bedloo's books, or to summon them in his Maties Name to answer their neglect at ye Next Genall Court of Assizes to be held in this City, beginning ye 4th day of ye next month in default att their Perills: when also you are to make a returne of this Warrt Given under my hand in New York this 25th of Sept. 1676.

To ye Constable and Overseers of Gravesend.

Andros

DOCUMENT BEARING AUTOGRAPH OF SIR EDMUND ANDROS

to have acted upon a consistent policy of not disturbing, except in cases of necessity, the state of things which he found. As a rule he retained in his service the old officials against whom no grave charges were brought ; and while the personality of Andros was not prepossessing, there can be no doubt as to his integrity.

Nicholson's career as royal governor of Maryland lasted until 1698, while Andros was having a hard time in Virginia trying to enforce with rigour the Navigation Act and to make life miserable for Dr. Blair. His conduct was far more moderate than it had been in New England, but he had his full share of trouble in Virginia. The moving cause of his hostility to the college of William and Mary is not distinctly assigned, but he is not unlikely to have believed, like many a dullard of his stripe, that education is apt to encourage a seditious and froward spirit. He did everything he could think of to thwart and annoy President Blair. At the election of burgesses he predicted that the establishment of a college would be sure to result in a terrible increase of taxes. He tried to persuade subscribers to withhold the payment of their subscriptions. He sought to arouse an absurd prejudice against Scotchmen, for which it was rather late in the day. Finally he connived at gross insults to the president and friends of the college. Among the young men to whom Andros showed especial favour was Daniel Parke, whose grandson, Daniel Parke Custis, is now remembered as the first husband of Martha Washington. This young Daniel did some things to which posterity could hardly point with pride. He is described as a "sparkish gentleman," or as some would say a slashing blade. He was an expert with the rapier and anxious to thrust it between the ribs of people who supported the college. His challenges were numerous, but clergymen could not be reached in such a way. So "he set up a claim to the pew in church in which Mrs. Blair sat, and one Sunday," as we are told, "with fury and violence he pulled her out of it in the presence of the minister and congregation,

Andros quarrels with Blair

who were greatly scandalized at this ruffian and profane action."[1]

This was going too far. The stout Scotchman had power-

COLONEL DANIEL PARKE

ful friends in London; the outrage was discussed in Lambeth Palace; and Sir Edmund Andros, for winking at such behaviour, was removed. He was evidently a slow-witted official. His experiences in Boston, with Parson Willard of the Old South, ought to have cured him of his propensity to quarrel with aggressive and resolute clergymen. For two or three years after going home, Sir Edmund governed the little channel island of Jersey, and the rest of his days were spent in retirement, until his death in 1714.

Removal of Andros

[1] *William and Mary College Quarterly*, i. 65.

The system of absentee governors, occasionally exemplified in such cases as those of Lord Delaware and Lord Howard, was now to be permanently adopted. A great favourite with William III. was George Hamilton Douglas, whose distinguished gallantry at the battle of the Boyne and other occasions had been rewarded with the earldom of Orkney. In 1697 he was appointed governor-in-chief of Virginia, and for the next forty years he drew his annual salary of £1200 without ever crossing the ocean. Henceforth the official who represented him in Virginia was entitled lieutenant-governor, and the first was Francis Nicholson, who was brought back from Maryland in 1698.

Earl of Orkney

One of Nicholson's achievements in Maryland, as we shall see in the next chapter, had been the change of the seat of government from St. Mary's to Annapolis. He now proceeded to make a similar change in Virginia. After perishing in Bacon's rebellion, Jamestown was rebuilt by Lord Culpeper, but in the last decade of the century it was again destroyed by an accidental fire, and has never since risen from its ashes. Of that sacred spot, the first abiding-place of Englishmen in America, nothing now is left but the ivy-mantled ruins of the church tower and a few cracked and crumbling tombstones. The site of the hamlet is more than half submerged, and unless some kind of sea-wall is built to protect it, the unresting tides will soon wash everything away.[1] Jamestown had always a bad reputation for malaria, and after its second burning people were

Return of Nicholson

[1] I leave this as it was first written a few years ago, and take pleasure in adding to it the following quotation from Mr. Bruce: "That the entire site of the town will not finally sink beneath the waves of the river will be due to the measures of protection which the National Government have adopted at the earnest solicitation of the *Association for the Preservation of Virginia Antiquities*. This organization is performing a noble and sacred work in rescuing so many of the ancient landmarks of the state from ruin, a work into which it has thrown a zeal, energy, and intelligence entitling it to the honour and gratitude of all who are interested in the history, not merely of Virginia, but of America itself." *Economic History of Virginia*, ii. 562.

not eager to restore it. Plans for moving the government elsewhere had been considered on more than one occasion. In 1699 the choice fell upon the site of Middle Plantation, half way between James and York rivers, with its salubrious air and wholesome water. It had already, in 1693, been selected as the site of the new college.[1] Nicholson called the place Williamsburg, and began building a town there with streets so laid out as to make W and M, the initials of the king and queen, a plan soon abandoned

Founding of Williamsburg

GEORGE HAMILTON DOUGLAS, EARL OF ORKNEY

as inconvenient. The town thus founded by Nicholson remained the capital of Virginia until 1780, when it was superseded by Richmond.

Nicholson was in full sympathy with President Blair as regarded the college, but occasions for disagreement between them were at hand. On the lieutenant-governor's arrival the wise parson read him a lesson upon the

Nicholson and Blair

[1] Hening's *Statutes*, iii. 122.

need for moderation in the display of his powers. The career of his predecessor Andros, in more than one colony, furnished abundant examples of the need for such moderation. Blair offered him some good advice tendered by the Bishop of London, whereupon Nicholson exclaimed, with a big round oath, "I know how to govern Virginia and Maryland better than all the bishops in England. If I had not hampered them in Maryland and kept them under, I should never have been able to govern them." The doctor replied: "Sir, I do not pretend to [speak for] Maryland, but if I know anything of Virginia, they are a good-natured [and] tractable people as any in the world, and you may do anything with them by way of civility, but you will never be able to manage them in that way you speak of, by hampering and keeping them under."[1] The eccentric governor did not profit by this advice. Of actual tyranny there was not much in his administration, but his blustering tongue would give utterance to extravagant speeches whereat company would sit "amazed and silent."

PIECE OF SIXTEENTH CENTURY ARMOR UNEARTHED AT JAMESTOWN

At last in a laughable way this blustering habit proved his ruin. Not far from Williamsburg lived Major Lewis Burwell, who had married a cousin of the rebel Bacon and had a whole houseful of blooming daughters. With one of these young ladies the worshipful governor fell madly in love, but to his unspeakable chagrin she promptly and decisively refused him. Poor Nicholson could not keep the matter to himself, but raved about it in public. He suspected that Dr. Blair's brother was a favoured rival and threatened the whole family with dire vengeance. He swore

A scolding swain

[1] *William and Mary College Quarterly*, i. 66.

that if Miss Burwell should undertake to marry anybody but himself, he would "cut the throats of three men: the bridegroom, the minister, and the justice who issued the license." This truculent speech got reported in London, and one of Nicholson's friends wrote him a letter counselling him not to be so unreasonable, but to remember that English women were the freest in the world, and that Virginia was not like those heathen Turkish countries where tender ladies were dragged into the arms of some pasha still reeking with the blood of their nearest relatives. But nothing could quiet the fury of a "governor scorned;" and one day when he suspected the minister of Hampton parish of being his rival, he went up to him and knocked his hat off. This sort of thing came to be too much for Dr. Blair; a memorial was sent to Queen Anne, and Nicholson was recalled to England in 1705. Afterwards we find him commanding the expedition which in 1710 captured the Acadian Port Royal from the French. He then served as governor of the newly conquered Nova Scotia and afterwards of South Carolina, was knighted, rose to the rank of lieutenant-general, and died in 1728.

Removal of Nicholson

Meanwhile the college of William and Mary, in which Nicholson felt so much interest, was flourishing. Unfortunately its first hall, designed by Sir Christopher Wren, was destroyed by fire in 1705, but it was before long replaced by another. Until 1712 the faculty consisted of the president, a grammar master, writing master, and an usher; in that year a professor of mathematics was added. By 1729 there were six professors. Fifty years later the departments of law and medicine were added, and the name "College" was replaced by "University."[1]

The college

As in the case of Harvard, it was hoped that this college might prove effective in converting and educating Indians. In 1723 Brafferton Hall was built for their use, from a fund

[1] *William and Mary College Quarterly*, ii. 65.

given by Robert Boyle, the famous chemist. It is still standing and used as a dormitory. We are told that the "Queen of Pamunkey" sent her son to college with a boy to wait upon him, and likewise two chiefs' sons, "all handsomely cloathed after the Indian fashion;"[1] but as to any effects wrought upon the barbarian mind by this Christian institution of learning, there is nothing to which we can point.

Indian students

The first Commencement exercises were held in the year 1700, and it is said that not only were Virginians and Indians present on that gala day, but so great was the fame of it that people came in sloops from Maryland and Pennsylvania, and even from New York.[2] The journals of what we may call the "faculty meetings" throw light upon the manner of living at the college. There is a matron, or housekeeper, who is thus carefully instructed: "1. That you never concern yourself with any of the Boys only when you have a Complaint against any of them, and then that you make it to his or their proper Master. — 2. That there be always both fresh and salt Meat for Dinner; and twice in the Week, as well as on Sunday in particular, that there be either Puddings or Pies besides; that there be always Plenty of Victuals; that Breakfast, Dinner, and Supper be serv'd up in the cleanest and neatest manner possible; and for this Reason the Society not only allow but desire you to get a Cook; that the Boys Suppers be not as usual made up of different Scraps, but that there be at each Table the same Sor[t]: and when there is cold fresh Meat enough, that it be often hashed for them; that when they are sick, you yourself see their Victuals before it be carry'd to them, that it be clean, decent, and fit for them; that the Person appointed to take Care of them be constantly with them, and give their Medicine regularly. The general Complaints of the Visitors, and other Gentlemen throughout the whole Colony, plainly shew the Necessity of a strict and

Instructions to the housekeeper

[1] *Williams and Mary College Quarterly*, i. 187.

[2] Cooke's *Virginia*, p. 306.

regular Compliance with the above Directions. . . . 4. That a proper Stocking-mender be procured to live in or near the college, and as both Masters and Boys complain of losing their Stockings, you are desired to look over their Notes given with their Linnen to the Wash, both at the Delivery and Return of them. . . . 5. That the Negroes be trusted with no keys; . . . that fresh Butter be look'd out for in Time, that the Boys may not be forced to eat salt in Summer. — 6. As we all know that Negroes will not perform their Duties without the Mistress' constant Eye, especially in so large a Family as the College, and as we all observe You going abroad more frequently than even the Mistress of a private Family can do without the affairs of her province greatly suffering, We particularly request it of you, that your

MEDAL PRESENTED BY JAMES II. TO THE "KING OF POTOWMACKS"

visits for the future in Town and Country may not be so frequent, by which Means we doubt not but Complaints will be greatly lessened." [1]

At another meeting it is ordered "y^{t} no scholar belonging to any school in the College, of w^{t} Age, Rank, or Quality, soever, do keep any race Horse at y^{e}. College, in ye Town — or any where in the neighbourhood — y^{t} they be not anyway concerned in making races, or in backing, or abetting, those made by others, and y^{t} all Race Horses, kept in ye neighbourhood of ye College & be-

Horse-racing prohibited

[1] *William and Mary College Quarterly*, iii. 263.

longing to any of ye scholars, be immediately dispatched & sent off, & never again brought back, and all of this under Pain of ye severest Animadversion and Punishment."

There is a stress in the wording of this order which makes one suspect that the faculty had encountered difficulty in suppressing horse-racing. Similar orders forbid students to take part in cock-fighting, to frequent "ye Ordinaries," to bet, to play at billiards, or to bring cards or dice into the college. Punishment is most emphatically threatened for any student who may "presume to go out of ye Bounds of ye College, particularly towards the mill pond" without express leave; but why the mill pond was to be so sedulously shunned, we are left to conjecture. Finally, "to ye End yt no Person may pretend Ignorance of ye foregoing . . . Regulations, . . . it is Ordered . . . yt a clear & legible copy of ym be posted up in every School of ye College."[1]

Other prohibitions

One of the brightest traditions in the history of the college is that which tells of the wooing and wedding of Parson Camm, a gentleman famous once, whose fame deserves to be revived. John Camm was born in 1718 and educated at Trinity College, Cambridge. He was a man of good scholarship and sturdy character, an uncompromising Tory, one of the leaders in that "Parsons' Cause" which made Patrick Henry famous.[2] He lived to be the last president of William and Mary before the Revolution. After he had attained middle age, but while he was as yet only a preacher and professor, and like all professors in those days at William and Mary a bachelor, there came to him the romance which brightened his life. Among those who listened to his preaching was Miss Betsy Hansford, of the family of Hansford the rebel and martyr. A young friend, who had wooed Miss Betsy without success, persuaded the worthy parson to aid him with his eloquence. But it was in vain that Mr. Camm besieged the young lady with texts

The story of Parson Camm

[1] *William and Mary College Quarterly*, ii. 55, 56.

[2] See my *American Revolution*, i. 17, 18.

from the Bible enjoining matrimony as a duty. She proved herself able to beat him at his own game when she suggested that if the parson would go home and look at 2 Samuel xii. 7, he might be able to divine the reason of her obduracy.

MRS. JAMES BLAIR

When Mr. Camm proceeded to search the Scriptures he found these significant words staring him in the face : "And Nathan said to David, *Thou art the man!*" The sequel is told in an item of the Virginia Gazette, announcing the marriage of Rev. John Camm and Miss Betsy Hansford.[1]

So, Virginia, too, had its Priscilla! In the words of the sweet mediæval poem :—

El fait que dame, et si fait bien,
Car sos ciel n'a si france rien

[1] This charming story is only one of many good things for which I am indebted to President L. G. Tyler; see *William and Mary College Quarterly*, i. 11.

Com est dame qui violt amer,
Quant Deus la violt à ço torner:
Deus totes dames beneie.[1]

But this marriage was an infringement of the customs of the college, and was rebuked in an order that *hereafter* the marriage of a professor should *ipso facto* vacate his office.

The college founded by James Blair was a most valuable centre for culture for Virginia, and has been remarkable in many ways. It was the first college in America to introduce teaching by lectures, and the elective system of study; it was the first to unite a group of faculties into a university; it was the second in the English world to have a chair of Municipal Law, George Wythe coming to such a professorship a few years after Sir William Blackstone; it was the first in America to establish a chair of History and Political Science; and it was one of the first to pursue a thoroughly secular and unsectarian policy. Though until lately its number of students at any one time had never reached one hundred and fifty, it has given to our country fifteen senators and seventy representatives in congress; seventeen governors of states, and thirty-seven judges; three presidents of the United States, — Jefferson, Monroe, and Tyler; and the great Chief Justice Marshall.[2] It was a noble work for America that was done by the Scotch parson, James Blair.

Some interesting facts about the college

As for Governor Nicholson who was so deeply interested in that work, he played a memorable part in the history of the United States, which deserves mention before we leave the subject of his connection with Virginia. When he was first transferred from the governorship of New York to that of the Old Dominion, with his head full of experiences gained in New York, he proposed a grand Union of the English colonies for mutual

Nicholson's schemes for a union of the colonies

[1] *Partonopeus de Blois*, 1250, ed. Crapelet, tom. i. p. 45. "She acts like a woman, and so does well, for under the heavens there is nothing so daring as the woman who loves, when God wills to turn her that way: God bless the ladies all!"

[2] *William and Mary College Annual Catalogue*, 1894–95.

defence against the encroachments of the French. King William approved the scheme and recommended it to the favourable consideration of the colonial assemblies. But a desire for union was not strong in any of these bodies, and as for Virginia, she was too remote from the Canadian border to feel warmly interested in it. The act of 1695, authorizing the governor to apply £500 from the liquor excise to the relief of New York, shows a notably generous spirit in the Virginia burgesses, but the pressure which was to drive people into a Federal Union was still in the hidden future. The attitude of the several colonies so exasperated Nicholson as to lead him to recommend that they should all be placed under a single viceroy and taxed for the support of a standing army. When this plan was submitted to Queen Anne and her ministers, it was rejected as unwise, and no British ministry ever ventured to try any part of such a policy until the reign of George III. Francis Nicholson should be remembered as one of the very first to conceive and suggest the policy that afterward drove the colonies into their Declaration of Independence.

CHAPTER XIII

MARYLAND'S VICISSITUDES

THE accession of William and Mary, which wrought so little change in Virginia, furnished the occasion for a revolution in the palatinate of Maryland. To trace the causes of this revolution, we must return to 1658, the year which witnessed the death of Oliver Cromwell and saw Lord Baltimore's government firmly set upon its feet through the favour of that mighty potentate. The compromises which were then adopted put an end to the conflict between Virginia and Maryland, and from that time forth the relations between the two colonies were nearly always cordial. For the next century the constitutional development of Maryland proceeded without interference from Virginia, although on many occasions the smaller colony was profoundly influenced by what went on in its larger neighbour, as well as by those currents of feeling that from time to time pervaded the English world and swayed both colonies alike. We shall presently see, for example, that marked effects were wrought in Maryland by Bacon's rebellion, and we shall observe what various echoes of the political situation in England were heard in all the colonies, from the wild scare of the Popish Plot in 1678 down to the assured triumph of William III. in 1691, and even later.

Virginia and Maryland

It will be remembered that when the Puritans of Providence, in March, 1658, gave in their assent to the compromises by which Lord Baltimore's authority was securely established in Maryland, only three years had elapsed since their victory at the Severn had given them supreme control over the country. While the defeated Governor Stone languished in jail, the victorious leader, William Fuller, exercised complete sway and for a moment could afford to laugh at the pretensions of Josias Fendall, the new governor whom Baltimore appointed in 1656. But this state of things came abruptly to an end when it was discovered that Lord Baltimore was upheld by Cromwell. Virginia, with her Puritan rulers, Bennett and Claiborne and Mathews, was thus at once detached from the support of Fuller, so that nothing was left for him but to come to terms. Fendall's policy toward his late antagonists was pacific and generous, so much so that in the assembly of 1659 we find the names of Fuller and other Puritan leaders enrolled among the burgesses. Associated with Fendall, and second to him in authority, was the secretary and receiver-general, Philip Calvert, younger brother of Cecilius, Lord Baltimore.

Fuller and Fendall

After the fires of civil dudgeon had briskly burned for so many years, it was not strange that their smouldering embers should send forth a few fitful gleams before dying. Apart from questions of religion or of loyalty, there were difficulties in regard to taxation that can hardly have been without their effect. There seems to have been more or less widely diffused a feeling of uneasiness upon which agitators could play. In 1647 the assembly had granted to the lord proprietor a duty of ten shillings per hogshead on all tobacco exported from the colony. This grant called forth remonstrances which seem to have had their effect, as in 1649 the act was replaced by another which granted to the proprietor for seven years a similar duty upon all tobacco exported on Dutch vessels if not bound to some English port.[1] This act seemed to carry with it the repeal of that of 1647, concerning which it was silent; if the first act continued in force, the second was meaningless. During the turbulence that ensued after 1650 it is not likely that the revenue laws were rigidly enforced. In 1659 Baltimore

The duty on tobacco

[1] See Sparks, "Causes of the Maryland Revolution of 1689," *Johns Hopkins University Studies*, vol. xiv. p. 501, a valuable contribution to our knowledge of the subject.

directed Fendall to have the act of 1647 explicitly repealed on condition that the assembly should grant him two shillings per hogshead on tobacco when shipped to British ports and ten shillings when shipped to foreign ports. Whether this demand was popular or not, we may gather from dates that are more eloquent than words. The act of 1647 was repealed by the assembly in 1660, but no grant in return was made to the proprietor until 1671, and then it was a uniform duty of two shillings. Unless the demand had been unpopular it would not have been resisted for eleven years.

When the assembly met on the last day of February, 1660, to consider this and other questions, memorable changes had occurred in England. The death of mighty Oliver, in September, 1658, threatened the realm with anarchy; and the prospect for a moment grew darker when in May, 1659, his gentle son Richard dropped the burden which he had not strength to carry. For nine months England seemed drifting without compass or helm. When our assembly met, one notable thing had just happened, early in February, when George Monk, "honest old George," entered London at the head of his army, and assumed control of affairs. The news of this event had not yet crossed the ocean, and even if it had, our Marylanders would not have understood what it portended. To some of them it seemed as if in this season of chaos whoever should seize upon the government of their little world would be likely to keep it. So Governor Fendall seems to have thought, and with him Thomas Gerrard, a member of the council and a Catholic, but disloyal to Baltimore. Why should not the government be held independently of the lord proprietor and all fees and duties to him be avoided? In this view of the case Fendall had two or three sympathizers in the council, and probably a good many in the House of Burgesses, especially among the Puritan members, who were in number three fourths of the whole.

Fendall's plot

In the course of the discussion over the tobacco duty the burgesses sent a message to Governor Fendall and the council, saying that they judged themselves to be a lawful assembly without dependence upon any other power now existing within the province, and if anybody had any objections to this view of the case they should like to hear them. The upper house answered by asking the lower house if they meant that they were a complete assembly without the upper house, and also that they were independent of the lord proprietor. These questions led to a conference, in which, among other things, Fendall declared it to be his opinion that laws passed by the assembly and published in the lord proprietor's name should at once be in full force. Two of the council, Gerrard and Utie, agreed with this view, while the secretary, Philip Calvert, and all the rest, dissented. In these proceedings the governor was plainly in league with the lower house, and this vote demonstrated the necessity of getting rid of the upper house. Accordingly the burgesses sent word to the governor and council, that they would not acknowledge them as an upper house, but they might come and take seats in the lower house if they liked. Secretary Calvert observed that in that case the governor would become president of the joint assembly, and the speaker of the burgesses must give place to him. A compromise was presently reached, according to which the governor should preside, with a casting vote, but the right of adjourning or dissolving the assembly should be exercised by the speaker. Hereupon Calvert protested, and demanded that his protest be put on record, but Fendall refused. Then Calvert and his most staunch adherent, Councillor Brooke, requested permission to leave the room. "You may if you please," quoth Fendall, "we shall not force you to go or stay." With the departure of these gentlemen the upper house was virtually abolished, and now Fendall quite threw off the mask by surrendering his commission from Lord Baltimore and accepting a new one from the assembly. Thus the palatinate government was overthrown, and it only remained for Fendall and his assembly to declare it felony for anybody in Maryland to acknowledge Lord Baltimore's authority.

Temporary overthrow of Baltimore's authority

These proceedings in Maryland become perfectly intelligible if we compare them with what was going on at the very same moment in Virginia. In March, 1660, the assembly at Jamestown, in view of the fact that there was no acknowledged supreme authority then resident in England, declared that the supreme power in Virginia was in the assembly, and that all writs should issue in its name, until such command should come from England as the assembly should judge to be lawful. This assembly then elected Sir William Berkeley to the governorship, and he accepted from it provisionally his commission.[1]

Superficial resemblance to the action of Virginia

Now in Maryland there was a superficial resemblance to these proceedings, in so far as the supreme power was lodged in the assembly and the governor accepted his commission from it. But there was a profound difference in the two situations, and while the people of Virginia read their own situation correctly, Fendall and his abettors did not. The assembly at Jamestown was predominantly Cavalier in its composition and in full sympathy with the expected restoration of the monarchy; and its proceedings were promptly sanctioned by Charles II., whose royal commission to Sir William Berkeley came in October of the same year. On the other hand, the assembly at St. Mary's was predominantly Puritan in its composition, and one of its most influential members was that William Fuller who five years before had defeated Lord Baltimore's governor in the battle of the Severn, and executed drumhead justice upon several of his adherents. The election had been managed in the interest of the Puritans, as is shown by Fuller's county, Anne Arundel, returning seven delegates, whereas it was only entitled to four. The collusion between Fuller and Fendall is unmistakable. For two years the Puritans had acquiesced in Lord Baltimore's rule, because they had not dared resist Cromwell. Now if Puritanism were to remain uppermost in England,

Profound difference in the situations

[1] See above, p. 17.

they might once more hope to overthrow him; if the monarchy were to be restored, the prospect was also good, for it did not seem likely that Charles II. would befriend the man whom Cromwell had befriended. Here was the fatal error of Fendall and his people. Charles II. had long ago recovered from his little tiff with Cecilius for appointing a Parliamentarian governor, and as a Romanist at heart he was more than ready to show favour to Catholics. Thus with rare good fortune — defended in turn by a king and a lord protector, and by another king, and aided at every turn by his own consummate tact, did Cecilius triumphantly weather all the storms. When the news of Fendall's treachery reached London it found Charles II. seated firmly on the throne. All persons were at once instructed to respect Lord Baltimore's authority over Maryland, and Sir William Berkeley was ordered to bring the force of Virginia to his aid if necessary; Cecilius appointed his brother Philip to the governorship; the rebellion instantly collapsed, and its ringleaders were seized. Vengeance was denounced against Fendall and Fuller and all who had been concerned in the execution of Baltimore's men after the battle of the Severn. Philip Calvert was instructed to hang them all, and to proclaim martial law if necessary, but on second thought so much severity was deemed impolitic. Such punishments were inflicted as banishment, confiscation, and loss of civil rights, but nobody was put to death. Such was the end of Fendall's rebellion. In the course of the year 1661, Cecilius sent over his only son, Charles Calvert, to be governor of the palatinate, while Philip remained as chancellor; and this arrangement continued for many years.

Fendall's error

Collapse of the rebellion

Fendall's administration had witnessed two events of especial interest, in the arrival of Quakers in the colony and of Dutchmen in a part of its territory. Quakers came from Massachusetts and Virginia, where they suffered so much ill usage, into Maryland, where they also got into trouble, though it does not appear that the objec-

The Quakers

tions against them were of a religious nature. The peculiar notions of the Quakers often brought them into conflict with governments on purely civil grounds, as when they refused to be enrolled in the militia, or to serve on juries, or give testimony under oath. For such reasons, two zealous Quaker preachers, Thurston and Cole, were arrested and tried in 1658, but it does not appear that they were treated with harshness or that at any time there was anything like persecution of Quakers in Maryland. When George Fox visited the country in 1672, his followers there were numerous and held regular meetings.

With the arrival of Quakers there appeared on the north-eastern horizon a menace from the Dutch, and incidents occurred that curiously affected the future growth of Lord Baltimore's princely domain. Since 1638 parties of Swedes had been establishing themselves on the western bank of the Delaware River, on and about the present sites of Newcastle and Wilmington. This region they called New Sweden, but in 1655 Peter Stuyvesant despatched from Manhattan a force of Dutchmen which speedily overcame the little colony. Stuyvesant then divided his conquest into two provinces, which he called New Amstel and Altona, and appointed a governor over each. It was now Maryland's turn to be aroused. The governor of New Netherland had no business to be setting up jurisdictions west of Delaware River. That whole region was expressly included in Lord Baltimore's charter. Accordingly the Dutch governors of New Amstel and Altona were politely informed that they must either acknowledge Baltimore's jurisdiction or leave the country. This led to Stuyvesant's sending an envoy to St. Mary's, to discuss the proprietorship of the territory in question. The person selected for this business was a man of no ordinary mould, a native of Prague, with the German name of Augustine Herman. He came to New Amsterdam at some time before 1647, in which year he was appointed one of the Nine Men whose business it was to advise the governor. This Herman

The Swedes and Dutch

Augustine Herman

was a man of broad intelligence, rare executive ability, and perfect courage. He was by profession a land surveyor and draughtsman, but in the course of his life he accumulated a great fortune by trade. His portrait, painted from life, shows

AUGUSTINE HERMAN

us a masterful face, clean shaven, with powerful jaw, firm-set lips, imperious eyes, and long hair flowing upon his shoulders over a red coat richly ruffled.[1] Such was the man whom Stuyvesant chose to dispute Lord Baltimore's title to the smiling fields of New Amstel and Altona. He well understood the wisdom of claiming everything, and when the discovery of North America by John Cabot was cited against him, he boldly set up the priority of Christopher Columbus as giving the Spaniards a claim upon the whole hemisphere.

[1] For this description of Herman I am much indebted to E. N. Vallandigham's paper on "The Lord of Bohemia Manor," reprinted in Lee Phillips, *Virginia Cartography*, Washington, 1896, pp. 37–41.

To the Dutch, he said, as victors over their wicked stepmother Spain, her claims had naturally passed! One is inclined to wonder if such an argument was announced without something like a twinkle in those piercing eyes. At all events, it was not long before the astute ambassador abandoned his logic and changed his allegiance. Romantic tradition has assigned various grounds for Herman's leaving New Amsterdam. Whether it was because of a quarrel with Stuyvesant, and whether the quarrel had its source in love of woman or love of pelf, we know not; but in 1660 Herman wrote to Lord Baltimore, asking for the grant of a manor, and offering to pay for it by making a map of Maryland. The proposal was accepted. The map, which was completed after careful surveys extending over ten years and was engraved in London in 1673, with a portrait of Herman attached, is still preserved in the British Museum. For this important service the enterprising surveyor received an estate on the Elk River, which by successive accretions came to include more than 20,000 acres.[1] It is still called by the name which Herman gave it, Bohemia Manor. There he grew immensely rich by trade with the Indians along the very routes which Claiborne had hoped to monopolize, and there in his great manor house, in spite of matrimonial infelicities like those of Socrates and the elder Mr. Weller, he lived to a good old age and dispensed a regal hospitality, in which the items of rum and brandy, strong beer, sound wines, and "best cider out of the orchard" were not forgotten. Herman's tomb is still to be seen hard by the vestiges of his house and his deer park. Six of his descendants succeeded him as lords of Bohemia Manor, until its legal existence

Bohemia Manor

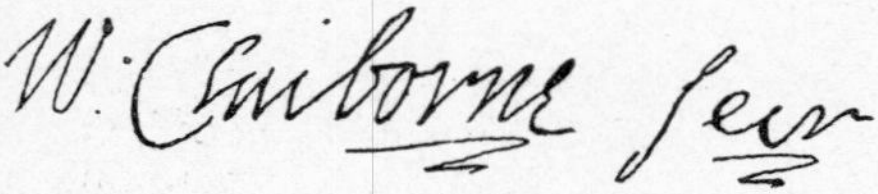

[1] To enable him to hold real estate in Maryland, Herman received letters of naturalization, the first ever issued in that province, and he is supposed by some writers to have been the first foreign citizen thus naturalized in America.

TUCKAHOE: SOUTH FRONT

came to an end in 1789. The fact is not without interest that Margaret Shippen, wife of Benedict Arnold, counted among her ancestors the sturdy Augustine Herman.[1]

A noteworthy episode in the history of Bohemia Manor is the settlement of a small sect of Mystics, known as Labadists, from the name of their French founder, Jean de Labadie. Their professed aim was to restore the simplicity of life and doctrine attributed to the primitive Christians. Their views of spiritual things were brightened by an inward light, their drift of thought was toward antinomianism, they held all goods in common, and their notions about marriage were thought to be such as to render them liable to be molested on civil grounds. The persistent recurrence of such little communities, age after age, each one ignorant of the existence of its predecessors and supremely innocent of all knowledge of the world, is one of the interesting freaks in religious history. Even in the tolerant atmosphere of Holland these Labadists led an uneasy life, and in 1679 two of their brethren, Sluyter and Dankers, came over to New York, to make fresh converts and find a new home. One of their first converts was Ephraim, the weak-minded son of Augustine Herman, and it may have been through the son's persuasion that the father was induced to grant nearly 4000 acres of his manor to the community. A company settled there in 1683 and were joined by persons from New York. As often happens in such communities, the affair ended in a despotism, in which the people were ruled with a rod of iron by Brother Sluyter and his wife, who set themselves up as a kind of abbot and abbess. On Sluyter's death in 1722 the sect seems to have come to an end, but to this day the land is known as "the Labadie tract."

The Labadists

Long before Augustine Herman's death, Lord Baltimore had granted him a second estate, called the manor of St. Augustine, extending eastward from Bohemia Manor to the shore of Delaware Bay; but to the greater part of it the Herman family never succeeded in making good their title,

[1] See Vallandigham, *loc. cit.*

for the territory passed out of Lord Baltimore's domain. Once more the heedlessness and bad faith of the Stuart kings, in their grants of American lands, was exhibited, and as Baltimore's patent had once encroached upon the Virginians, so now he was encroached upon by the Duke of York and presently by William Penn. The province of New Netherland, which Charles II. took from the Dutch in 1664 and bestowed upon his brother as lord proprietor, extended from the upper waters of the Hudson down to Cape May at the entrance to Delaware Bay, but did not include a square foot of land on the west shore of the bay, since all that was expressly included in the Maryland charter. It was not to be expected that Swedes or Dutchmen would pay any heed to that English charter; but it might have been supposed that Charles II. and his brother James would have shown some respect for a contract made by their father. Not so, however. The little Swedish and Dutch settlements on the west shore were at once taken in charge by officers of the Duke of York, as if they had belonged to his domain of New Netherland, while the southern part of that domain was granted by him, under the name of New Jersey, to his friends, Lord Berkeley and Sir George Carteret.

The Duke of York takes possession of the Delaware settlements

Nothing more of consequence occurred for several years, in the course of which interval, in 1675, Cecilius Calvert died and was succeeded by his son Charles, third Lord Baltimore. Not long afterward William Penn appeared on the scene, at first as trustee of certain Quaker estates in New Jersey, but presently as ruler over a princely domain of his own. The Quakers had been ill treated in many of the colonies; why not found a colony in which they should be the leaders? The suggestion offered to Charles II. an easy way of paying an old debt of £16,000 owed by the crown to the estate of the late Admiral Penn, and accordingly William was made lord proprietor of a spacious country lying west of the Delaware River and between Maryland to the south and the Five Nations to the north. His charter created a government very similar to Lord Baltimore's but far less independent, for laws passed in Pennsylvania must be sent to England for the royal assent, and the British government, which fifty years before had expressly renounced the right to lay taxes upon Marylanders, now expressly asserted the right to lay taxes upon Pennsylvanians. This change marks the growth of the imperial and anti-feudal sentiment in England, the feeling that privileges like those accorded to the Calverts were too extensive to be enjoyed by subjects.

Charter of Pennsylvania

According to Lord Baltimore's charter his northern boundary was the fortieth parallel of latitude, which runs a little north of the site of Philadelphia. The latitude was marked by a fort erected on the Susquehanna River, and when the crown lawyers consulted with Baltimore's attorneys, they were informed that all questions of encroachment would be avoided if the line were to be run just north of this fort, so as to leave it on the Maryland side.[1] Penn made no objection to this, but when the charter was drawn up no allusion was made to the Susquehanna fort. Penn's southern boundary was made to begin twelve miles north of Newcastle, thence to curve northwestward to the fortieth parallel and follow that parallel. Measurement soon showed that such a boundary would give Penn's province inadequate access to the sea. His position as a royal favourite enabled him to push the whole line twenty miles to the south. Even then he was disappointed in not gaining the head of Chesapeake Bay, and, being bent upon securing somewhere a bit of seacoast, he persuaded the Duke of York to give him the land on the west shore of Delaware Bay which the Dutch had once taken from the

Boundaries between Penn and Baltimore

[1] See Browne's *Maryland*, p. 137.

Swedes. By further enlargement the area of this grant became that of the present state of Delaware, the whole of which was thus, in spite of vehement protest, carved out of the original Maryland. In such matters there was not much profit in contending against princes.

In the course of this narrative we have had occasion to mention the grants of Bohemia and other manors. In order

WILLIAM PENN

that we should understand the course of Maryland history before and after the Revolution of 1689, some description of the manorial system is desirable. One of the most interesting features in the early history of English America is the way in which different phases of English institutions were reproduced in the differ-

Old manors in Maryland

ent colonies. As the ancient English town meeting reached a high development in New England, as the system of close vestries was very thoroughly worked out in Virginia, so the old English manor was best preserved in Maryland. In 1636 Lord Baltimore issued instructions that every grant of 2000 acres or more should be erected into a manor, with court baron and court leet. "The manor was the land on which the lord and his tenants lived, and bound up with the land were also the rights of government which the lord possessed over the tenants, and they over one another."[1] Such manors were scattered all over tidewater Maryland. Mr. Johnson, in his excellent essay on the subject, cites at random the names of "George Evelin, lord of the manor of Evelinton, in St. Mary's county; Marmaduke Tilden, lord of Great Oak Manor, and Major James Ringgold, lord of the manor on Eastern Neck, both in Kent; Giles Brent, lord of Kent Fort, on Kent Island; George Talbot, lord of Susquehanna Manor, in Cecil county," and he mentions a sale, in 1767, of "twenty-seven manors, embracing 100,000 acres."

Life in the manors

In the life upon these manors there was a kind of patriarchal completeness; each was a little world in itself. There was the great house with its generous dining-hall, its panelled wainscot, and its family portraits; there was the chapel, with the graves of the lord's family beneath its pavement and the graves of common folk out in the churchyard; there were the smoke-houses, and the cabins of negro slaves; and here and there one might come upon the dwellings of white freehold tenants, with ample land about them held on leases of one-and-twenty years. In establishing these manors, Lord Baltimore had an eye to the military defence of his colony. It was enacted in 1641 that the grant of a manor should be the reward for every settler who should bring with him from England twenty able-bodied men, each armed with a musket, a sword and belt, a bandelier and flask, ten pounds of powder, and forty pounds of bullets and shot.

[1] Johnson, "Old Maryland Manors," *Johns Hopkins University Studies*, vol. i.

DOUGHOREGAN MANOR, MARYLAND

These manors were little self-governing communities. The court leet was like a town meeting. All freemen could take part in it. It enacted by-laws, elected constables, bailiffs, and other local officers, set up stocks and pillory, and sentenced offenders to stand there, for judicial and legislative functions were united in this court leet. It empanelled its jury, and with the steward of the manor presiding as judge, it visited with fine or imprisonment the thief, the vagrant, the poacher, the fraudulent dealer.

The court leet

Side by side with the court leet was the court baron, an equally free institution in which all the freehold tenants sat as judges determining questions of law and of fact. This court decided all disputes between the lord and his tenants concerning such matters as rents, or trespass, or escheats. Here actions for debt were tried, and transfers of land were made with the ancient formalities.

The court baron

These admirable manorial institutions were brought to Maryland in precisely the same shape in which they had long existed in England. They were well adapted for preserving liberty and securing order in rural communities before the days of denser population and more rapid communication. In our progress away from those earlier times we have gained vastly, but it is by no means sure that we have not also lost something. In the decadence of the Maryland manors there was clearly an element of loss, for that decadence was chiefly brought about by the growth of negro slavery, which made it more profitable for the lord of the manor to cultivate the whole of it himself, instead of leasing the whole or parts of it to tenants. Slavery also affixed a stigma upon free labour and drove it off the field, very much as a debased currency invariably drives out a sound currency. From these causes the class of freehold tenants gradually disappeared, "the feudal society of the manor" was transformed into "the patriarchal society of the plantation," [1] and the arbitrary fiat of a master was substituted for the argued judgments of the court leet.

Changes wrought by slavery

[1] Johnson, *op. cit.* p. 21.

Among the people of Lord Baltimore's colony, as among English-speaking people in general, one might observe a fierce spirit of political liberty coupled with engrained respect for law and a disposition to achieve results by argument rather than by violence. Such a temper leads to interminable parliamentary discussion, and in the reign of Charles II. the tongues of the Maryland assembly were seldom quiet. As compared with the stormy period before 1660, the later career of Cecilius and that of his son Charles down to the Revolution of 1689 seem peaceful, and there are writers who would persuade us that when the catastrophe arrived, it came quite unheralded, like lightning from a cloudless sky. A perusal of the transactions in the Maryland assembly, however, shows that the happy period was not so serene as we have been told, but there were fleecy specks on the horizon, with now and then a faint growl of distant thunder.

A fierce spirit of liberty

That the proprietary government had many devoted friends is not to be denied, and it is clear that some of the opposition to it was merely factious. There is no doubt as to the lofty personal qualities of the second Lord Baltimore, his courage and sagacity, his disinterested public spirit, his devotion to the noble ideal which he had inherited. As for Charles, the third lord, he seems to have been a paler reflection of his father, like him for good intentions, but far inferior in force. The period of eight-and-twenty years which we are considering, from 1661 to 1689, is divided exactly in the middle by the death of Cecilius in 1675. Before that date we have Charles administering the affairs of Maryland subject to the approval of his father in London; after that date Charles is supreme.

Cecilius and Charles

Now the circumstances were such that father and son would have had to be more than human to carry on the government without serious opposition. In the first place, they were Catholics, ruling a population in which about one twelfth part were Catholics, while one sixth belonged to the Church of England, and three fourths were

Sources of discontent

dissenting Puritans. To most of the people the enforced toleration of Papists must have seemed like keeping on terms of polite familiarity with the devil. In the second place, the proprietor was apt to appoint his own relatives and trusted friends to the highest offices, and such persons were usually Catholics. As these high officers composed the council, or upper house of the assembly, the proprietor had a permanent and irreversible majority in that body. When we read the minutes of a council composed of Governor Charles Calvert, his uncle Philip, his cousin William, Mr. Baker Brooke, who had married cousin William's sister, Mr. William Talbot, who was another cousin, and Mr. Henry Coursey, who was uncle Philip's bosom friend, we seem to be assisting at a pleasant little family party. Again, when the governor marries a widow, and each of his five stepchildren marries, and we are told that "every one who became related to the family soon obtained an office,"[1] we begin to realize that there was coming to be quite a clan to be supported from the revenues of a small province. Nepotism may not be the blackest of crimes, but it is pretty certain to breed trouble.

The family party

The governing power opposed to this family party was the House of Burgesses, or lower house of assembly. Those freeholding tenants and small proprietors who had brought with them from England their time-honoured habits of self-government in court leet and court baron, represented the democratic element in the constitution of Maryland, as the upper house represented the oligarchical element. The history of the period we are considering is the history of a constitutional struggle between the two houses. We have seen that it was not a part of the proprietor's original scheme that the assembly should take an initiative in legislation, and that on this ground he refused his assent to the first group of laws sent to him in 1635 for his signature. Apparently it was his idea that his burgesses should simply comment on acts passed by their betters, as

Conflict in the assembly

[1] F. E. Sparks, *op. cit.* p. 65.

on old Merovingian fields of March the magnates legislated while the listening warriors clashed their shields in token of approval. If such was the first notion of Cecilius he promptly relinquished it and gracefully conceded the claim of the assembly to take the initiative in legislation. But the veto power, without any limitation of time, was a prerogative which he would not give up. At any moment he could use this veto power to repeal a law, and this was felt by the colonists to be a grievance. On such constitutional matters, when we read of antagonism between the proprietor and the assembly, it is the burgesses that we are to understand as in opposition, since the council was almost sure to uphold the proprietor.

Rights of the burgesses

One point upon which the upper house always insisted was that the burgesses were not a house of commons with inherent rights of legislation, but that they owed their existence to the charter, with powers that must be limited as strictly as possible. But this point the burgesses would never concede. They were Englishmen, with the rights and privileges of Englishmen, and it was an inherent right in English representatives to make laws for their constituents; accordingly they insisted that they were, to all intents and purposes, a house of commons for Maryland.[1] On one occasion a clergyman, Charles Nichollet, preached a sermon, in which he warned the burgesses not to forget that they had no real liberty unless they could pass laws that were agreeable to their conscience; as a house of commons they must keep their hand upon the purse strings and consider if the taxes were not too heavy. The family party of the upper house called such talk seditious, and the parson was roundly fined for preaching politics.

Cessation Act of 1666

But it would be grossly unfair to the proprietor to overlook the fact that on some important occasions he took sides with the representatives of the people against his own little family party. As an instance may be cited the act of 1666 concerning the "Cessation of Tobacco." As

[1] *Archives of Maryland: Assembly*, ii. 64.

the fees of public officials were paid in tobacco, a large crop was liable to diminish their value, and accordingly the upper house wished to contract the currency by an act stopping all planting of tobacco for one year. The lower house objected to this, but after a long dispute was induced to give consent, provided Virginia should pass a similar act. The speaker, however, wrote to Cecilius urging him to veto the act, and he did so.[1]

The occasions of difference between the two houses were many and various. One concerned the relief of Quakers. In Rhode Island, New Jersey, and Jamaica, they were allowed to make affirmations instead of taking oaths. When the Quakers of Maryland petitioned for a similar relief, the burgesses granted it, but the council refused to concur. A more important matter was the appointment of sheriffs. In addition to the ordinary functions of the sheriff, with which we are familiar in more modern times, these officers collected all taxes, superintended all elections, and made out the returns. These were formidable powers, for a dishonest or intriguing sheriff might alter the composition of the House of Burgesses. Sheriffs were appointed by the governor, and were in no way responsible to the county courts. The burgesses tried to establish a check upon them by enacting that the county court should recommend three persons out of whom the governor should choose one, and that the sheriff thus selected should serve for one year; but the upper house declared that such an act infringed the proprietor's prerogative. No check upon the sheriffs, therefore, was left to the people except the regulating of their fees, and upon this point the burgesses were stiff.

Sheriffs

In 1669 the disputes between the houses were more stormy than usual, and in the election of the next year the suffrage was restricted to freemen owning plantations of fifty acres or more, or possessed of personal property to the amount of £50 sterling. This restriction was not accomplished by legislation; it must have been a

Restriction of suffrage, 1670

[1] *Archives of Maryland: Council*, ii. 18.

sheer assertion of prerogative, either by Cecilius or by Charles acting on his own responsibility. All that is positively known is that the sheriffs were instructed to that effect in their writs. It is worthy of note that a similar restriction of suffrage had just occurred in Virginia. Perhaps Charles Calvert was imprudently taking a lesson from Berkeley. But still worse, in summoning to the assembly the members who had been elected, he omitted a few names, presumably those of persons whose opposition was likely to prove inconvenient. When the burgesses demanded the reason for this omission, Charles made a shuffling explanation which they saw fit to accept for the moment, and thus a precedent was created of which he was not slow to avail himself, and from which endless bickering ensued. For the present a house of burgesses was obtained which was much to the governor's liking; accordingly, instead of allowing its term to expire at the end of a year, he simply adjourned it, and thus kept it alive until 1676, — another lesson learned from Berkeley.

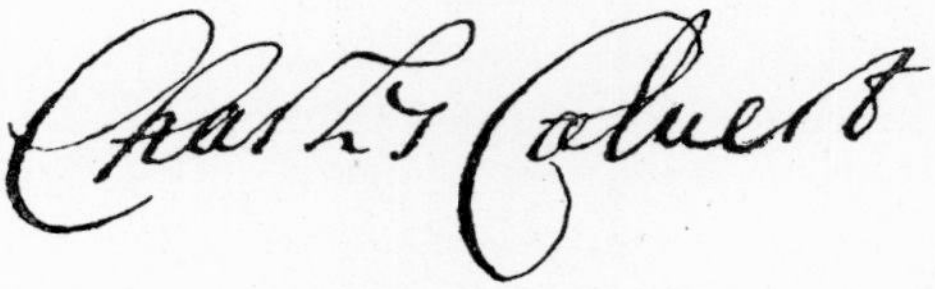

It was this comparatively submissive assembly that in 1671 passed the act which for eleven years had been resisted, granting to the proprietor a royalty of two shillings on every hogshead of tobacco exported. In return for this grant, however, the lower house obtained some concessions. With the death of Cecilius, in 1675, the situation was certainly changed for the worse. Now for the first time the people of Maryland had their lord proprietor dwelling among them and not in England; but Charles was narrower and less public-spirited than his father, his measures were more arbitrary, and the feeling that the country was governed in the interests of a small coterie of Papists rapidly increased. In 1676 Maryland seemed on the point of following Virginia into rebellion.

Death of Cecilius, 1675

Lord Baltimore went to England in the spring, and by midsummer it had become evident that Bacon had able sympathizers in Maryland. A set of manuscript archives, recently recovered from long oblivion,[1] make it probable that but for Bacon's sudden death in October and the collapse of the movement in Virginia, there would have been bloodshed in the sister colony. In August a seditious paper was circulated, alleging grievances similar to those of Virginia, and threatening the proprietor's government. Two gentlemen named Davis and Pate, with others, gathered an armed force in Calvert county with the design of intimidating the governor and council, and extorting from them sundry concessions. When the governor, Thomas Notley, ordered them to disband, promising that their demands should be duly considered at the next assembly, they refused on the ground that the assembly had been tampered with and no longer represented the people. As Notley afterward wrote to Lord Baltimore, never was there a people "more replete with malignancy and frenzy than our people were about August last, and they wanted but a monstrous head to their monstrous body." But this incipient Davis and Pate rebellion derived its strength from the Bacon rebellion, and the collapse of the one extinguished the other. Davis and Pate were hanged, at which Notley tells us the people were "terrified," and so peace was preserved.

Rebellion of Davis and Pate, 1676

Execution of Davis and Pate

An episode which occurred before the final catastrophe throws some light upon the relations of parties at the time. An Irish kinsman of Lord Baltimore's, by name George Talbot, obtained in 1680 an extensive grant of land on the Susquehanna River, where he lived in feudal style, with a force of Irish retainers at his beck and call, hunting venison, drinking strong waters, browbeating Indians, and picking quarrels with William Penn's newly

George Talbot

[1] *MSS. Archives of Maryland, Liber R. R. and R. R. R. and Council Books* 1677–1683, *of the Council Proceedings :* Maryland Historical Society.

TUCKAHOE, SOUTH STAIR

arrived followers. In 1684 Lord Baltimore went again to England, leaving his son, Benedict Calvert, in the governorship; and as Benedict was a mere boy, there was a little regency of which George Talbot was the head. Now the exemption of Maryland from king's taxes did not extend to custom-house duties. These were collected by crown officers and paid into the royal treasury; and the collectors were apt to behave themselves, as in all ages and countries, like enemies of the human race. Between them and the proprietary government there was deep-seated antipathy. They accused Lord Baltimore of hindering them in their work, and this complaint led the king to pounce upon him with a claim for £2500 alleged to have been lost to the revenue through his interferences. One of these collectors, Christopher Rousby, was especially overbearing, and some called him a rascal. Late in 1684 a small ship of the royal navy was lying at St. Mary's, and one day, while Rousby was in the cabin drinking toddies with the captain, Talbot came on board, and a quarrel ensued, in the course of which Talbot drew a dagger and plunged it into Rousby's heart. The captain refused to allow Talbot to go ashore to be tried by a council of his relatives; he carried him to Virginia and handed him over to the governor, Lord Howard of Effingham. Talbot was imprisoned not far from the site where once had stood the red man's village, Werowocomoco, where he was in imminent danger of the gallows, or perhaps of having to pay his whole fortune as a bribe to the greedy Howard. But Talbot's brave wife, with two trusty followers, sailed down the whole length of Chesapeake Bay and up York River in a boat. On a dark winter's night they succeeded in freeing Talbot from his jail, and returning as they came, carried him off exulting to Susquehanna Manor. For the sake of appearances his friends in the Maryland council thought it necessary to proclaim the hue and cry after him, and there is a local tradition that he was for a while obliged to hide in a cave, where a couple of his trained hawks kept him alive by fetching him game — canvas-back ducks, perhaps, and terrapin — from the river! It is not likely, however, that the search for him was zealous or thorough. For some time he stayed unmolested in his manor house, but presently deemed it prudent to go and surrender himself. The council refused to bring him to trial in any court held in the king's name, until a royal order came from England to send him over there for trial, but before this was done Lord Baltimore interceded with James II. and secured a pardon.

The general effect of this Talbot affair was to weaken the palatinate government by making it appear lukewarm in its allegiance and remiss in its duties to the crown. The custom-house became a subject of hot discussion, and the charges of defrauding the royal revenue were reiterated with effect. Some time before this a remarkable pamphlet had appeared with the title, "Complaint from Heaven with a Huy and Crye and a

A "Complaint from Heaven"

petition out of Virginia and Maryland." It was evidently written by some Puritan friend of Fendall's. After a bitter denunciation of the palatinate administration some measures of relief were suggested, one of which was that the king should assume the government of Maryland and appoint the governors. The time was now at hand when this suggestion was to bear fruit.

The anti-Catholic panic

The forced abdication of James II. in 1688, with his flight to France, was the occasion of an anti-Catholic panic throughout the greater part of English America. It was as certain as anything future could be that the antagonism between Louis XIV. and William of Orange would at once break out in a great war, in which French armies from Canada would invade the English colonies. There was a widespread fear that Papists in these colonies would turn traitors and assist the enemy. It was in this scare that Leisler's rebellion in New York originated, although there too a conflict between democracy and oligarchy was concerned, somewhat as in Maryland. Everywhere the ordinary dread of Papists became more acute. It was soon after this time that the clause of an act depriving Roman Catholics of the franchise found its way into the Rhode Island statutes, the only instance in which that commonwealth ever allowed itself to depart from the noble principles of Roger Williams.[1]

Causes of the panic

While there were absurdities in this anti-Catholic panic, it contained an element that was not unreasonable. Throughout the century the Papist counter-reformation had made alarming progress. In France, the strongest nation in the world, it had just scored a final victory in the expulsion of the Huguenots. In Germany the Thirty Years' War had left Protestantism weaker than it had been at the death of Martin Luther. England had barely escaped from having a Papist dynasty settled upon her; nor was it yet

[1] See Arnold's *History of Rhode Island*, ii. 490–494.

sure that she had escaped. A caprice of fortune might drive King William out as suddenly as he had come. Ireland still held out for the Stuarts, and there in May, 1689, James II. landed with French troops, in the hope of winning back his crown. The officer who held Ireland for James was Richard Talbot, Duke of Tyrconnel, a distant relative and intimate friend of Lord Baltimore. Under these circumstances a panic was natural. There were absurd rumours of a plot between Catholics and Indians to massacre Protestants. More reasonable was the jealous eagerness with which men watched the council to see what it would do about proclaiming William and Mary. Lord Baltimore was prompt in sending from London directions to the council to proclaim them; whatever his political leanings might have been, he could in prudence hardly do less. But the messenger died on the voyage, and a second messenger was too late.

Meanwhile, in April, 1689, there was formed "An Association in arms for the defence of the Protestant Religion, and for asserting the right of King William and Queen Mary to the Province of Maryland and all the English Dominions." The president of this association was John Coode, who had married a daughter of that Thomas Gerrard who took a part in Fendall's rebellion. Another leader, who had married another daughter of Gerrard, was Nehemiah Blackiston, collector of customs, who had been foremost in accusing the Calverts of obstructing his work. Others were Kenelm Cheseldyn, speaker of the house, and Henry Jowles, colonel of the militia. As the weeks passed by, and news of the proclaiming of William and Mary by one colony after another arrived, and still the council took no action in the matter, people grew impatient and the association kept winning recruits. At last, toward the end of July, Coode appeared before St. Mary's at the head of 700 armed men. No resistance was offered. The council fled to a fort on the Patuxent River, where they were besieged and in a few days surrendered. Coode detained all outward-bound ships until he had prepared an

Coode's *coup d'état*, 1689

account of these proceedings to send to King William in the name of the Protestant inhabitants of Maryland. Like the insurrection in Boston, three months earlier, which overthrew Sir Edmund Andros, this bold stroke wore the aspect of a rising against the deposed king in favour of the king

WILLIAM III

actually reigning. William was asked to undertake the government of Maryland, and the whole affair met with his approval. He issued a *scire facias* against the Baltimore charter, and before a decision had been reached in the court of chancery he sent out Sir Lionel Copley in 1691, to be royal governor of Maryland. In such wise was the palatinate overturned.

Overthrow of the palatinate, 1691

Oppressive enactments

If any party in Maryland expected the millennium to follow this revolution, they were disappointed. Taxes were straightway levied for the support of the Church of England, the further immigration of Catholics

was prohibited under heavy penalties, and the public celebration of the mass was strictly forbidden within the limits of the colony. When Governor Nicholson arrived upon the scene, in 1694, he summoned his first assembly to meet at the Anne Arundel town formerly known as Providence; and in the course of that session it was decided to move the seat of government thither from St. Mary's. The purpose was to deal a blow at the old capital, the social and political centre of Catholicism in Maryland. Bitter indignation was felt at St. Mary's, and a petition signed by the mayor and other municipal officers, with a number of the freemen, was sent to the assembly, praying that the change might be reconsidered. The House of Burgesses returned an answer, brutal and vulgar in tone, which shows the wellnigh incredible virulence of political passion in those days.[1] The blow was final, so far as St. Mary's was concerned. Her civic life had evidently depended upon the presence of the government. At one time, with its fifty or sixty houses, the little city founded by Leonard Calvert was much larger than Jamestown; but after the removal it dwindled till little was left save a memory. The name of the new capital on the Severn was doubtless felt to be cumbrous, for it was presently changed to Annapolis,[2] the first of a set of queer hybrid compounds with which the map of the United States is besprinkled. Nicholson wished to crown the work of founding a new capital by establishing a school or college there, and accordingly in 1696 King William School was founded. For many years the income for supporting this and other free schools was derived from an export duty on furs.[3]

Removal of the capital to Annapolis, 1694

[1] The petition and answer are given in Scharf's *History of Maryland*, i. 345–348.

[2] Probably in honour of Princess Anne, the heiress presumptive, afterward Queen Anne.

[3] Every bearskin paid 9d., elk 12d., deer or beaver 4d., raccoons 3 farthings, muskrats 4d. per dozen, etc. Scharf, i. 352.

The change of the capital was perhaps bewailed only by the Catholics and others who were most strongly attached to the proprietary government. But the change in ecclesiastical policy disgusted everybody. Taxation for the support of the Episcopal church, of which only a small part of the population were members, was as unpopular with Puritans as with Papists. The Puritans, who had worked so zealously to undermine the proprietary government, had not bargained for such a result as this. The manner in which the church revenue was raised was also extremely irritating. The rate was forty pounds of tobacco per poll, so that rich and poor paid alike. A more inequitable and odious measure could hardly have been devised. The statute, however, with the dulness that usually characterizes the work of legislative bodies, forgot to specify the quality of tobacco in which the rates should be paid. Naturally, therefore, they were paid in the vilest unmarketable stuff that could be found, and the Episcopal clergymen found it hard to keep the wolf from the door. There was thus no inducement for competent ministers to come to Maryland, and those that were sent from England were of the poorest sort which the English Church in that period of its degradation could provide. Dr. Thomas Chandler, of New Jersey, who visited the eastern shore of Maryland in 1753, wrote to the Bishop of London as follows: "The general character of the clergy . . . is wretchedly bad. . . . It would really, my lord, make the ears of a sober heathen tingle to hear the stories that were told me by many serious persons of several clergymen in the neighbourhood of the parish where I visited; but I still hope that some abatement may be fairly made on account of the prejudices of those who related them."[1] The Swedish botanist, Peter Kalm, who visited Maryland about the same time, tells us that it was a common trick with a

Unpopularity of the establishment of the Episcopal church

Episcopal parsons

[1] Meade's *Old Churches*, ii. 352. Bishop Meade adds: "My own recollection of statements made by faithful witnesses . . . accords with the above."

parson, when performing the marriage service for a poor couple, to halt midway and refuse to go on till a good round fee had been handed over to him.[1] On such occasions it may be presumed that the tobacco was of unimpeachable quality.

The last decade of the seventeenth century was a period of ceaseless wrangling over church matters. Almost every year saw some new act passed from which its opponents succeeded in causing the assent of the crown to be withheld. The government of William III. was not ill-disposed toward a policy of toleration, except toward Papists. Accordingly, although the act of 1692 remained substantially in force until the American Revolution, it was so qualified in 1702 as to exempt Quakers and other Protestant Dissenters from civil disabilities, and to allow them the free exercise of public worship in their own churches or meeting-houses. They were not exempted, however, from the poll tax for the maintenance of the Episcopal church.

Exemption of Protestant Dissenters from civil disabilities

For the Catholics there was neither exemption nor privilege; they were shamefully insulted and vexed. In the autumn of 1704 two priests were summoned before the council: the one, William Hunter, was accused of consecrating a chapel, which he answered with a plea that was in part denial and in part "confession and avoidance;" the other, Robert Brooke, acknowledged the truth of the charge that he had said mass at the chapel of St. Mary's. The request of these gentlemen for legal counsel was refused. As the complaint against them was a first complaint, they were let off with a reprimand, which the

Seymour's reprimand to the Catholic priests

[1] Alexander Graydon tells us that in his early days any jockeying, fiddling, wine-bibbing clergyman, not over-scrupulous as to stealing his sermons, was currently known as a "Maryland parson." Graydon's *Memoirs*, Edinburgh, 1822, p. 102. This was in Pennsylvania, and any sneering remark or phrase current in any of our states with reference to its next neighbours is entitled to be taken *cum grano salis*. But there was doubtless justification for what Graydon says.

newly installed governor, John Seymour, thus politely administered: "It is the unhappy temper of you and all your tribe to grow insolent upon civility and never know how to use it, and yet of all people you have the least reason for considering that, if the necessary laws that are made were let loose, they are sufficient to crush you, and which (if your arrogant principles have not blinded you) you must need to dread. You might, methinks, be content to live quietly as you may, and let the exercise of your superstitious vanities be confined to yourselves, without proclaiming them at public times and in public places, unless you expect by your gaudy shows and serpentine policy to amuse the multitude and beguile the unthinking, . . . an act of deceit well known to be amongst you. But, gentlemen, be not deceived. . . . In plain and few words, if you intend to live here, let me hear no more of these things; for if I do, and they are made good against you, be assured I 'll chastise you. . . . I 'll remove the evil by sending you where you may be dealt with as you deserve. . . . Pray take notice that I am an English Protestant gentleman, and can never equivocate." After this fulmination the governor ordered the sheriff of St. Mary's county to lock up the Catholic chapel and "keep the key thereof;" and for all these proceedings the House of Burgesses declared themselves "cheerfully thankful" to his excellency, whom they found "so generously bent to protect her majesty's Protestant subjects here against insolence and growth of Popery." [1]

Cruel laws against Catholics

From 1704 to 1718 several ferocious acts were passed against Catholics. A reward of £100 was offered to any informer who should "apprehend and take" a priest and convict him of saying mass, or performing any of a priest's duties; and the penalty for the priest so convicted was perpetual imprisonment. Any Catholic found guilty of keeping a school, or taking youth to educate, was to spend the rest of his life in prison. Any person sending his child abroad to be educated as a Catholic

[1] Scharf, i. 368.

DRAWING-ROOM AT DOUGHOREGAN MANOR

was to be fined £100. No Catholic could become a purchaser of real estate. Certain impossible test oaths were to be administered to every Papist youth within six months after his attaining majority, and if he should refuse to take them he was to be declared incapable of inheriting land, and his nearest kin of Protestant faith could supplant him. The children of a Protestant father might be forcibly taken away from their widowed mother and placed in charge of Protestant guardians. When extra taxes were levied for emergencies, Catholics were assessed at double rates.[1]

These atrocities of the statute book were a symptom of the inflammatory effect wrought upon the English mind by the gigantic war against Louis XIV., and immediately afterward by the wild attempt of the so-called James III. to seize the crown of Great Britain. From the accession of William and Mary to the end of the reign of Anne, war against France was perpetual except for the breathing spell after the Peace of Ryswick. This state of things brought a fresh burden

[1] Scharf, i. 370, 383.

Crown requisitions

upon Maryland. War between France and Great Britain meant war between the Algonquin tribes and the English colonies aided by the Five Nations. The new situation was heralded in the Congress which met at New York in 1690, at Leisler's invitation, when Maryland was called upon to contribute men and money toward the invasion of Canada. With the advent of the royal government came royal requisitions for military purposes; and although this new burden was due to the new continental situation rather than to the change in the provincial government, it was one thing the more to make Marylanders look back with regret to the days of the proprietary rule.

Benedict Calvert becomes a Protestant

For four-and-twenty years after 1691 the third Lord Baltimore lived in England in the full enjoyment of his private rights and revenues, though deprived of his government. His son, Benedict Leonard Calvert, was a prince who took secular views of public policy, like the great Henry of Navarre. He preferred his palatinate to his church, and abjured the Catholic faith, much to the wrath and disgust of his aged father, who at once withdrew his annual allowance of £450. Benedict was obliged to

apply to the crown for a pension, which was granted by Anne and continued by George I. until on February 20, 1715, the situation was completely changed by the father's death. On the petition of Benedict, fourth Lord Baltimore, the proprietary government of Maryland was revived in his behalf. But Benedict survived his father only six weeks, and on April 5 his son

Revival of the palatinate, 1715

Charles Calvert became fifth Lord Baltimore. As Charles was a lad of sixteen, whose Romanist faith had been forsworn with his father's, he was forthwith proclaimed Lord Proprietor of Maryland, and royal governors no more vexed that colony.

Despite all troubles it had thriven under their administration. The population had doubled within less than twenty years, and on Charles's accession it was reckoned at 40,700 whites and 9500 negroes.[1] Oppressive statutes had not prevented the Catholics from increasing in numbers and the influence which ability and character always wield. They were preëminently the picked men of the colony. Entire suppression of their forms of worship had been recognized as impracticable. An act of 1704 had allowed priests to perform religious services in Roman Catholic families, though not in public. From this permission advantage was taken to build chapels as part of private mansions, so that the family with their guests might worship God after their manner, relying upon the principle that an Englishman's house is his castle. By some of these people it was hoped that the restoration of the palatinate would revive their political rights and privileges. But this

Change in the political situation

[1] The following estimate of the population of the twelve colonies in 1715 (from Chalmers's *American Colonies*, ii. 7) may be of interest: —

	White.	Black.	Total.
Massachusetts	94,000	2,000	96,000
Virginia	72,000	23,000	95,000
Maryland	40,700	9,500	50,200
Connecticut	46,000	1,500	47,500
Pennsylvania / Delaware	43,300	2,500	45,800
New York	27,000	4,000	31,000
New Jersey	21,000	1,500	22,500
South Carolina	6,250	10,500	16,750
North Carolina	7,500	3,700	11,200
New Hampshire	9,500	150	9,650
Rhode Island	8,500	500	9,000
	375,750	58,850	434,600

renewal of the palatinate was far from restoring the old state of things. The position of the fifth Lord Baltimore was very different from that of the second and third. They were Catholic princes, and were steadily supported by two Catholic kings of England. The new proprietor was a Protestant, dependent upon the favour of a Protestant king. The features of the old palatinate government, therefore, which lend the chief interest to its history, were never restored. Catholic citizens remained disfranchised, and continued to be taxed for the support of a church which they disapproved.

CARROLL ARMS

An interesting project was entertained about this time, by Charles Carroll and other Catholic gentlemen, of leading a migration to the Mississippi valley, thus transferring their allegiance from Great Britain to France. Mr. Carroll, a descendant of the famous Irish sept of O'Carrolls, and one of the foremost citizens of Maryland, had long been agent and receiver of rents for the third Lord Baltimore. The scheme which he was now contemplating might have led to curious results, but it was soon abandoned. A grant of territory by the Arkansas River was sought from the French government,[1] but it proved impossible to agree upon terms, and that region remained a wilderness until several questions of world-wide importance had been settled.

Charles Carroll

Though the accession of the fifth Lord Baltimore did not reinstate the Catholics in their civil rights, it nevertheless did much to mitigate the operation of the oppressive statutes against them. An early symptom of Charles's temper was shown by his reappointment of Carroll as his agent. He went on to do such justice to Catholics as was in his power, and under his mild and equitable rule the fierceness of polit-

[1] Scharf, i. 390.

ical passion was much abated. The proprietary government retained its popularity until it came to an end with the Declaration of Independence. But the interval of crown

Seeds of revolution

government from 1691 to 1715 had for the first time made the connection with Great Britain seem oppressive, and had planted the seeds of future sympathy with the revolutionary party in Massachusetts and Virginia. As the long struggle with France increased in dimensions, the political questions at issue in the several colonies became more and more continental in character. All were more or less assimilated one to another, and thus the way toward federation was prepared. Thus the discussions in Maryland came more and more to deal with the rights of the colonial legislature and British interference with them. At the same time Maryland had a grievance of her own in the poll tax for maintaining a foreign and hated church. In 1772 an assault upon that tax was the occasion of one of the most remarkable legal controversies in American annals; and the leader in that assault, Charles Carroll's grandson and namesake, Charles Carroll of Carrollton, soon afterward signed his name to the Declaration of Independence.

In 1751, after a tranquil reign, only two years of which were spent in Maryland, Charles Calvert died in London, and was succeeded by his son Frederick, sixth and last Lord Baltimore. After a series of Antonines, at last came the Commodus. Frederick was a miserable debauchee, unworthy scion of a noble race. For Maryland he cared nothing except to spend its revenues in riotous living in London. One adventure of his, for which he was tried and acquitted on a mere technicality, fills one of the most loathsome chapters of the Newgate Calendar.[1] But this villain was represented in Maryland by two excellent governors, Horatio Sharpe from 1753 to 1768, and then Sir Robert Eden, who had married Frederick's younger sister. Eden remained in authority until June 24, 1776, when he embarked for England with the good wishes of the people. The wretched Frederick died in 1771, without legitimate children, and the barony of Baltimore became extinct. By the will of Charles, the fifth baron, the proprietorship of Maryland was now vested in Frederick's elder sister, Louisa, wife of John Browning. But Frederick had also left a will, in which he devised the province to an illegitimate son, called Henry Harford. This young man laid claim to the proprietorship, but before the chancery suit was ended the Palatinate of Maryland had become one of the thirteen United States.

End of the palatinate

[1] Knapp and Baldwin, *Newgate Calendar*, ii. 385–397; Pelham, *Chronicles of Crime*, i. 213–220.

CHAPTER XIV

SOCIETY IN THE OLD DOMINION

A LEARNED son of Old Virginia, who is fond of wrapping up a bookful of meaning in a single pithy sentence, has declared that "a true history of tobacco would be the history of English and American liberty." This remark occurs near the beginning of Mr. Moncure Conway's dainty volume printed for the Grolier Club, entitled "Barons on the Potomack and the Rappahannock." When construed liberally, as all such sweeping statements need to be, it contains a kernel of truth. It was tobacco that planted an English nation in Virginia, and made a corporation in London so rich and powerful as to become a formidable seminary of sedition; it was the desire to monopolize the tobacco trade that induced Charles I. to recognize the House of Burgesses; discontent with the Navigation Act and its effect upon the tobacco trade was potent among the causes of Bacon's Rebellion; and so on down to the eve of Independence, when Patrick Henry won his first triumph in the famous Parsons' Cause, in which the price of tobacco furnished the bone of contention, the Indian weed has been strangely implicated with the history of political freedom.

Tobacco and liberty

Furthermore, when we reflect upon the splendid part played by Virginia in winning American independence and bringing into existence the political framework of our Federal Republic; when we recollect that of the five founders of this nation who were foremost in constructive work — Washington, Hamilton, Madison, Jefferson, and Marshall — four were Virginians, — it becomes interesting to go back and study the social features of the community in which such leaders of men were produced. The economic basis of that community was the cultivation of tobacco on large plantations, and from that single economic circumstance resulted most of the social features which we have now to pass in review.

We have seen in a previous chapter how important was the cultivation of tobacco in setting the infant colony at Jamestown upon its feet in 1614 and the following years. In the rapid development of the colony during the reign of Charles I. other kinds of agriculture thrived, there were good crops of wheat, and Indian corn was exported. But tobacco culture increased rapidly and steadily until in the latter part of the century it nearly extinguished all other kinds of activity, except the raising of domestic animals and vegetables needed for food. Long before this result was reached, the tendency was deplored by the colonists themselves. To use a modern political phrase, it was "viewed with alarm." This is quite intelligible. "We know now that tobacco, though not strictly a necessary of life, is one of those articles whose consumption may be looked on as certain and permanent. In the seventeenth century, men could hardly be blamed if they regarded the use of tobacco as a precarious fashion."[1] It was also felt that in case of war it would be dangerous for Virginia to be forced to rely upon importing the manufactured necessaries of life. Moreover, the absorption of the colony's industry in the production of a single staple made it especially easy for the home government to depress that industry by stupid legislation, as in the reign of Charles II., when the Navigation Act so seriously diminished the purchasing power of tobacco. For these various reasons many attempts were made to check the cultivation of the Indian weed. The legislation of the seventeenth century was full of instances. It was attempted to establish rival industries and to produce silk, cotton, and iron; laws were made forbidding any planter to raise more than 2000 plants in one year's crop, and so on. All such attempts proved futile; in

Rapid growth of tobacco culture

Attempts to check it

[1] Doyle's *Virginia*, p. 192.

spite of everything that could be done, tobacco drove all competitors from the field.

This tobacco was generally cultivated upon large estates. The policy of making extensive grants of land as an inducement to settlers was begun at an early date, and all that was needed to develop the system was an abundance of cheap labour. English yeomanry, such as came to New England, was too intelligent and enterprising to furnish the right sort. English yeomanry, coming to Virginia, came to own estates for itself, not to work them for others. It soon became necessary to have recourse to servile labour. We have seen negro slaves first brought into the colony from Africa in 1619, but their numbers increased very slowly, and it was only toward the end of the century that they began to be numerous. In the early period the demand for servile labour was supplied from other sources. Convicted criminals were sent over in great numbers from the mother country, as in later times they were sent to Botany Bay. On their arrival they were indented as servants for a term of years. Kidnapping was also at that time in England an extensive and lucrative business. Young boys and girls, usually but not always of the lowest class of society, were seized by press-gangs on the streets of London and Bristol and other English seaports, hurried on board ship, and carried over to Virginia to work on the plantations or as house servants. These poor wretches were not, indeed, sold into hopeless slavery, but they passed into a state of servitude which might be prolonged indefinitely by avaricious or cruel masters. The period of their indenture was short, — usually not more than four years; but the ordinary penalty for serious offences, such as were very likely to be committed, was a lengthening of the time during which they were to serve. Among such offences the most serious were insubordination or attempts to escape, while of a more venial character were thievery, or unchaste conduct,[1] or attempts to make money on their own account.

Need for cheap labour

Indented white servants

[1] For runaways additional terms of from two to seven years were

Their lives were in theory protected by law, but where an indented servant came to his death from prolonged ill-usage, or from excessive punishment, or even from sudden violence, it was not easy to get a verdict against the master. In those days of frequent flogging, the lash was inflicted upon the indented servant with scarcely less compunction than upon the purchased slave; and in general the condition of the former seems to have been nearly as miserable as that of the latter, save that the servitude of the negro was perpetual, while that of the white man was pretty sure to come to an end. For him, Pandora's box had not quite spilled out the last of its contents.

Notion that Virginians are descended from convicts

In England the notion presently grew up that the aristocracy of Virginia was recruited from the ranks of these kidnapped paupers and convicts. This impression may have originated in statements, based upon real but misconstrued facts, such as we find in Defoe's widely read stories, "Moll Flanders"[1] and "Colo-

sometimes prescribed. The birth of a bastard was punished by an additional term of from one and a half to two and a half years for the mother and a year for the father. See Ballagh, "White Servitude in the Colony of Virginia," *Johns Hopkins Univ. Studies*, xiii. 315.

[1] "Among the rest, she often told me how the greatest part of the inhabitants of that colony came thither in very indifferent circumstances from England; that, generally speaking, they were of two sorts: either, 1st, such as were brought over by masters of ships to be sold as servants; or, 2nd, such as are transported after having been found guilty of crimes punishable with death. When they come here . . . the planters buy them, and they work together in the field till their time is out. . . . [Then] they have a certain number of acres of land allotted them by the country, and they go to work to clear and cure the land, and then to plant it with tobacco and corn for their own use; and as the merchants will trust them with tools and necessaries upon the credit of their crop before it is grown, so they again plant every year a little more [etc.]. . . . Hence, child, says she, many a Newgate-bird becomes a great man, and we have . . . several justices of the peace, officers of the trained bands, and magistrates of the towns they live in, that have been burnt in the hand. . . . You need not think such a thing strange; . . . some of the best men in the country are burnt in the hand, and they are not ashamed to own it; there 's Major ——, says she, he was an eminent

THE

Widdow Ranter

OR,

The HISTORY of

Bacon in Virginia.

A

TRAGI-COMEDY.

Acted by their Majesties Servants.

Written by Mrs. *A*. *Behn*.

LONDON, Printed for *James Knapton* at the Crown in St. *Paul's* Church-Yard. 1690.

TITLE OF MRS. APHRA BEHN'S "WIDOW RANTER"

nel Jack." So, too, in Mrs. Aphra Behn's comedy, "The Widow Ranter, or, The History of Bacon in Virginia," one of the personages, named Hazard, sails to Virginia, and on arriving at Jamestown suddenly meets an old acquaintance, named Friendly, whereupon the following conversation ensues:—

Hazard. This unexpected happiness o'erjoys me. Who could have imagined to have found thee in Virginia? . . .

Friendly. My uncle dying here left me a considerable plantation. . . . But prithee what chance (fortunate to me) drove thee to this part of the New World?

Hazard. Why, 'faith, ill company and that common vice of the town, gaming. . . . I had rather starve abroad than live pitied and despised at home.

Friendly. Would [the new governor] were landed; we hear he is a noble gentleman.

Hazard. He has all the qualities of a gallant man. Besides, he is nobly born.

Friendly. This country wants nothing but to be peopled with a well-born race to make it one of the best colonies in the world; but for want of a governor we are ruled by a council, some of whom have been perhaps transported criminals, who having acquired great estates are now become Your Honour and Right Worshipful, and possess all places of authority.[1]

It is not only in novels and plays, however, that we encounter such statements. Malachy Postlethwayt, author of several valuable and scholarly treatises on commerce, tells us: "Even your transported felons, sent to Virginia instead of Tyburn, thousands of them, if we are not misinformed, have, by turning their hands to industry and improvement, and (which is best of all) to honesty, become rich, substantial planters and merchants, settled large families, and been famous in the country; nay, we have seen many of them made magistrates, officers of

Malachy Postlethwayt

pickpocket; there's Justice B—— was a shoplifter, . . . and I could name you several such as they are." *Moll Flanders*, p. 66.

[1] *Plays written by the late ingenious Mrs. Behn*, London, 1724, iv. 110–112.

WESTOVER

militia, captains of good ships, and masters of good estates."[1] Either from the study of Postlethwayt, or perhaps simply from reading "Moll Flanders," we may suppose that Dr. Johnson got the notion to which he gave vent in 1769 when quite out of patience because the ministry seemed ready to make some concessions to the Americans. "Why, they are a race of convicts," cried the irate doctor, "and ought to be thankful for anything we allow them short of hanging!"[2] Thus we witness the progress of generalization: first it is some Virginians that are jail-birds, or offspring of jail-birds, then it is all Virginians, finally it is all Americans. A few years ago, in the time of our Civil War, one used to find this grotesque notion still surviving in occasional polite statements of European newspapers, informing their readers that the citizens of the United States are the "offspring of the vagabonds and felons of Europe."[3]

Dr. Johnson

The statement of the worthy Postlethwayt seems based partly on observation, partly on information, and has unquestionably been the source of inferences much more sweeping than facts will sustain. In order to arrive at clear views of the subject, we must distinguish between two questions: —

The real question

1. What sort of people, on the whole, were the indented white servants in Virginia?

2. How far did they ever succeed, as freedmen, in attaining to high social position in the colony?

In answering the first question, a mere reference to "felons" and "convicts" will carry us but little way. A considerable proportion of the indented white servants were

[1] Postlethwayt's *Dictionary of Commerce*, 3d. ed., London, 1766, vol. ii. fol. 4 M, 2 *recto*, col. 1.

[2] Boswell's *Life of Johnson*, ed. Birkbeck Hill, ii. 312. Professor James Butler, in an excellent paper on "British Convicts shipped to American Colonies," *American Historical Review*, ii. 12–33, suggests that Johnson's impression may have been derived from his long connection with the *Gentleman's Magazine*, wherein the lists of felons, reprieved from the gallows and sent to America were regularly published.

[3] Whitmore, *The Cavalier Dismounted*, p. 17.

poor but honest persons who sold themselves into slavery for a brief term to defray the cost of the voyage from England. The ship-owner received from the planter the passage-money in the shape of tobacco, and in exchange he handed over the passenger to be the planter's servant until the debt was wiped out. Indented servants of this class were known as "redemptioners," and many of them were eminently industrious and of excellent character. Such redemptioners came in large numbers to Virginia, Maryland, and the middle colonies, and much more rarely to New England, where the demand for any kind of servile labour was but small.

Redemptioners

Again, among the transported convicts were many who had been sentenced to death for what would now be considered trivial offences; the poor woman who stole a joint of meat to relieve her starving children was not necessarily a hardened criminal, yet if the price of the joint were more than a shilling she incurred the death penalty. For counterfeiting a lottery ticket, or for personating the holder of a stock and receiving the dividends due upon it, the punishment was the same as for wilful murder.[1] The favourite remedy prescribed in law was the gallows, as in medicine the lancet. Yet many judges and officers of state were conscious of the excessive severity of the system, and welcomed the device of sending the less hardened offenders out of the kingdom instead of putting them to death. There is reason for believing that murderers, burglars, and highwaymen continued to be summarily sent to Tyburn, while for offences of a lighter sort and in cases with extenuating circumstances the death penalty was often commuted to transportation. As a rule it was not the worst sort of offenders who were sent to the colonies.

Punishments for crime

The practice of sending rogues beyond sea began soon after the founding of Virginia, and continued until it was cut short in America by the War of Independence; thereafter the Australasian colonies were made a receptacle for them

[1] Pike, *History of Crime in England*, ii. 447.

until the practice came to an end soon after the middle of the nineteenth century. It has been estimated that between 1717 and 1775 not less than 10,000 "involuntary emigrants" were sent from the Old Bailey alone;[1] and possibly the total number sent to America from the British islands in the seventeenth and eighteenth centuries may have been as high as 50,000.[2] In the lists of such offenders their particular destinations are apt to be very loosely and carelessly indicated; the name Virginia, for example, is often used so vaguely as to include the West Indies.[3] The destinations most commonly specified are Virginia, Maryland, Barbadoes, and Jamaica, but it is certain that all English colonies outside of New England received considerable numbers of convicts. Very few were brought to New England, because the demand for such labour was less than elsewhere, and therefore the prisoners would not fetch so high a price.[4] Stringent laws were made against bringing in such people. In 1700 Massachusetts enacted that every master of a ship arriving with passengers must hand to the custom-house officer a written certificate of the "name, character, and circumstances" of each passenger, under penalty of a fine of £5 for every name omitted; and the custom-house officer was obliged to deliver to the town clerk the full list of names with the accompanying certificates.[5] The existence of this wholesome statute indicates that undesirable persons had been brought into the colony; and the reënactment of it in 1722, with the fine raised from £5 to £100, is clear proof that the nuisance was not yet

Number and distribution of convicts

[1] *American Historical Review*, ii. 25.

[2] *Penny Cyclopædia*, xxv. 138.

[3] *Report of Royal Historical MSS. Commission*, xiii. 605.

[4] The only specific mention which Professor Butler has been able to find of a criminal sent to New England is that of Elizabeth Canning, who was sent out for seven years under penalty of death if she returned to England during that time. She was brought to Connecticut in 1754, married John Treat two years afterward, and died in Wethersfield in 1773. *American Historical Review*, ii. 32.

[5] *Massachusetts Acts and Resolves*, i. 452; ii. 245.

A
DECLARATION
OF THE STATE OF
the COLONY and Affaires
in *VIRGINIA.*
WITH
The Names of the Aduenturors,
and Summes aduentured in
that Action.

By his Maiesties Counseil for VIRGINIA.
22. *Iunij* 1620.

LONDON:
Printed by *Thomas Snodham* 1620.

TITLE OF THE COUNCIL'S REPORT FOR 1620

abated. Nevertheless, partly because of such vigilant measures of prevention, but much more because of the economic reason above alleged, the four New England colonies received but few convicts.

A very different class of transported persons consisted of those who were not criminals at all, but merely political offenders, or even prisoners of war. For example, of the Scotch prisoners taken at Dunbar in 1650, Cromwell sent about 150 to Boston. The next year orders were issued for sending 1610 of the Worcester captives to Virginia, but very few of them seem to have arrived there.[1] In 1652 a party of 272 men captured at Worcester were landed in Boston, but so small was the demand for their labour that they were soon exported southward, — perhaps to the West Indies in exchange for sugar or rum. After the restoration of the monarchy so many non-conformists were sold into servitude in Virginia as to lead to an insurrection in 1663, followed by legislation designed to keep all convicts out of the colony.[2] On the whole, the number of political offenders brought to those colonies that have since become the United States was certainly much smaller than the number of criminal convicts, while the latter were in all probability much less numerous than the redemptioners. During the seventeenth century the demand for wholesale servile white labour was much greater in Virginia and Maryland than elsewhere, and there are many indications that they received more convicts and redemptioners than the other colonies. In the eighteenth century, however, the middle colonies, especially Pennsylvania, probably received at least as large a share.

Prisoners of war

[1] Bruce, *Economic History of Virginia*, i. 609; Gardiner, *History of the Commonwealth*, i. 464. It is commonly said that many of the prisoners condemned for taking part in Monmouth's rebellion, 1685, were sent to Virginia (see Bancroft, *Hist. of U. S.* i. 471; Ballagh, *J. H. U. Studies*, xiii. 293). But an examination of the lists shows that nearly all were sent to Barbadoes, and probably none to Virginia. See Hotten, *Original Lists of Persons of Quality*, *Emigrants*, *Religious Exiles*, *Political Rebels*, etc. pp. 315–344.

[2] Hening's *Statutes*, ii. 50.

Careers of white freedmen

Our survey shows that in the class of indented white servants there was a wide range of gradation, from thrifty redemptioners[1] and gallant rebels at the one extreme down to ruffians and pickpockets at the other. Bearing this in mind, we come to our second question, How far did white freedmen succeed in attaining to high social position in such a colony as Virginia? There is no doubt that, as Postlethwayt declares, some of the best of them did work their way up to the ownership of plantations. In the seventeenth century they were occasionally elected to the House of Burgesses. The composition of that assembly for 1654 affords an interesting example. One of the two members for Warwick was the worthy Samuel Mathews, soon to be elected governor; and one of the four members for Charles City was Major Abraham Wood, who, as a child of ten years, had been brought from England in 1620, and had been a servant of Mathews. John Trussel, the member for Northumberland, and William Worlidge, one of the two members for Elizabeth City, had been servants brought over in 1622, aged respectively nineteen and eighteen.[2] Whether these lads had been offenders against the law does not

[1] Mr. Bruce has well said that in the seventeenth century the white servant was "the main pillar of the industrial fabric" of Virginia, and "performed the most honourable work in establishing and sustaining" that colony. There can be no doubt, as he goes on to say, that the work of colonization which has been performed by the people of England surpasses, both in extent and beneficence, that of any other race which has left an impression upon universal history, and the part the manual labourers have taken in this work is not less memorable than the part taken by the higher classes of the nation." *Economic History of Virginia*, i. 573, 582.

[2] Neill's *Virginia Carolorum*, p. 279; Hotten's *Original Lists*, pp. 207, 233, 254; Hening's *Statutes*, i. 386.

appear, nor do we know whether the child had come with parents not mentioned, or as the victim of kidnappers. We only know that all three were servants,[1] and, if the word is to be understood in the ordinary sense, it was much to their credit that they rose to be burgesses. Cases of ordinary indented servants thus rising were certainly exceptional in the seventeenth century, and still more so in the eighteenth. Nothing can be more certain than that the representative families of Virginia were not descended from convicts, or from indented servants of any sort. Although family records were until of late less carefully preserved than in New England, yet the registered facts abundantly prove that the leading families had precisely the same sort of origin as the leading families in New England. For the most part they were either country squires, or prosperous yeomen, or craftsmen from the numerous urban guilds; and alike in Virginia and in New England there was a similar proportion of persons connected with English families ennobled or otherwise eminent for public service.

Representative Virginia families are not descended from white freedmen

As for the white freedmen, those of the better sort often acquired small estates, while some became overseers of white servants and black slaves. The kind of life which they led is described in Defoe's "Colonel Jack" with that great writer's customary minuteness of information. The class of small proprietors always remained in Virginia, and included many other persons beside freedmen. With the increasing tendency toward the predominance of great estates in tidewater Virginia, there was a tendency for the smaller proprietors to move westward into the Piedmont region or southward into North Carolina, as will appear in the next chapter.

Some white freedmen became small proprietors

[1] In the absence of detailed specific knowledge it is unsafe to base inferences upon the word "servant," inasmuch as in the seventeenth century it included not only menials but clerks and apprentices, even articled students in a lawyer's or doctor's office, etc. See *William and Mary College Quarterly*, i. 22; Bruce, *Economic History*, i. 573-575; ii. 45.

While it was true that "the convicts . . . sometimes prove very worthy creatures and entirely forsake their former follies,"[1] it was also true that many of them "have been and are the poorest, idlest, and worst of mankind, the refuse of Great Britain and Ireland, and the outcast of the people."[2] These degraded freedmen were apt to be irreclaimable vagabonds. According to Bishop Meade, they gave the vestrymen a great deal of trouble. "The number of illegitimate children born of them and thrown upon the parish led to much action on the part of the vestries and the legislature. The lower order of persons in Virginia in a great measure sprang from those apprenticed servants and from poor exiled culprits. It is not wonderful that there should have been much debasement of character among the poorest population, and that the negroes of the first families should always have considered themselves a more respectable class. To this day [1857] there are many who look upon poor white folks (for so they call them) as much beneath themselves; and, in truth, they are so in many respects."[3] Indeed, the fact that manual labour was a badge of servitude, while the white freedmen of degraded type were by nature and experience unfitted to perform any work of a higher sort, was of itself enough to keep them from doing any work at all, unless driven by impending starvation. As manual labour came to be more and more entirely relegated to men of black and brown skins, this wretched position of the mean whites grew worse and worse. The negro slave might take a certain sort of pride in belonging to the grand establishment of a powerful or wealthy master, and from this point of view society might be said to have a place for him, even though he possessed no legal rights. There was no such haven of security for the mean whites. If the negro was like a Sudra, they were simply Pariahs. Crimes against person and property were

Some became "mean whites"

[1] "Tour through the British Plantations," *London Magazine*, 1755.

[2] Hugh Jones, *Present State of Virginia*, 1724, p. 114.

[3] Meade's *Old Churches*, i. 366.

usually committed by persons of this class. They were loungers in taverns and at horse-races, earning a precarious livelihood, or violent death by gambling and thieving; or else they withdrew from the haunts of civilization to lead half-savage lives in the backwoods. In these people we may recognize a strain of the English race which has not yet on American soil become extinct or absorbed. There can be little doubt that the white freedmen of degraded type were the progenitors of a considerable portion of what is often called the "white trash" of the South. Originating in Virginia and Maryland, the greater part of it seems to have been gradually sifted out by migration to wilder regions westward and southward, much to the relief of those colonies. As to the probable manner of its distribution, something will be said in the next chapter.

Long before the end of the seventeenth century, Virginia and Maryland had begun to protest against the policy of sending criminals from England,[1] and as negro slaves became more numerous white servitude was greatly diminished. The rapid increase of negroes began toward the end of the century, and an immense impetus was given it by the *asiento* clause of the treaty of Utrecht in 1713. By way of indemnifying herself for the cost of the War of the Spanish Succession, victorious England bade Spain and France keep their hands off from Africa, while she monopolized for herself the slave trade. We are reminded by Mr. Lecky that this was the one clause in the treaty that seemed to give the most general satisfaction; and while an eminent prelate affixed his name to the treaty and a magnificent *Te Deum* by Handel was sung in

Development of negro slavery; treaty of Utrecht

[1] Before the Revolution this grievance had come to awaken fierce resentment. A letter printed in 1751 exclaims: "In what can Britain show a more sovereign contempt for us than by emptying their gaols into our settlements, unless they would likewise empty their offal upon our tables? . . . And what must we think of those merchants who for the sake of a little paltry gain will be concerned in importing and disposing of these abominable cargoes!" — *Virginia Gazette*, May 24, 1751.

A briefe and true report of the new found land of Virginia: of *the commodities there found and to be raysed, as well mar*chantable, as others for victuall, building and other necessa*rie vses for those that are and shalbe the planters there; and of the na*ture and manners of the naturall inhabitants: Discouered by the *English Colony there seated by* Sir Richard Greinuile *Knight in the* yeere 1585. which remained vnder the gouernment of Rafe Lane Esqui*er, one of her Maiesties Equieres, during the space of twelue monethes: at* the speciall charge and direction of the Honourable SIR WALTER RALEIGH Knight, Lord Warden of the stanneries; who therein hath beene fauoured and authorised by her Maiestie and her letters patents:

Directed to the Aduenturers, Fauourers, *and Welwillers of the action, for the inhabiting and planting there:*

By *Thomas Hariot*; seruant to the abouenamed *Sir Walter, a member of the Colony, and there imployed in discouering.*

Imprinted at London 1588.

TITLE OF THOMAS HARIOT'S BOOK

the churches, it occurred to nobody to denounce as unchristian a national scheme for kidnapping thousands of black men and selling them into slavery.[1] Before 1713 the part which English ships had taken in the slave trade was comparatively small; and it is curious now to look back and think how Marlborough and Eugene at Blenheim were unconsciously cutting out work for Grant and Sherman at Vicksburg. In 1700 there were probably 60,000 Englishmen and 6000 negroes in Virginia; by 1750 there were probably 250,000 whites and 250,000 blacks, while during that same half century the peopling of the Carolinas was rapidly going on.[2] This portentous increase of the slave population presently began to awaken serious alarm in Virginia. Attempts were made to restrict the importation of negroes, and at the time of the Revolutionary War the humanitarian spirit of the eighteenth century showed itself in the rise of a party in favour of emancipation. In 1784 Thomas Jefferson announced the principle upon which Abraham Lincoln was elected to the presidency in 1860, the prohibition of slavery in the national domain; Jefferson attempted to embody this principle in an ordinance for establishing territorial government west of the Alleghanies. In 1787 George Mason denounced the "infernal traffic" in flesh and blood with phrases quite like those which his grandchildren were to resent when they fell from the lips of Wendell Phillips. The life of the anti-slavery party in Virginia was short. After the abolition of the African slave trade in 1808 had increased the demand for Virginia-bred slaves in the states farther south, the very idea of emancipation faded out of memory.

Anti-slavery sentiment in Virginia

I have already remarked upon the approval with which negro slavery was by many people regarded in the days of

[1] Lecky, *History of England*, i. 127.

[2] Smyth's *Tour in the United States*, London, 1784, i. 72. In 1748 Maryland had 98,357 free whites, 6870 redemptioners, 1981 convicts, and 42,764 negroes. See Williams, *History of the Negro Race in America*, i. 247.

Queen Elizabeth. To bring black heathen within the pale of Christian civilization was deemed a meritorious business.[1] But there were people who took a lower and coarser view of the matter. They denied that the negro was strictly human; it was therefore useless to try to make him a Christian, but it was right to make him a beast of burden, like asses and oxen.[2] This point of view was illustrated in the remark made by a lady of Barbadoes, noted for her exemplary piety, to Godwyn, the able author of "The Negro's and Indian's Advocate;" she told him that "he might as well baptize puppies as negroes."[3] This line of thought was pursued to all sorts

Theory that negroes were non-human

[1] See above, vol. i. p. 18.

[2] At the famous meeting in the Tabernacle at New York, in May, 1850, when Isaiah Rynders and his ruffians made a futile attempt to silence Garrison, one of the speakers maintained "that the blacks were not men, but belonged to the monkey tribe." *William Lloyd Garrison: the Story of his Life, told by his Children*, iii. 294. Defenders of slavery at that time got much comfort from Agassiz's opinion that the different races of men had distinct origins. It was perhaps even more effective than the favourite "cursed be Canaan" argument.

[3] Bruce, *Economic History*, ii. 94. About 1854 (I am not quite sure as to the date) it was reported in Middletown, Conn., that the "horrid infidel," Rev. Theodore Parker, had, on a recent Sunday in the Boston Music Hall, brought forward sundry cats and dogs and baptized them in the name of Father, Son, and Holy Ghost!!! I shall never forget the chill of horror which ran through the neighbourhood at this tale of wanton blasphemy. In 1867 I found the belief in the story still surviving among certain persons in Middletown with a tenacity that no argument or explanation could shake. The origin of the ridiculous tale was as follows: The famous abolitionist, Parker Pillsbury, made a speech in which he quoted what the lady said to Godwyn, that "he might as well baptize puppies as negroes." In passing from mouth to mouth the report of this incident underwent an astounding transformation. First the speaker's name was exchanged for that of another famous abolitionist, the strong and lovely Christian saint, Theodore Parker; and then the figure of speech was developed into an act and clothed with circumstance. Thus from the true statement, that Parker Pillsbury told a story in which an allusion was made to baptizing puppies, grew the false statement that Theodore Parker actually baptized cats and dogs. A great deal of what passes current as history has no better foundation than this outrageous calumny.

GATE AT WESTOVER

of grotesque conclusions. Some held that mulattoes were made half human by the infusion of white blood, and might accordingly be baptized. Others deemed it poor economy to baptize the slave, since it would be incumbent on the master to feed Christians better than heathen, and to flog them less. And there were yet others who had heard the doctrine that Christians ought not to be held in bondage, and feared lest baptism should be judged equivalent to emancipation.[1] This notion was at first so prevalent in Virginia that in 1667 it was enacted: "Whereas some doubts have risen whether children that are slaves by birth, and by the charity and piety of their owners made partakers of the blessed sacrament of baptisme, should by vertue of their baptisme be made ffree; It is enacted and declared by this grand assembly and the authority thereof, that the conferringe of baptisme doth not alter the condition of the person as to his bondage or ffreedom; that diverse masters, ffreed from this doubt, may more carefully endeavour the propagation of christianity by permitting children, though slaves, or

[1] Bruce, *op. cit.* ii. 96–98.

those of greater growth if capable, to be admitted to that sacrament." [1]

During the seventeenth century the slave was regarded as personal property, but a curious statute of 1705 declared him to be for most purposes a kind of real estate. He could be sold, however, without the registry of a deed; he could be recovered by an action of trover; and he was not reckoned a part of the property qualification which entitled his master to the political privileges of a freeholder.[2]

Negroes as real estate

In the system of taxation white servants and negro slaves played an important part. The primary tax upon all landholders was the quit-rent of a shilling for every fifty acres, payable at Michaelmas. This quit-rent was at first collected in the name of the Company, but after 1624 in the King's name; and the proceeds were devoted to various public uses. It was always an unpopular tax, inasmuch as there was no feasible way (as now-a-days with our blessed tariffs) of making dullards believe that "the foreigner paid it," and there were frequent complaints of delinquency. Another tax was the duty of two shillings upon every hogshead of tobacco exported. A third was the tax upon slaves and servants. At the close of the seventeenth century adult negroes were valued at from £25 to £40, and children at £10 or £12; there seems to have been little if any difference between the prices of men and women.[3] The taxation of slave property was equitable, inasmuch as it bore most heavily upon those best able to pay.

Taxes on slaves

VIRGINIA HALF PENNY

[1] Hening's *Statutes*, ii. 260.

[2] Hening, iii. 333–335.

[3] For many of these details concerning slavery I am indebted to Bruce's *Economic History of Virginia*, chap. xi., — a book which it would be difficult to praise too highly.

It is generally admitted that the treatment of slaves by their masters was mild and humane. There were instances of cruelty, of course. Cruelty forever lurks as a hideous possibility in the mildest system of slavery; it is part of its innermost essence. In every community there are brutes unfit to have the custody of their fellow-creatures. Such a ruffian was the Rev. Samuel Gray, who

Treatment of slaves

COLONEL JOHN PAGE

had his runaway black boy tied to a tree and flogged to death. Separation of families also occurred, though much less frequently than in later times. But cases of cruelty were on the whole rare. The cultivation of tobacco was not such a drain upon human life as the cultivation of sugar in the West Indies, or the raising of indigo and rice in South Carolina. It created a kind of patriarchal society in which the master felt a genuine interest in the welfare of his slaves. "The solicitude exhibited by John Page of York was not uncommon: in his will he instructed his heirs to provide for the old age of all the negroes who descended to them from him, with as much care in point of food, clothing, and other necessaries as if they were still capable of the most profitable labour."[1] The historian, Robert Beverley, writing in 1705, tells us that "the male servants and the slaves of both sexes are employed together in tilling and manuring the ground, in sowing and planting corn, tobacco, etc. Some distinction indeed is made between them in their clothes and food; but the work of both is no other than

what the overseers, the freemen, and the planters themselves do. . . . And I can assure you with a great deal of truth that generally their slaves are not worked near so hard, nor so many hours in a day, as the husbandmen and day-labourers in England." As for cruelty, he exclaims, with honest fervour, "no people more abhor the thoughts of such usage than the Virginians, nor take more precaution to prevent it."[2]

Nevertheless, a state of enforced servitude is something which human nature does not willingly endure. A slaveholding community must provide for catching runaways and suppressing or preventing insurrections. It is one of the

[1] Bruce, *op. cit.* ii. 107.

[2] Beverley, *History and Present State of Virginia*, London, 1705, part iv. pp. 36–39. The historian was son of Major Robert Beverley mentioned above, on p. 95 of the present volume.

remarkable facts in American history that there have been so few insurrections of negroes. There have been, however, occasional instances and symptoms which have kept slave-owners in dread and given rise to harsh legislation. In 1687 a conspiracy among the blacks on the Northern Neck was detected just in time to prevent the explosion.[1] In 1710 a similar plot in Surry County was betrayed by one of the conspirators, whom the assembly proceeded to reward by giving him his freedom with permission to remain in the colony.[2] The fears engendered by such discoveries are revealed in the statute book. Slaves were not allowed to be absent from their plantations without a ticket-of-leave signed by their master. The negro who could not show such a passport must receive twenty lashes, and was liable to be treated as a fugitive or "outlying" slave. Such runaways were formally outlawed; a proclamation issued by two justices of the peace was read on the next Sunday by the parish clerk from the door of every church in the county, after which anybody might seize the fugitive and bring him home, or kill him if he made any resistance. In the latter event the master was indemnified from the public funds. At the discretion of the county court, such mutilation might be inflicted upon the outlying negro as to protect white women against the horrible crime which then as now he was prone to commit.[3] In 1701 we find an act of the assembly directed against "one negro man named Billy," who "has severall years unlawfully absented himselfe from his masters services, lying out and lurking in obscure places, . . . devouring and destroying stocks and crops, robing the houses of and committing and threatening other injuryes to

Fears of insurrection

Cruel laws

[1] Burk's *History of Virginia*, Petersburg, 1805, ii. 300.

[2] Hening's *Statutes*, iii. 537. For the loss of this slave by emancipation his master was indemnified by a payment of £40 from the colonial treasury.

[3] Hening, iii. 461; vi. 111. In England in the Middle Ages such mutilation was a common punishment for rape; sometimes, in addition, the culprit's eyes were put out. See Pollock and Maitland, *History of English Law before the Time of Edward I.* ii. 489.

severall of his majestye's good and leige people." It was enacted that whosoever should bring in the said Billy alive or dead should receive a thousand pounds of tobacco in reward, and if dead, his master's loss should be repaired with four thousand pounds. Anybody who should aid or harbour Billy was to be adjudged guilty of felony.[1] No penalty was attached to the murder of a slave by his master; but if he were killed by any one else, the master could recover his value, just as in case of damage done to a dog or a horse. Slaves were not allowed to have fire-arms or other weapons in their possession; "and whereas many negroes, under pretence of practising physic, have prepared and exhibited poisonous medicines, by which many persons have been murdered, and others have languished under long and tedious indispositions, and it will be difficult to detect such pernicious and dangerous practices if they should be permitted to exhibit any sort of medicine," it was enacted that any slave who should prepare or administer any medicine whatsoever, save with the full knowledge and consent of the master or mistress, should suffer death.[2] The testimony of a slave could not be received in court except when one of his own race was on trial for life; then, if he should be found to testify falsely, he was to stand for an hour with one ear nailed to the pillory, and then be released by slicing off the ear; the same process was then repeated with the other ear, after which the ceremony was finished at the whipping-post with nine-and-thirty lashes on the bare back, "well laid on." [3] Stealing a slave from a plantation was a capital offence.[4] No master was allowed to emancipate one of his slaves, except for meritorious services, in which case he must obtain a license from the governor and council. If a slave were set free without such a license, the church-wardens could forthwith arrest him and sell him at auction, appropriating the proceeds for the parish funds, and thereby lightening the taxes.[5] When a license was granted, the

[1] Hening, iii. 210.
[2] Id. vi. 105.
[3] Id. 107.
[4] Id. v. 558.
[5] Id. vi. 112.

master received the usual indemnity, and by an act of 1699 the freedman was required to quit the colony within six months;[1] for obviously the presence of a large number of free blacks in the same community with their enslaved brethren was a source of danger. They were apt, moreover, to become receivers of stolen goods, and their shiftless habits made them paupers.[2] Nevertheless there were some free negroes in the colony, and at one time they even appear to have had the privilege of voting, for an act of 1723 deprived them of it; but no free negroes, whether men or women, were exempt from taxation.[3]

Taking slaves to England

Since gentlemen from the North American colonies and from the West Indies not unfrequently visited England, and sometimes remained there for months or years, it was quite natural that they should take with them household slaves to whose personal attendance they were accustomed. In course of time the question thus arose whether the arrival of a slave upon the free soil of England worked his emancipation. According to Virginia law it did not.[4] The opinion expressed in 1729 by Lord Talbot, the attorney-general, and supported by Lord Hardwicke, agreed with the Virginia theory. These eminent lawyers held that mere arrival in England was not enough to free a slave without some specific act of emancipation, but Chief Justice Holt expressed a contrary opinion. Meanwhile masters kept carrying negroes to London until in 1764 the "Gentleman's Magazine" asserted (surely with wild exaggeration) that no less than 20,000 were domiciled there. Escape was so easy for them that their owners felt obliged to put collars on them, duly inscribed with name and address. In 1685 the "London Gazette" advertised Colonel Kirke's runaway black boy, upon whose silver collar the colonel's arms and cipher were engraved; in 1728 the "Daily Journal" informs us that a stray negro has on his collar the inscription, "My Lady Bromfield's black in Lincoln's Inn Fields;" and in the

[1] Hening, iii. 87, 88.
[2] Bruce, *op. cit.* ii. 129.
[3] Hening, iv. 133, 134.
[4] Id. ii. 448, act of 1705.

"London Advertiser," 1756, a goldsmith in Westminster announces that he makes "silver padlocks for Blacks' or Dogs' collars." Colonel Kirke and Lady Bromfield were not American visitors, but residents in London, and there is evidence, not abundant but sufficient, that negroes were now and then bought and sold there for household service. When the forger John Rice was hanged at Tyburn in 1763, his effects were sold at auction, and a black boy brought £32. A similar sale at Richmond in 1771 was mentioned in terms of severe condemnation by the "Stamford Mercury."[1] However the English people may have sanctioned the establishment of slavery beyond sea, they were not disposed to tolerate it at home; and in the sixty years withal since the treaty of Utrecht, the public conscience had grown tender on the subject. The days of Clarkson and Wilberforce were at hand. A cry was raised by the press, a test case was brought before the King's Bench, and in 1772 Lord Mansfield pronounced the immortal decision that "as soon as a slave sets foot on the soil of the British islands he becomes free."

Lord Mansfield's decision

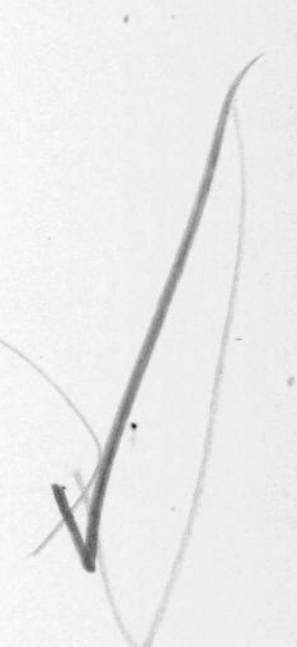

It is not long after this that we find Thomas Jefferson — himself the kindest of masters, and familiar with slavery in its mild Virginia form — thus writing about it: "The whole commerce between master and slave is a perpetual exercise of the most boisterous passions, the most unremitting despotism on the one part, and degrading submissions on the other. Our children see this, and learn to imitate it. . . . The man must be a prodigy who can retain his manners and morals undepraved by such circumstances. . . . With the morals of the people their industry also is destroyed. For in a warm climate no man will labour for himself who can make another labour for him. This is so true that of the proprietors of slaves a very small proportion, indeed, are ever seen to labour. And can the liberties of the nation be thought secure when we have removed their only

Jefferson on slavery

[1] See Larned's excellent *History for Ready Reference*, iv. 2921, where the case is ably summed up.

firm basis, a conviction in the minds of the people that these liberties are of the gift of God? that they are not to be violated but with his wrath? Indeed, I tremble for my country when I reflect that God is just."[1]

Sexual immoralities

In no respect was the system of slavery more reprehensible than in the illicit sexual relations that grew out of it. The extent of the evil may be realized when we simply reflect that the numerous race of mulattoes and quadroons did not originate from wedlock. In 1691 it was enacted that any white man or woman, whether bond or free, intermarrying with a negro, mulatto, or Indian, should be banished for life. In 1705 the penalty was changed to fine and imprisonment, and for any minister who should dare to perform the ceremony there was prescribed a fine nearly equal to his whole year's salary.[2] Yet the "abominable mixture and spurious issue," against which these statutes were aimed, went on, unsanctioned by law and unblessed by the church. Usually mulattoes were the children of negresses by white fathers, but it was not always so. Some of the wretched women from English jails seem to have had fancies as unaccountable as those of the frail sultanas of the Arabian Nights. In such cases the white mother, if free, was fined £15, or in default thereof was sold into servitude for five years; if she were a bondwoman, the church-wardens waited for her term of service to expire, and then sold her for five years; her child was bound to service until thirty years of age.[3] The case of the bastards of negresses was very simply disposed of by enacting that the legal status of children was the same as that of their mother.[4] This made them all slaves,

OLD WOOD CARVING OF LEE ARMS

[1] Jefferson's *Notes on Virginia*, 1782, Query xviii.
[2] Hening, iii. 87, 454. [3] Id. 87. [4] Id. ii. 170, act of 1662.

from the prognathous and platyrrhine creature with woolly hair to the handsome and stately octoroon, and secured their labour to the master. At first the illicit relations between masters and their female slaves were frowned at, and in some instances visited with church discipline or punished by fines.[1] But public opinion seems to have lost its sensitiveness in the presence of a custom which lasted until slavery was abolished.[2] With the signal advance in refinement which the nineteenth century ushered in, there is reason to believe that in many a southern home there were earnest hearts that deplored the dreadful evil, and welcomed at last the downfall of the system that sustained it.

Classes in Virginia society

Some writers divide Old Virginia society into four classes, — the great planters, the small planters, the white servants and freedmen, and the negro slaves. The division is sound, provided we remember that between the two upper classes no hard and fast line can be drawn. Already in England the classes of rural gentry and yeomen shaded into one another; in Virginia both alike became land-holders and slave-owners, they mingled together in society, and their families intermarried. A typical instance is that of the parents of Thomas Jefferson. His paternal ancestors were yeomanry who in Virginia developed into country squires. The first Jefferson in Virginia was a member of the first House of Burgesses in 1619; Thomas's father, who was also a burgess and county lieutenant, owned about thirty slaves. Thomas's mother, Jane Randolph, whose grandfather migrated to Virginia in 1674, belonged to a family that had been eminent in England since the thirteenth century, including among its members a baron of the exchequer, a number of knights, a foreign ambassador, a head of one of the colleges at Oxford, etc.

[1] See Bruce, *Economic History*, ii. 109, where we are told that Jamestown was sorely scandalized by the loose behaviour of "thoughtful Mr. Lawrence."

[2] "The gain from the African labour outweighed all fears of evil from the intermixture." Foote's *Sketches of Virginia*, i. 23.

There can be no doubt that the white blood of tidewater Virginia was English almost without admixture until the end of the seventeenth century, and of the very slight admixture nearly all was from the British islands. There was a desultory sprinkling of Protestant Frenchmen, Walloons, and Dutch, scarcely appreciable in

Huguenots in tide-water Virginia

SIR JOHN RANDOLPH

the mass of the population. But after the revocation of the Edict of Nantes, in 1685, Virginia received a small part of the Huguenot exodus from France. The largest company, more than seven hundred in number, led by the Breton nobleman, Olivier, Marquis de la Muce, arrived in the year

1700, and settled in various places, more particularly at Monacan Town in Henrico County. A part of this company were Waldenses from Piedmont, who had taken refuge in Switzerland, and thence made their way through Alsace and the Low Countries to England.[1] Other parties came from time to time, adding to Virginia many estimable citizens whom France could ill afford to lose. Among the Huguenot names in Virginia, the reader will recognize Maury, Flournoy, Jouet, Moncure, Fontaine, Marye, Bertrand, and others.[2] Dabneys (*D'Aubigné*) and Bowdoins (*Baudouin*) came to

LADY RANDOLPH

Virginia as well as to Boston. Such was the principal foreign admixture while Virginia was still tidewater Virginia, before the crossing of the Blue Ridge. The advent of Germans and Scotch-Irish will be treated in a future chapter.

[1] Baird, *History of the Huguenot Emigration to America*, ii. 178.

[2] Brock, *Documents relating to the Huguenot Emigration to Virginia*, Va. Hist. Soc. Coll. N. S. v.; cf. Hayden's *Virginia Genealogies*, Wilkes-Barré, 1891.

Having thus considered the composition of society in its different strata, as connected with wholesale tobacco culture, let us observe one of the most conspicuous results of this industry as influenced by the physical geography of the country. One might suppose that the necessity for exporting the enormous crops of tobacco would have called into existence a large class of thriving merchants, who would naturally congregate at points favourable for shipping, and thus give rise to towns. In most countries that is what would have happened. But the manner in which the Virginia planter disposed of his crops was peculiar. Most of the large plantations lay on or near the wide and deep rivers of that tidewater country;[1] and each planter would have his own wharf, from which his own slaves might load the tobacco on to the vessels that were to carry it to England. If the plantation lay at some distance from a navigable river, the tobacco was conveyed to the nearest creek and tied down upon a raft of canoes, and so floated and paddled down stream until some head of navigation was reached, where a warehouse was ready to receive it. The vessels which carried away this tobacco usually paid for it in all sorts of manufactured articles that might be needed upon the plantations. Every manufactured article that required skill or nicety of workmanship was brought from England, in ships of which the owners, masters, and

Influence of the rivers upon society

[1] Chesapeake Bay, says Rev. Francis Makemie, is "a bay in most respects scarce to be outdone by the universe, having so many large and spacious rivers, branching and running on both sides; . . . and each of these rivers richly supplied, and divided into sundry smaller rivers, spreading themselves . . . to innumerable creeks and coves, admirably carved out and contrived by the omnipotent hand of our wise Creator, for the advantage and conveniency of its inhabitants; . . . so that I have oft, with no small admiration, compared the many rivers, creeks, and rivulets of water . . . to veins in human bodies." *A Plain and Friendly Perswasive*, London, 1705, p. 5. "One receives the impression in reading of colonial Virginia that all the world lived in country-houses on the banks of rivers. And the Virginia world did live very much in this way." Miss Rowland's *Life of George Mason*, i. 90.

crews were for the most part either natives of the British islands or of New England. Such a ship would unload upon the planter's wharf some part of its motley cargo of mahogany tables, chairs covered with russia leather, wines in great

WHARF AT UPPER BRANDON

variety from the Azores and Madeira,[1] brandy, Gloucester cheeses, linens and cottons, silks and dimity, quilts and feather-beds, carpets, shoes, axes and hoes, hammers and nails, rope and canvas, painters' white lead and colours, saddles, demijohns, mirrors, books, — pretty much everything.[2] If she came from a New England port she was likely to bring salted cod and mackerel, with fragrant rum, either out of the distilleries at Newport and Boston,[3] or imported from

[1] The Huguenots seem to have preferred a French wine, for one of the first things they did (in 1704) was to "begin an essay of wine, which they made of the wild grapes gathered in the woods; the effect of which was noble, strong-bodied claret, of a curious flavour." Beverley, *History of Virginia*, London, 1705, part iv. p. 46. This has the earmark of truth. American clarets are to this day strong-bodied, with a curious flavour!

[2] Bruce, *Economic History of Virginia*, ii. 340–342.

[3] Weeden, *Economic and Social History of New England*, ii. 501.

Antigua or Jamaica. Sometimes the rum came from Barbadoes, along with sugar and molasses, and occasionally ginger and lime-juice, in return for which the ship often carried away some of the planter's live hogs or packed pork, as well as butter, and corn, and tanned leather. The landing of rum was sometimes private and confidential, for there were duties on it which lent a charm to evasion.

Some exports and imports

It would be too much to say that there was no manufacturing done in colonial Virginia. There were probably few if any plantations where the spinning-wheel and hand-loom were not busy. Female slaves and white servants wove coarse cloth and made it up into suits of clothes [1] for people of their sort, and doubtless for some of the small planters. Such artisans as blacksmiths, carpenters, and coopers, shipwrights, tailors, tanners, and shoemakers were often to be found among the indentured servants. Boys of this class were sometimes upon their arrival made apprentices in these crafts. Occasionally negro slaves became more or less skilled as workmen, especially as coopers and joiners. There must always have been some demand for the labour of white freedmen acquainted with any of the mechanical arts, and in fact instances of free labourers in these departments are found. There can be no doubt, however, that the style of work thus attained was apt to be unsatisfactory; for we find such planters as Colonel Byrd and Colonel Fitzhugh, late in the seventeenth century, sending to England for skilled workmen, and offering to pay very high wages, on the ground that it was wasting money to employ such workmen as were to be had in the colony.[2]

Some domestic industries

The historian Beverley, who sometimes indulged himself (like the late Matthew Arnold) in upbraiding his fellow-countrymen for their own good, says of the Virginians in

[1] Bruce, *op. cit.* ii. 471, where we are also told that "in many cases the wealthy planters imported from England the clothes worn by these servants and slaves."

[2] Bruce, *op. cit.* ii. 395, 399, 403, 405.

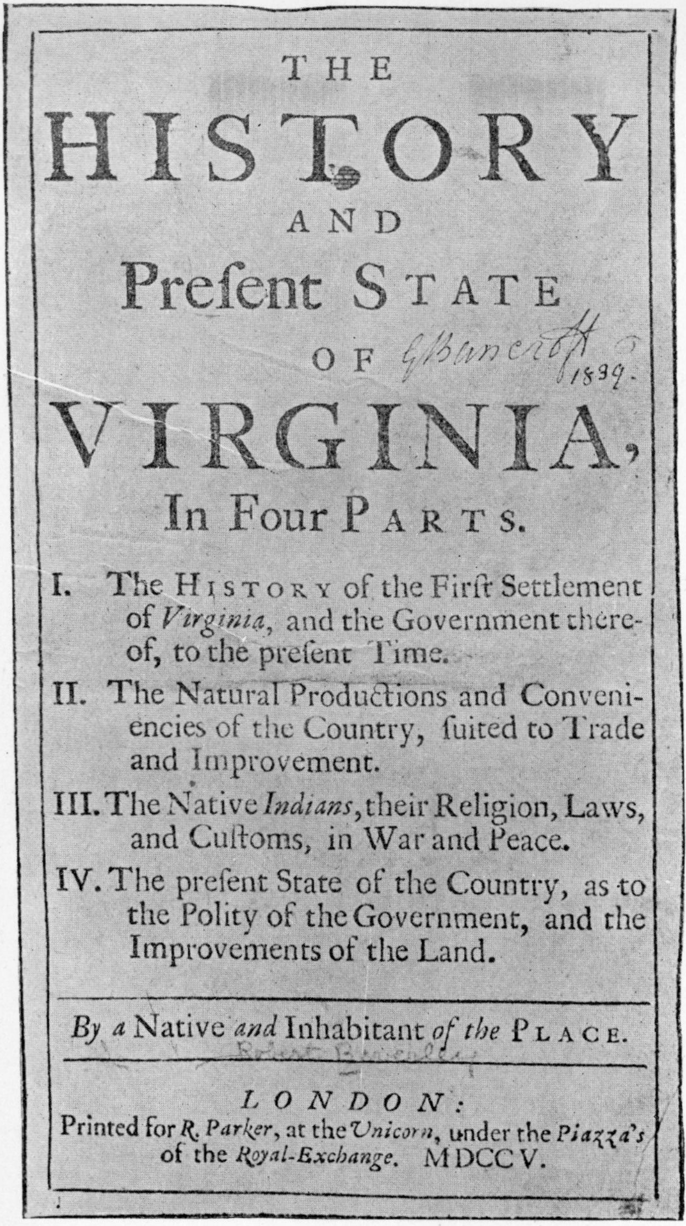

THE

HISTORY

AND

Preſent STATE

OF

VIRGINIA,

In Four PARTS.

I. The HISTORY of the Firſt Settlement of *Virginia*, and the Government thereof, to the preſent Time.

II. The Natural Productions and Conveniencies of the Country, ſuited to Trade and Improvement.

III. The Native *Indians*, their Religion, Laws, and Cuſtoms, in War and Peace.

IV. The preſent State of the Country, as to the Polity of the Government, and the Improvements of the Land.

By a Native *and* Inhabitant *of the* PLACE.

LONDON:

Printed for *R. Parker*, at the *Unicorn*, under the *Piazza's* of the *Royal-Exchange*. MDCCV.

TITLE OF ROBERT BEVERLEY'S HISTORY OF VIRGINIA

Beverley's complaint against his countrymen

1705: "They have their Cloathing of all sorts from *England*, as Linnen, Woollen, Silk, Hats, and Leather. Yet Flax and Hemp grow no where in the World, better than there; their Sheep yield a mighty Increase, and bear good Fleeces, but they shear them only to cool them. The Mulberry-Tree, whose Leaf is the proper Food of the Silk-worm, grows there like a Weed, and Silk-worms have been observ'd to thrive extreamly, and without any hazard. The very Furrs that their Hats are made of, perhaps go first from thence; and most of their Hides lie and rot, or are made use of, only for covering dry Goods, in a leaky House. Indeed some few Hides with much adoe are tann'd, and made into Servants Shoes; but at so careless a rate, that the Planters don't care to buy them, if they can get others; and sometimes perhaps a better manager than ordinary, will vouchsafe to make a pair of Breeches of a Deer-Skin. Nay, they are such abominable Ill-husbands, that tho' their Country be over-run with Wood, yet they have all their Wooden Ware from *England;* their Cabinets, Chairs, Tables, Stools, Chests, Boxes, Cart-wheels, and all other things, even so much as their Bowls, and Birchen Brooms, to the Eternal Reproach of their Laziness. . . . Thus they depend altogether upon the Liberality of Nature, without endeavoring to improve its Gifts, by Art or Industry. They spunge upon the Blessings of a warm Sun, and a fruitful Soil, and almost grutch the Pains of gathering in the Bounties of the Earth. I should be asham'd to publish this slothful Indolence of my Countrymen, but that I hope it will rouse them out of their Lethargy, and excite them to make the most of all those happy Advantages which Nature has given them; and if it does this, I am sure they will have the Goodness to forgive me." [1]

It was not, however, as Mr. Bruce reminds us, from any "inherent repugnance" that Englishmen in Virginia did not take kindly to manufactures, and perhaps the good Bever-

[1] Beverley, *History and Present State of Virginia*, book iv. pp. 58, 83.

COUNTY COURT-HOUSE, DUKE OF GLOUCESTER STREET, WILLIAMSBURG

ley's reproachful tone is a trifle overdone. When the planter could get sharp knives, well-made boots, and fine blankets at his own wharf, simply by handing over to the skipper a few hogsheads of tobacco, he was not greatly to be blamed for preferring them to such dull knives, clumsy boots, and coarse blankets as could be made by the workmen within reach. Many inconveniences, however, grew out of the absence of local means for supplying local needs, and I have little doubt that sundry trades and crafts could have been made to flourish much better than they did, had it not been for the baneful effects of a tobacco currency, which we shall presently have to consider.

True state of the case

The most conspicuous result of the absorption of all activities in tobacco-planting, and the absence of developed arts and trades, was the non-existence of town life. At the beginning of the eighteenth century there was hardly so much as a village in Virginia, unless we make an exception in honour of Williamsburg, the new seat of government and of the college. By the middle of the century Williamsburg contained about 200 houses, chiefly wooden, and its streets were unpaved. Richmond, founded in 1737,

Absence of town life

had a population of 3761 in the census of 1790. The growth of Norfolk, founded in 1705, was exceptional. The trade with the West Indies, for sugar, molasses, and rum, tended to become concentrated there, and the proximity of North Carolina made it a mart for lumber at a time when Virginia forests in the lower tidewater region had been largely cleared away. Colonel Byrd in 1728 says of the Norfolk people: "They have a pretty deal of lumber from the borderers on the Dismal, who make bold with the king's land thereabouts, without the least ceremony." Besides boards and shingles, they sent beef and pork to the West Indies, and it was not unusual to see a score of sloops and brigantines riding in the noble harbour. Under these favourable circumstances the population of Norfolk had come by 1776 to be about 6000. At that time Philadelphia had some 35,000 inhabitants, and New York 25,000, though the population of their two states taken together scarcely equalled that of Virginia.

The lack of urban life was deplored by the legislators at Jamestown and Williamsburg, and assiduous efforts were made to correct the evil; but neither bounties nor orders to build were of avail. To make towns on paper was as easy as to make a promissory note, but nobody would go and settle in the towns. Most of the county seats consisted simply of the court-house, flanked by the jail, the dismal country inn, and the nondescript country "store," where the roving peddler sometimes replenished his pack on his route through the plantations. Among the legislative acts designed to encourage the building of towns, three were especially important. The act of 1662 ordered that thirty-two brick houses should be erected at Jamestown, and forbade the building or repairing of wooden houses there; all tobacco grown in the three counties of James City, Charles City, and Surry was to be sent to Jamestown and stored there for shipping, and the penalty for disobedience of this order was a fine of 1000 lbs. of tobacco; every ship, moreover, ascending the river above Mulberry Island, must land its cargo at Jamestown and

Futile attempts to make towns by legislation

nowhere else, under penalty of forfeiting the cargo. Half of these fines was to be paid to the town, the other half to the informer.[1] The statute of 1680, commonly known as the Cohabitation Act, undertook in somewhat similar fashion to establish a town in every county; and the attempt was renewed on a larger scale in 1691.[2] But all these acts were either disregarded or suspended. When the Surry planter could effect an exchange at his own wharf, without incidental expense or risk, it was useless to command him to load his crop on shallops and send it to Jamestown, with a charge for freight, a chance of capsizing, and warehouse dues at the end of the journey. The skipper withal had no wish to be saddled with port dues, or to be hindered from stopping and trading wherever a customer hove in sight. So skipper and planter had their way, and towns refused to grow.[3] When Thomas Jefferson entered William and Mary College in 1760, a lad of seventeen years, he had never seen so many as a dozen houses grouped together.

The country store

The country store was an important institution in Old Virginia. Under some conditions it would have formed a nucleus around which a town would have been developed, but in Virginia the store seems to have been regarded as a kind of rival against which the town could not compete.[4] It furnished a number of petty centres which did away with the need for larger centres. The store was

[1] Hening, ii. 172–176.

[2] Id. 471–478; iii. 53–69.

[3] There was much strong feeling and vehement writing on the subject by those who were disgusted at the prevalent state of things: "I always judged such as are averse to towns to be three sorts of persons: 1. Fools, who cannot, neither will see their own interest and advantage in having towns. 2. Knaves, who would still carry on fraudulent designs and cheating tricks in a corner or secret trade, afraid of being exposed at a public market. 3. Sluggards, who rather than be at labour and at any charge in transporting their goods to market, though idle at home, and lose double thereby rather than do it. To which I may add a fourth, which are Sots, who may be best cured of their disease by a pair of stocks in town." Makemie's *Plain and Friendly Perswasive*, London, 1705, p. 16.

[4] *Present State of Virginia*, 1697, p. 12.

apt to be an appendage to a plantation, unless its size became such as to reverse the relationship, after the manner of Dundreary's dog. It might be a room in a planter's house, or it might be a detached barn-like building on the estate. Mr. Bruce tells us that to enumerate its contents would be to mention pretty much every article for which Virginians had any use. For example, the inventory of the Hubbard store in York County, taken in 1667, "contained lockram, canvas, dowlas, Scotch cloth, blue linen, oznaburg, cotton, holland, serge, kersey, and flannel in bales, full suits for adults and youths, bodices, bonnets, and laces for women, shoes, . . . gloves, hose, cloaks, cravats, handkerchiefs, hats, and other articles of dress, . . . hammers, hatchets, chisels, augers, locks, staples, nails, sickles, bellows, froes,[1] saws, axes, files, bed-cords, dishes, knives, flesh-forks, porringers, sauce-pans, frying-pans, grid-irons, tongs, shovels, hoes, iron posts, tables, physic, wool-cards, gimlets, compasses, needles, stirrups, looking-glasses, candlesticks, candles, funnels, 25 pounds of raisins, 100 gallons of brandy, 20 gallons of wine, and 10 gallons of aqua vitæ. The contents of the Hubbard store were valued at £614 sterling, a sum which represented about $15,000 in our present currency."[2] One can imagine how dazzling to youthful eyes must have been the miscellaneous variety of desirable things. Not only were the manufactured articles pretty sure to have come from England, but everything else, to be salable, must be labelled English, "insomuch that fanciers used to sell the songsters unknown to England, if they sang particularly well, as *English mocking-birds*."[3]

We have seen how the rivers and creeks were used as highways of traffic; for a long time they were the only highways, and the sloop or the canoe was the only kind of vehicle, public or private, in which it was possible to get about with ease and safety.[4] Until after the middle of the eigh-

[1] A kind of cleaver. [2] Bruce, *Economic History*, ii. 382, 383.

[3] Conway, *Barons of the Potomack and the Rappahannock*, p. 116.

[4] Though the attempts to stimulate shipbuilding met with little suc-

teenth century there were but few roads save bridle-paths, and such as there were became impassable in rainy weather. There were also but few bridges, and these were very likely to be unsound, while the ferry-boats were apt to be leaky. It was often necessary for the traveller to swim across the stream, with a fair chance of getting drowned, and more than a fair chance of losing his horse. The course of the bridle-path often became so obscure that it was necessary to blaze the trees. It was not uncommon for people to lose their way and find themselves obliged to stay overnight in the woods, perhaps with the howls of the wolf and panther sounding in their ears. The highway robber was even a more uncomfortable customer to meet than such beasts of prey; and in those days, when banking was in its infancy and travellers used to carry gold coins sewed under the lining of their waistcoats, the highwayman enjoyed opportunities which in this age of railways and check-books are denied him. Nevertheless crime was far less common than in England or France, and travelling was much safer than one might suppose. This was true of the whole colonial period. In 1777 a young Rhode Island merchant, Elkanah Watson, armed with a sabre and pair of pistols, journeyed from Providence to Charleston in South Carolina, with several hundred pounds sterling in gold quilted into his coat. In seventy days he accomplished the distance of 1243 miles, partly on horseback and partly in a sulky, without encountering any more serious mishaps than being arrested for a British spy in Pennsylvania, and meeting a large bear in North Carolina; and he has left us a narrative of his journey, which is as full of instruction as of interest.[1]

Roads

The traveller in Old Virginia, however, was not likely to carry large sums of money concealed on his person, for he dealt in a circulating medium too bulky for that. In

cess, the manufacture of barges, pinnaces, and shallops was sustained by imperative necessity. See Bruce, *op. cit.* ii. 426–439.

[1] Elkanah Watson, *Men and Times of the Revolution*, 2d ed., New York, 1856, chap. ii.

the course of this book we have had frequent occasions to observe that the Virginian's current money was tobacco. The prices of all articles of merchandise were quoted in pounds of tobacco. In tobacco taxes were assessed and all wages and salaries were paid. This use of tobacco as a circulating medium and as a standard of values was begun in the earliest days of the colony, when coin was scarce, and the structure of society was simple enough to permit a temporary return toward the primitive practice of barter. Under such circumstances tobacco was obviously the article most sure to be used as money. It was exchangeable for whatever anybody wanted in the shape of service or merchandise, and it was easily procured from the bountiful earth. But as time went on this ease of attainment made it an extremely vicious currency. In the course of our narrative we have encountered some of the disastrous financial and social results that flowed from the use of so cheap a substitute for money. Many reasons have been alleged for the scarcity of coin throughout the whole colonial period in Virginia;[1] but assuredly the chief reason was the fact that tobacco was currency. The bad money drove away the good money, as it always does. There are indications that there was always a small stock of coin in the colony, but it was hoarded or sent to other colonies or to England in the settlement of trade balances. Yet it was not easy to demonetize tobacco without a radical revolution in the industrial system and in the commercial relations of the colony.

Tobacco as currency

The nature of the currency evidently had much to do with the ill success of the attempts to encourage manufactures. The carpenter or shoemaker, after doing his work, must wait for his pay until the year's crop of tobacco was gathered and cured. Meanwhile he had nothing to live on unless he raised it for himself; he might either plant grain and rear cattle, or else grow tobacco wherewith to buy things. But the time consumed in these agricultural operations was time taken from his handicraft. The

Effect upon crafts and trades

[1] See Ripley's *Financial History of Virginia*, pp. 119–124.

evil was attacked by legislation. "In 1633 brickmakers, carpenters, joiners, sawyers, and turners were expressly forbidden to take part in any form of tillage." In 1662 tradesmen and artisans were exempted from all taxes except church-rates, on condition that they should abstain from all interest, direct or indirect, in the growing of tobacco. But the evil was not cured.[1]

Further disaster came from the fact that tobacco was a highly speculative crop. The fluctuations in its value were liable to be great and sudden, and they affected the price of every article that was bought and sold throughout the colony. No one could estimate from one year to another, with any approach to accuracy, what the purchasing power of his income was going to be. The inevitable results of this were extravagance in living and chronic debt. The planter was drawn into a situation from which it was almost impossible to extricate himself. "The system of keeping open accounts in London was calculated to encourage extravagance; and these accounts were habitually overdrawn. Many of the merchants even made it a rule to encourage this indebtedness, so as to assure the continuance of their customers. It gave them a certain advantage in all their dealings with the planters."[2] They charged nearly twice as much for their goods sent to Norfolk or Williamsburg as for the same goods sent to New York.[3] In all this they were aided by the Navigation Act.

Effect upon planters' accounts

Extravagance in living was further stimulated by the regal hospitality for which the great planters early became famous. Although the life upon their estates was much more busy than some writers seem to suppose, yet the drudgery of business did not consume all their time; and in their rural isolation, with none of the diversions of town life, the entertainment of guests by the month together

Hospitality

[1] Bruce, *op. cit.* ii. 411–416.

[2] Ripley, *Financial History of Virginia*, p. 122; cf. Bruce, *op. cit.* ii. 368.

[3] McMaster, *History of the People of the United States*, i. 273.

was regarded both as a duty and as a privilege; and the example set by the large plantations was followed by the smaller. Even the keeper of an inn, if he wished to make a charge for food and shelter, must notify the guest upon his arrival, for a statute of 1663 declared that in the absence of such preliminary understanding not a penny could be recovered from the guest, however long he might have staid in the house.[1] As a rule, no person whose company was at all desirable was allowed to stop at an inn, for the neighbours vied with one another in offering hospitality. Every planter kept open house, and provided for his visitors with unstinted hand.

[1] Hening, ii. 192. An old satirical writer mentions the same custom at a Maryland inn, where, however, he did not seem in all respects to relish his supper: —

> So after hearty Entertainment
> Of Drink and Victuals without Payment;
> For Planters Tables, you must know,
> Are free for all that come and go.
> While Pon and Milk, with Mush well stoar'd,
> In Wooden Dishes grac'd the Board;
> With Homine and Syder-pap,
> (Which scarce a hungry dog would lap)
> Well stuff'd with Fat from Bacon fry'd,
> Or with *Mollossus* dulcify'd.
> Then out our Landlord pulls a Pouch
> As greasy as the Leather Couch
> On which he sat, and straight begun
> To load with Weed his *Indian* Gun. . . .
> His Pipe smoak'd out, with aweful Grace,
> With aspect grave and solemn pace,
> The reverend Sire walks to a Chest; . . .
> From thence he lugs a Cag of Rum.

The night had for our traveller its characteristic American nuisance: —

> Not yet from Plagues exempted quite,
> The Curst Muskitoes did me bite;
> Till rising Morn and blushing Day
> Drove both my Fears and Ills away;

but the morning meal seems to have made amends: —

> I did to Planter's Booth repair,
> And there at Breakfast nobly Fare
> On rashier broil'd of infant Bear:
> I thought the Cub delicious Meat,
> Which ne'er did ought but Chesnuts eat.

Ebenezer Cook, *The Sot-Weed Factor; or, a Voyage to Maryland*, London, 1708, pp. 5, 9.

Let us put ourselves into the position of one of these visitors, and get some glimpses of life upon the old plantation. Our host we may suppose to be a vestryman, justice of the peace, and burgess, dwelling upon a plantation of five or six thousand acres, with his next neighbours at a distance of two or three miles.[1] The space is in great part cleared for the planting of vast

Visit to a plantation; the negro quarter

FIREPLACE IN A SLAVE'S KITCHEN

fields of tobacco, but here and there are extensive stretches of woodland and coppice, with noble forest trees and luxuriant undergrowth, much rougher and wilder than an English park. The cabins for slaves present the appearance of a hamlet. These are wooden structures of the humblest sort, built of logs or undressed planks, and afflicted with chronic dilapidation. An inventory of 1697 shows us that the cabin might contain a bed and a few chairs, two or three pots and kettles, "a pair of pot-racks, a pot-hook, a frying-pan, and a beer barrel;" and advertisements for runaways describe Cuffy and Pompey as clad in red cotton, with canvas drawers, waistcoat, and wide-brimmed black hat. Their victuals, of

[1] For the description of the planter's house and its surroundings I am much indebted to the admirable work of Mr. Bruce, chap. xii.

"hog and hominy" with potatoes and green vegetables, were wholesome and palatable. If there were white servants on the estate, they were commonly but not necessarily somewhat better housed and clothed.

Leaving the negro quarters, with their grinning mammies and swarms of woolly pickaninnies, one would presently come upon other outbuildings; the ample barns for tobacco and granaries for corn, the stable, the cattle-pens, a hen-coop and a dove-cot, a dairy, and in some cases a malt-house, or perhaps, as we have seen, a country store. There were brick ovens for curing hams and bacon; and the kitchen likewise stood apart from the mansion, which was thus free from kitchen odours and from undue heating in summer time. There was a vegetable garden, with "all the culinary plants that grow in England, and in far greater perfection," besides "roots, herbs, vine-fruits, and salad-flowers peculiar to themselves," and excellent for a relish with meat.[1] Nearer to the house, among redolent flower-beds gay with varied colours, some vine-clad arbour afforded shelter from the sun. A short walk across the mown space shaded by large trees, called, as in New England, the yard, would bring us to the mansion, very commonly known as the Great House. From this epithet no sure inference can be drawn as to the size of the building, for it simply served to contrast it with its dependent cabins and outhouses. It was often called the Home House. It was apt to stand upon a rising ground, and from its porch you might look down at the blue river and the little wharf, known as "the landing," with pinnaces moored hard by and canoes lying lazily on the bank or suddenly darting out upon the water. Turning away from the river, the eye would rest upon an orchard bearing fruits in great variety, and a pasture devoted to horses of some special breed.

Other appurtenances

The Great House

The planter's mansion might be built of wood or brick, but was comparatively seldom of stone. In tidewater Vir-

[1] Beverley, *History and Present State of Virginia*, book iv. p. 56.

ginia, good stone for building purposes was not readily found, but there was an abundance of red clay from which excellent and durable brick could be made. A number of brick houses were built in the seventeenth century, but wood was much more commonly used, since the work of clearing away the forests furnished great quantities of timber of the finest quality. Among the many articles that were imported from England, bricks are not to be reckoned.[1] Brickmaking went on from the earliest days of the colony, and much of this work was done by white servants and freedmen. In course of time there came to be many brick houses, and chimneys were regularly of this material. For roofs the strong and durable cypress shingle was the material most commonly used. Partition walls, covered first with a tenacious clay and then whitewashed, were very firm and solid. The glass windows, for protection against storms of a violence to which Englishmen had not been accustomed, had stout wooden shutters outside, which gave the house somewhat the look of a stronghold.

Brick and wooden houses

During the seventeenth century not much architectural beauty was attained. To any criticisms on this score the planters would have replied, as the early settlers did to Captain Butler, that their houses were for use and not for ornament.[2] During the eighteenth century some progress was made in this respect, but for the architectural effect of the mansions not much is to be said, though they were often highly picturesque. The earliest type, the house of greater width than depth, with an outside chim-

House architecture

[1] One often hears it said, of some old house or church in Virginia, that it was built of bricks imported from England; but, according to Mr. Bruce, all bricks used in Virginia during the seventeenth century seem to have been made there. Bricks were 8 shillings per 1000 in Virginia when they were 18s. 8¼d. in London, to which the ocean freight would have had to be added. It is not strange, therefore, that Virginia exported bricks to Bermuda. As early as the Indian massacre of 1622 some of the Indians were driven away with brickbats. See Bruce, *Economic History*, ii. 134, 137, 142.

[2] See above, vol. i. p. 201.

ney at each end, is familiar to every one, at least in pictures. It was as characteristic of Old Virginia as the house of huge central chimney and small entryway with transverse staircase was characteristic of early New England. Both are slightly modified types of the smaller English manor-houses of the Tudor period. A more picturesque style, and somewhat more stately, is that of Gunston Hall, the homestead of the Mason family; while scarcely less attractive, and still

STRATFORD HALL

more capacious, is that of Stratford Hall, the home of the Lees. The well-known Mount Vernon shows a further departure from English models; while in Monticello both the name and the house present symptoms of the beginning of that so-called classical revival when children were baptized Cyrus and Marcellus, and dwelt in the shade of porticoes that simulated those of Greek temples.[1]

[1] The Marquis de Chastellux, who visited Monticello in 1782, says: "We may safely aver that Mr. Jefferson is the first American who has consulted the fine arts to know how he should shelter himself from the weather." See Randall's *Life of Jefferson*, i. 373.

The differentiation of rooms for specific uses had by no means proceeded so far as in modern houses. One mediæval English feature which was retained was the predominance of the Hall, or Great Room, used for meals and for general purposes. Along with the hall, there might be as few as five or six rooms, or as many as eighteen or twenty, upstairs and down. Stratford Hall, built about 1725–30, contained eighteen large rooms, exclusive of the central hall,[1] whereas Governor Berkeley's house at Green Spring, built three quarters of a century earlier, had but six rooms altogether. Beside the central hall, there might be a hall parlour, equivalent to reception room and family sitting-room combined, and in this there might be chests and a bed; the others were simply bedrooms. Beds were such as we are still familiar with; their ticking might be stuffed with feathers or hair or straw, but feathers were much more commonly used than now, as they are now more commonly used in chilly England than in the fiery summers and hot-house winters of America. With sheets, blankets, and counterpane, pillows, curtains, and valances, the bed was dressed as at present, save that curtains are now departing along with the brass warming-pans, bequests from higher latitudes. Already the Virginia bed often had a protection for which England could have no use, the mosquito net. For such members of the household as were lazily inclined in the daytime there was a couch, which might be plainly covered with calico, or more expensively with russia leather or embroidered stuffs. The chairs might be upholstered likewise, or be seated with cane, wicker, or rush-work. In every bedroom was a chest for storing clothes not

The rooms

Bedrooms and their furniture

CHAIR OF GOVERNOR GOOCH

[1] *Lee of Virginia*, p. 116.

in immediate use. There were also the ewer and basin, and the case of drawers with looking-glass. If one of the big chimneys was accessible, there was a fireplace for wooden logs, supported on andirons of iron or brass, and guarded by iron or tin fenders; otherwise there was an open brazier, such as we see to-day in Italy. Floors were usually ill-made in those days, and woollen carpets faithfully accumulated dirt; so that the sunbeam straggling through the dimity or printed calico window-curtains would often gild long dusty rays.

In the Hall, or Great Room, the principal feature was the long dining-table of walnut or oak or cedar, flanked either by benches or by chairs. For daily use it was covered with a cloth of unbleached linen, known as holland, while on extra occasions a damask cloth was used. Napkins were abundant, and often of a fine fabric delicately embroidered. Forks, on the other hand, were in the earlier days scarce. Before the seventeenth century, forks were nowhere in general use, save in Italy. Queen Elizabeth ate with her fingers. A satirical pamphlet, aimed at certain luxurious favourites of Henry III. of France, derides them for conveying bits of meat to their mouths on a little pronged implement, rather than do it in the natural way.[1] Forks are nowhere mentioned in Shakespeare. In 1608, while travelling in Italy, one Thomas Coryat took a liking to them and introduced the fashion into England, for which he was jocosely nicknamed *Furcifer*.[2] Naturally the use of forks narrowed the functions of napkins.[3] Spoons

The dinner-table

Napkins and forks

1 Larousse, *Dictionnaire universel*, viii. 668.

2 A *double entendre*, either "fork-bearer" or "gallows-bird."

3 *Meercraft*. — Have I deserved this from you two, for all
My pains at court to get you each a patent?
Gilthead. — For what?
Meercraft. — Upon my project o' the forks.
Sledge. — Forks? what be they?
Meercraft. — The laudable use of forks,
Brought into custom here, as they are in Italy,
To the sparing o' napkins.

Ben Jonson, *The Devil is an Ass*, act v. scene 3.

were in much more common use, and, in the New World as in the Old, were of iron or pewter in the poor man's house, and of silver in the rich man's. The dishes and plates were of earthenware or pewter, but in the eighteenth century the use of chinaware increased. Pewter cups and mugs were everywhere to be seen, and now and then a drinking-horn. Well-to-do planters had silver tankards, sometimes marked with the family arms, as well as silver salt-cellars, candlesticks, and snuffers. A cupboard with glass doors, or light drapery, displayed the store of cups and dishes; while about the walls sometimes hung family portraits, and more rarely paintings of other sorts. This central hall retained many marks of its mediæval miscellaneousness of use; capacious linen-chests, guns and pistols, powder-horns, swords, saddles, bridles, and riding-whips, in picturesque and cosy confusion. In the eighteenth century a luxurious elegance was developed quite similar to that of the "colonial mansions" at the North, such as the Philipse manor-house on the Hudson River, or Colonel Vassall's house in Cambridge, where Washington dwelt for a few months, and Longfellow for many years. Panelled wainscots of oak and carved oaken chimney-pieces were common; the walls were hung with tapestry; and artistic cabinets, screens, and clocks adorned the spacious room. In the Lee homestead at Stratford the hall added to its other functions that of library. The ceiling was very high and vaulted, and parts of the panelled walls had bookshelves set into them.[1] Such rooms were warmed by huge logs of hickory or oak, burning in open fireplaces. They were lighted by candles, which might be made of beef tallow or deer suet, but the favourite material was a wax obtained by boiling the berries of a myrtle that grew profusely in marshy land. It was extremely cheap and burned with a pleasant fragrance, giving a brilliant light.

Silver plate

Wainscots and tapestry

The central object in the kitchen was, of course, the fireplace, which was sometimes very large. At Stratford it was

[1] *Lee of Virginia*, p. 116.

"twelve feet wide, six high, and five deep, evidently capable of roasting a fair-sized ox."[1] In the days when pains were taken not to spoil good meat with bad cooking, your haunch of venison, saddle of mutton, or stuffed turkey was not baked to insipidity in an oven meant for better uses, but was carefully turned about on an iron spit, catching rich aroma from the caressing flame, while the basting was judiciously poured from ladles, and dripping-pans caught the savoury juices. Then there was the great copper boiler imbedded in brick and heated from underneath; there were the kettles and saucepans, the swinging iron pot, the gridirons and frying-pans, and the wooden trays for carrying the cooked dishes to the dining-hall.

The kitchen

The settlers in the strange wilderness of the Powhatans had once had their Starving Time, but it would be hard to point to any part of the earth more bountifully supplied with wholesome and delicious food than civilized Old Virginia. Venison, beef, and dairy products were excellent and cheap. Mutton was less common, and was highly prized. The pork in its various forms was pronounced equal to that of Yorkshire or Westphalia. Succulent vegetables and toothsome fruits were grown in bewildering variety. Good Henry of Navarre's peasant, had he lived in this favoured country, might have had every day a fowl in his pot; while, as for game and fish, the fame of Chesapeake Bay is world-wide for its canvas-backs, mallards, and redheads, its terrapin, its soles, bass, and shad, and, last not least, its oysters. The various cakes which the cooks of the Old Dominion could make from their maize and other grains have also won celebrity.

Abundance of food

To wash down these native viands the Virginian had divers drinks, whereof all the best were imported. Englishmen could not in a moment leave off beer-drinking, but the generous, full-bodied and delicate-flavoured ale of the mother country has never been successfully imitated on this side of the Atlantic, and indeed seems

Beverages, native and imported

[1] *Lee of Virginia, loc. cit.*

hardly adapted to our sweltering summers. Concerning the beer brewed in Old Virginia opinions varied; but since barley soon ceased to be cultivated, and attempts were made to supply its place with maize or pumpkins or persimmons,

OLD DOORWAY AT OATLANDS

we need not greatly regret that we were not there to be regaled with it. Cider, with its kindred beverages, was abundant,[1] and doubtless of much better quality. Apple-

[1] For Planters' Cellars, you must know,
Seldom with good *October* flow,
But Perry Quince and Apple Juice
Spout from the Tap like any Sluce.
Cook's *Sot-Weed Factor*, p. 22.

jack and peach brandy were distilled. Other beverages were imported, most commonly sack, of which Falstaff was so fond; the name was applied to such dry (Spanish *seco*) and strong wines as sherry and madeira. In the cellars of wealthy planters were often found choice brands of red wine from Bordeaux and white wine from the Rhineland. Cognacs were also imported, and of rum we have already spoken. Evidently our friends, the planters, had sturdy tipplers among them.[1] Fortunately for them, the manufacture of coarse whiskey from maize and rye had not yet come into vogue, while of the less harmful peaty "mountain dew" from Ireland or Scotland we hear nothing.

Of the daily life of a rich planter we have a graphic account from John Ferdinand Smyth, a British soldier who travelled through Virginia and other colonies, and sojourned for some years in Maryland, about the middle of the eighteenth century. I cite the description, because so much has been made of it: "The gentleman of fortune rises about nine o'clock; he may perhaps make an excursion to walk as far as his stable to see his horses, which is seldom more than fifty yards from his house; he returns to breakfast between nine and ten, which is generally tea or coffee, bread-and-butter, and very thin slices of venison, ham, or hung beef. He then lies down on a pallet on the floor, in the coolest room in the house, in his shirt and trousers only, with a negro at his head and another at his feet, to fan him and keep off the flies; between twelve and one he takes a draught of bombo, or toddy, a liquor composed of water, sugar, rum, and nutmeg, which is made weak and kept cool; he dines between two and three, and at every table, whatever else there may be, a ham and greens, or cabbage, is always a standing dish. At dinner he drinks cider, toddy, punch, port, claret, and madeira, which is generally excellent here; having drank [*sic*] some few glasses of wine after dinner, he returns to his pallet, with his two blacks to

Smyth's picture of a planter

[1] A minute account of the beverages and their use is given in Bruce, *op. cit.* ii. 211–231.

fan him, and continues to drink toddy, or sangaree, all the afternoon; he does not always drink tea. Between nine and ten in the evening he eats a light supper of milk and fruit, or wine, sugar, and fruit, etc., and almost immediately retires to bed for the night. This is his general way of living in his family, when he has no company. No doubt many differ from it, some in one respect, some in another; but more follow it than do not."[1]

This extract seems to show that Rev. Samuel Peters was not the only writer who liked to entertain his trustful British friends with queer tales about their American cousins.[2] No doubt Mr. Smyth wrote it with his tongue in his cheek; but if he meant what he said, we must remember that the besetting sin of travellers is hasty generalization. We will take Mr. Smyth's word for it that one or more gentlemen were in the habit of passing their days in the way he describes, and we may freely admit that a good many gentlemen might thus make shift to keep alive through some furious attack of the weather fiend in August; but his concluding statement, that this way of living was customary, is not to be taken seriously. An extract from the manuscript recollections of General John Mason, son of the illustrious George Mason, gives a different picture:—

"It was very much the practice with gentlemen of landed and slave estates . . . so to organize them as to have considerable resources within themselves; to employ and pay but few tradesmen, and to buy little or none of the coarse stuffs and materials used by them. . . . Thus my father had among his slaves carpenters, coopers, sawyers, blacksmiths, tanners, curriers, shoemakers, spinners, weavers, and knitters, and even a distiller. His

The mode of life at Gunston

[1] Smyth's *Tour in the United States*, London, 1784, i. 41.

[2] Samuel Peters, a Tory refugee, published in London, in 1781, an absurd "History of Connecticut," in which he started the story of the "Blue Laws" of the New Haven Colony, which most people allude to incorrectly as "Blue Laws of Connecticut." These "Blue Laws" were purely an invention of the mendacious Peters. There never were any such laws. See my *Beginnings of New England*, p. 136.

woods furnished timber and plank for the carpenters and coopers, and charcoal for the blacksmith; his cattle killed for his own consumption and for sale supplied skins for the tanners, curriers, and shoemakers; and his sheep gave wool and his fields produced cotton and flax for the weavers and spinners, and his orchards fruit for the distiller. His carpenters and sawyers built and kept in repair all the dwelling-houses, barns, stables, ploughs, harrows, gates, etc., on the plantations, and the outhouses at the house. His coopers made the hogsheads the tobacco was prized in, and the tight casks to hold the cider and other liquors. The tanners and curriers, with the proper vats, etc., tanned and dressed the skins as well for upper as for lower leather to the full amount of the consumption of the estate, and the shoemakers made them into shoes for the negroes. A professed shoemaker was hired for three or four months in the year to come and make up the shoes for the white part of the family. The blacksmiths did all the ironwork required by the establishment, as making and repairing ploughs, harrows, teeth, chains, bolts, etc. The spinners, weavers, and knitters made all the coarse cloths and stockings used by the negroes, and some of finer texture worn by the white family, nearly all worn by the children of it. The distiller made every fall a good deal of apple, peach, and persimmon brandy. The art of distilling from grain was not then among us, and but few public distilleries. All these operations were carried on at the home house, and their results distributed as occasion required to the different plantations. Moreover, all the beeves and hogs for consumption or sale were driven up and slaughtered there at the proper seasons, and whatever was to be preserved was salted and packed away for after distribution.

"My father kept no steward or clerk about him. He kept his own books and superintended, with the assistance of a trusty slave or two, and occasionally of some of his sons, all the operations at or about the home house above described. . . . To carry on these operations to the extent required, it will be seen that a considerable force was necessary, besides the house servants, who for such a household, a large family and entertaining a great deal of company, must be numerous;

Martha Washington

and such a force was constantly kept there, independently of any of the plantations, and besides occasional drafts from them of labour for particular occasions. As I had during my youth constant intercourse with all these people, I remember them all, and their several employments as if it was yesterday."[1]

Now when we consider that Colonel Mason had some 500 persons on his estate, and was known to have sent from his private wharf as many as 23,000 bushels of wheat in a single shipment, it is clear that no gentleman who spent the day lolling on a couch and sipping toddy could have superintended the details of business which his son describes. George Mason was, no doubt, a fair specimen of his class, and their existence was clearly not an idle one. With the public interests of parish, county, and commonwealth to look after besides, they surely earned the leisure hours that were spent in social entertainments or in field sports.

A glimpse of the life of a planter's wife, which Bishop Meade declares to be typical, is given in a letter from Mrs. Edward Carrington to her sister, about 1798. Colonel Carrington and his wife were visiting at Mount Vernon. After telling how Washington and the Colonel sat up together until midnight, absorbed in reminiscences of bivouac and hard-fought field, she comes to Mrs. Washington, who alluded to her days of public pomp and fashion as "her lost days." Then Mrs. Carrington continues: "Let us repair to the old lady's [Mrs. Washington's] room, which is precisely in the style of our good old aunt's, — that is to say, nicely fixed for all sorts of work. On one side sits the chambermaid, with her knitting; on the other, a little coloured pet, learning to sew. An old, decent woman is there, with her table and shears, cutting out the negroes' winter clothes, while the good old lady directs them all, incessantly knitting herself. She points out to me several pairs of nice coloured stockings and gloves she had just

A glimpse of Mount Vernon

[1] Miss Rowland's *Life of George Mason*, i. 101, 102. This Mason, author of the Virginia Bill of Rights, and member of the Federal Convention of 1787, was great-grandson of the George Mason who figured in Bacon's rebellion. His son John, whose narrative I here quote, was father of James Murray Mason, author of the Fugitive Slave Law of 1850, and one of the Confederacy's commissioners taken from the British steamer Trent by Captain Wilkes in 1861.

finished, and presents me with a pair half done, which she begs I will finish and wear for her sake." At this domestic picture Bishop Meade exclaims: "If the wife of General Washington, having her own and his wealth at command, should thus choose to live, how much more the wives and mothers of Virginia with moderate fortunes and numerous

MARY WASHINGTON

children! How often have I seen, added to the above-mentioned scenes of the chamber, the instruction of several sons and daughters going on, the churn, the reel, and other domestic operations all in progress at the same time, and the mistress, too, lying on a sick-bed!"[1]

[1] Meade's *Old Churches*, i. 98.

HOME OF MARY WASHINGTON

Although Mrs. Carrington may have finished and worn the pair of knit gloves, yet most articles of dress for well-to-do men and women were imported. London fashions were strictly followed. In the time of Bacon's rebellion, your host would have appeared, perhaps, in a coat and breeches of olive plush or dark red broadcloth, with embroidered waistcoat, shirt of blue holland, long silk stockings, silver buttons and shoe-buckles, lace ruffles about neck and wrists, and his head encumbered with a flowing wig; while the lady of the house might have worn a crimson satin bodice trimmed with point lace, a black tabby[1] petticoat and silk hose, with shoes of fine leather gallooned; her lace headdress would be secured with a gold bodkin, and she would be apt to wear earrings, a pearl neck-

Dress of planters and their wives

[1] A rich Oriental silk, usually watered, first made in the *Attabiya* quarter of Bagdad, whence its name.

lace, and finger-rings with rubies or diamonds, and to carry a fan.[1]

The ordinary chances for the ladies to exhibit their garments of flowered tabby, and beaux their new plush suits, were furnished by the Sunday services at the parish church, and by the frequent gatherings of friends at home. Weddings, of course, were high times, as everywhere and always; and the gloom of funerals was relieved by feasting the guests, who were likely to have come long distances over which they must return.[2] These journeys, like the journeys to church and to the court-house, might be made in boats; on land they were made on horseback. Carriages were very rare in the seventeenth century, but became much more common before the Revolution. In their fondness for horses the Virginians were true children of England. In the stables of wealthy planters were to be

Weddings and funerals.

[1] Mr. Bruce gives many inventories taken from county records, of which the following may serve as a specimen: "The wardrobe of Mrs. Sarah Willoughby, of Lower Norfolk, consisted of a red, a blue, and a black silk petticoat, a petticoat of India silk and of worsted prunella, a striped linen and a calico petticoat, a black silk gown, a scarlet waistcoat with silver lace, a white knit waistcoat, a striped stuff jacket, a worsted prunella mantle, a sky-coloured satin bodice, a pair of red paragon bodices, three fine and three coarse holland aprons, seven handkerchiefs, and two hoods." *Economic History*, ii. 194.

[2] The following specimen of a bill of funeral expenses is given in Bruce, *op. cit.* ii. 237: —

	lbs. tobacco.
Funeral sermon	200
For a briefe	400
" 2 turkeys	80
" coffin	150
2 geese	80
1 hog	100
2 bushels of flour	90
Dunghill fowle	100
20 lbs. butter	100
Sugar and spice	50
Dressing the dinner	100
6 gallon sider	60
6 " rum	240

found specimens of the finest breeds, and the interest in racing was universal. Common folk, however, were not allowed to take part in the sport, except as lookers-on. One of the earliest references to horse-racing is an order of the county court of York in 1674: "James Bullocke, a Taylor, haveing made a race for his mare to runn w'th a horse belonging to Mr. Mathew Slader for twoe thousand pounds of tobacco and caske, it being contrary to Law for a Labourer to make a race, being a sport only for Gentlemen, is fined for the same one hundred pounds of tobacco and caske."[1] Half a century later, Hugh Jones tells us that the Virginians "are such lovers of riding that almost every ordinary person keeps a horse; and I have known some spend the morning in ranging several miles in the woods to find and catch their horses only to ride two or three miles to church, to the court-house, or to a horse-race."[2] After 1740 there was a systematic breeding from imported English thoroughbreds.[3] Thirty years later, we are told that "there are races at Williamsburg twice a year; that is, every spring and fall, or autumn. Adjoining to the town is a very excellent course for either two, three, or four mile heats. Their purses are generally raised by subscription, and are gained by the horse that wins two four-mile heats out of three; they amount to an hundred pounds each for the first day's running, and fifty pounds each every day after, the races commonly continuing for a week. There are also matches

Horse-racing

Hugh Jones

[1] *Virginia Magazine*, ii. 294; cf. *William and Mary College Quarterly*, iii. 136.

[2] Jones's *Present State of Virginia*, London, 1724, p. 48.

[3] Mr. W. G. Stanard, in an admirable paper on this subject, gives some names of famous horses then imported, "many of them being ancestors of horses on the turf at the present day;" such as "Aristotle, Bolton, Childers, Dabster, Dottrell, Fearnaught, Jolly Roger, Juniper, Justice, Merry Tom, Sober John, Vampire, Whittington, James, Sterling, Valiant, etc." *Virginia Magazine*, ii. 301.

and sweepstakes very often for considerable sums. Besides . . . there are races established annually almost at every town and considerable place in Virginia; and frequent matches, on which large sums of money depend. . . . Very capital horses are started here, such as would make no despicable figure at Newmarket; nor is their speed, bottom, or blood inferior to their appearance. . . . Indeed, nothing can be more elegant and beautiful than the horses here, either for the turf, the field, the road, or the coach; . . . but their carriage horses seldom are possessed of that weight and power which distinguish those of the same kind in England."[1]

Fox-hunting

Since the Virginians were excellent horsemen, it was but natural that they should enjoy hunting. No sport was more dear than chasing the fox. Washington's extreme delight in riding to the hounds is well known; he kept it until his sixty-third year, when a slight injury to his back made such exercise uncomfortable. Washington was a true Virginian in his love for his dogs, to whom he gave such pretty names as Mopsey, Truelove, Jupiter, Juno, Rover, Music, Sweetlips, Countess, Lady, and Singer. Shooting and fishing were favourite diversions with Washington; when he was President of the United States, the newspapers used to tell of his great catches of blackfish and sea-bass.[2] In these tastes his neighbours were like him. Less wholesome sports were cock-fighting, and gambling with cards. The passion for gambling was far too strong among the Virginians. Laws were enacted against it; gambling debts were not recoverable; innkeepers who permitted any game of cards or dice, except backgammon, were subject to a heavy fine besides forfeiting their licenses.[3]

Gambling

An interesting newspaper notice, in the year 1737, shows

[1] Smyth's *Tour in the United States*, i. 20.

[2] Ford, *The True George Washington*, pp. 194–198.

[3] Hening, v. 102, 229–231; vi. 76–81. Washington was very fond of playing at cards for small stakes, also at billiards; and he sometimes bet moderately at horse-races. See Ford, *loc. cit.*

that some of the innocent open-air sports of mediæval England still survived: "We have advice from Hanover County, that on St. Andrew's Day there are to be Horse Races and several other Diversions, for the entertainment of the Gentlemen and Ladies, at the Old Field, near Captain John Bickerton's, in that county (if permitted by the Hon. Wm. Byrd, Esquire, Proprietor of said land), the substance of which is as follows, viz.: It is proposed that 20 Horses or Mares do run round a three miles' course for a prize of five pounds.

A rural entertainment

"That a Hat of the value of 20*s* be cudgelled for, and that after the first challenge made the Drums are to beat every Quarter of an hour for three challenges round the Ring, and none to play with their Left hand.

"That a violin be played for by 20 Fiddlers; no person to have the liberty of playing unless he bring a fiddle with him. After the prize is won they are all to play together, and each a different tune, and to be treated by the company.

"That 12 Boys of 12 years of age do run 112 yards for a Hat of the cost of 12 shillings.

"That a Flag be flying on said Day 30 feet high.

"That a handsome entertainment be provided for the subscribers and their wives; and such of them as are not so happy as to have wives may treat any other lady.

"That Drums, Trumpets, Hautboys, &c., be provided to play at said entertainment.

"That after dinner the Royal Health, His Honour the Governor's, &c., are to be drunk.

"That a Quire of ballads be sung for by a number of Songsters, all of them to have liquor sufficient to clear their Wind Pipes.

"That a pair of Silver Buckles be wrestled for by a number of brisk young men.

"That a pair of handsome Shoes be danced for.

"That a pair of handsome silk Stockings of one Pistole[1] value be given to the handsomest young country maid that

[1] About four dollars.

appears in the Field. With many other Whimsical and Comical Diversions too numerous to mention.

"And as this mirth is designed to be purely innocent and void of offence, all persons resorting there are desired to behave themselves with decency and sobriety; the subscribers being resolved to discountenance all immorality with the utmost rigour." [1]

The part played by violins in this quaint programme reminds us that fiddling was an accomplishment highly esteemed in the Old Dominion. As an accompaniment for dancing it was very useful in the home parties on the plantations. The philosophic Thomas Jefferson, as a dead shot with the rifle, a skilful horseman, and a clever violinist, was a typical son of Virginia. As boys learned to play the violin, and sometimes the violoncello, girls were taught to play the virginal, which was an ancestral form of the piano. Virginals, and afterward harpsichords, were commonly to be found in the houses of the gentry, and not unfrequently hautboys, flutes, and recorders.[2] The music most often played with these instruments was probably some form of dance or the setting of a popular ballad; but what is called "classical music" was not unknown. Among the effects of Cuthbert Ogle, a musician at Williamsburg, who died in 1755, we find Handel's "Acis and Galatea," and "Apollo's Feast," four books of instrumental scores of his oratorios, and ten books of his songs; also a manuscript score of Corelli's sonatas, and concertos by the English composers,

Music

[1] *Virginia Gazette*, October, 1737, cited in Rives's *Life of Madison*, i. 87, and Lodge's *History of the English Colonies*, pp. 84, 85.

[2] The recorder was a member of the flute family, and its name may be elucidated by Shakespeare's charming lines (*Pericles*, act iv., prologue): —

To the lute
She sang, and made the night-bird mute
That still records with moan.

Mr. Bruce (*op. cit.* ii. 175) mentions *cornets* as in use in Old Virginia, but this of course means an obsolete instrument of the hautboy family, not the modern brass cornet, which has so unhappily superseded the noble trumpet.

William Felton and Charles Avison, now wellnigh forgotten.[1]

After 1716 there was a theatre at Williamsburg, and during the sessions of the assembly, when planters with their families came from far and wide, there was much gayety. At other seasons the monotony of rural life was varied by the recreations above described, with an occasional picnic in the woods, or a grand barbecue in honour of some English victory or the accession of a new king.

Other recreations.

Some time was found for reading. The inventories of personal estates almost always include books, in some instances few and of little worth, in others numerous and valuable. The library of Ralph Wormeley, of Rosegill, contained about four hundred titles. Wormeley, who had been educated at Oriel College, Oxford, was president of the council, secretary of state, and a trustee of William and Mary College; he died in 1701. Among his books were Burnet's "History of the Reformation," a folio history of Spain, an ecclesiastical history in Latin, Camden's "Britannia," Lord Bacon's "History of Henry VII.," and his "Natural History," histories of Scotland, Ireland, France, the Netherlands, and the West Indies, biographies of Richard III., Charles I., and George Castriot, Plutarch's Lives, Burnet's "Theory of the Earth," Willis's "Practice of Physick," Heylin's "Cosmography," "a chirurgical old book," "the Chyrurgans mate," Galen's "Art of Physick," treatises on gout, pancreatic juice, pharmacy, scurvy, and many other medical works, Coke's Reports and his "Institutes," collections of Virginia and New England laws, a history of tithes, "The Office of Justice of the Peace," a Latin treatise on maritime law, and many other law books, Usher's "Body of Divinity," Hooker's "Ecclesiastical Polity," Poole's "Annotations to the Bible," "A Reply to the Jesuits," Fuller's "Holy State" and his "Worthies," a concordance to the Bible, Jeremy Taylor's "Holy Living and Dying," "The

Wormeley's library

[1] The inventory is printed in *William and Mary College Quarterly*, iii. 251.

Whole Duty of Man," a biography of St. Augustine, Baxter's "Confession of Faith," and many books of divinity, a liberal assortment of dictionaries and grammars of English, French, Spanish, Latin, and Greek, the essays of Montaigne and other French books, Cæsar, Virgil, Horace, Ovid, Thucydides, Josephus, Quintus Curtius, Seneca, Terence, "Æsop's Fables," "Don Quixote," "Hudibras," Quarles's poems, George Herbert's poems, Howell's "Familiar Letters," Waller's poems, the plays of Sir William Davenant, "ffifty Comodys & tragedies in folio," "The Displaying of Supposed Witchcraft," "An Embersee from ye East India Comp^a to ye Grand Tartar," "The Negro's and Indian's Advocate," "A Looking Glass for the Times," and so on.[1] Though not the library of a scholar, it indicates that its owner was a thoughtful man and fairly well informed.

Libraries of Byrd and Lee

A more remarkable library was that of William Byrd, of Westover. It contained 3625 volumes, classified nearly as follows: History, 700; Classics, etc., 650; French, 550; Law, 350; Divinity, 300; Medicine, 200; Scientific, 225; Entertaining, etc., 650.[2] This must have been one of the largest collections of books made in the colonial period. That of the second Richard Lee, who died in 1715, contained about 300 titles, among which we notice many more Greek and Latin writers than in Wormeley's, especially such names as Epictetus, Aristotle de Anima, Diogenes Laertius, Lucian, Heliodorus, Claudian, Arrian, and Orosius, besides such mediæval authors as Albertus Magnus and Laurentius Valla.[3]

Such libraries were of course exceptional. In most planters' houses you would probably have found a few English classics, with perhaps "Don Quixote" and "Gil Blas," and an assortment of books on divinity, manuals for magistrates, and helps in farming. Virginia was not eminent as a literary

[1] The full list is given in *William and Mary College Quarterly*, iii. 170–174.

[2] See Lyman Draper, in *Virginia Historical Register*, iv. 87–90.

[3] *William and Mary College Quarterly*, iii. 247–249.

or bookish community. There was no newspaper until the establishment of the "Virginia Gazette" in 1736. As for schools, the Lords Commissioners of Plantations sent over a series of interrogatories to Sir William Berkeley in 1671, and asked him, among other things, what provision was made for public instruction. His reply was characteristic: "I thank God there are no free

Schools and printing

William Berkeley

schools nor printing, and I hope we shall not have these hundred years; for learning has brought disobedience and heresy and sects into the world, and printing has divulged them, and libels against the best government. God keep us from both!"[1] Lord Culpeper seems to have been much of Berkeley's way of thinking, for we read that, "February 21, 1682, John Buckner [was] called before the Lord Culpeper and his council for printing the laws of 1680 without his excellency's license, and he and the printer [were] ordered to enter into bond in £100 *not to print anything* thereafter until his majesty's pleasure should be known."[2] The pleasure of Charles II. was, that nobody should use a printing-press in Virginia, and so he instructed the next governor, Lord Howard, in 1684.

The establishment of a system of schools such as flourished in New England was prevented by the absence of town life and the long distances between plantations. When Berkeley said there were no free schools in Virginia, he may have had in mind the contrast with New England. No such schools were founded in Virginia by the assembly, but there were instances of free schools founded by individuals; as, for example, the Symms school in 1636, Captain Moon's school in 1655, Richard Russell's in 1667,

Private free schools

[1] Hening, ii. 517.

[2] Id. ii. 518.

Merchants of Virginia.

THe Company of Merchants, called *Merchants of Virginia*, *Bermudas*, or *Summer-Ilands*, for (as I heare) all these additions are given them. I know not the time of their incorporating, neither by whom their Armes, Supporters, and Crest were granted, and therefore am compelled to leaue them abruptly.

SEAL OF COLONY OF VIRGINIA

Mr. King's in 1669, the Eaton school some time before 1689, and Edward Moseley's in 1721.[1] Indeed, there was after 1646[2] a considerable amount of compulsory primary education in Virginia, much more than has been generally supposed, since the records of it have been buried in the parish vestry-books. In the eighteenth century we find evidences that pains were taken to educate coloured people.[3] It was not unusual for the plantation to have among its numerous outbuildings a school conducted by some rustic dignitary of the neighbourhood. In the "old field schools" little more was taught than "the three Rs," but these humble institutions are not to be despised; for it was in one of them, kept by "Hobby, the sexton," that George Washington learned to read, write, and cipher. His father and his elder brother Lawrence had been educated at Appleby School, in England; George himself, after an interval with a Mr. Williams, near Wakefield, finished his school-days at an excellent academy in Fredericksburg, of which Rev. James Marye was master. The sons of George Mason studied two years at an academy in Stafford County kept by a Scotch parson named Buchan, "a pious man and profound classical scholar." Afterwards John Mason was

Academies and tutors

[1] *Virginia Magazine*, i. 326, 348; *William and Mary College Quarterly*, v. 113. Allusion has already been made, on page 5 of the present volume, to the school founded by Benjamin Symms, or Symes.

[2] Hening, i. 336.

[3] President Tyler cites from the vestry-book of Petsworth Parish, in Gloucester County, an indenture of October 30, 1716, wherein Ralph Bevis agrees to "give George Petsworth, a molattoe boy of the age of 2 years, 3 years' schooling, and carefully to Instruct him afterwards that he may read well in any part of the Bible, also to Instruct and Learn him ye sd molattoe boy such Lawfull way or ways that he may be able, after his Indented time expired, to gitt his own Liveing, and to allow him sufficient meat, Drink, washing, and apparill, until the expiration of ye sd time, &c., and after ye finishing of ye sd time to pay ye sd George Petsworth all such allowances as ye Law Directs in such cases, as also to keep the aforesd Parish Dureing ye aforesd Indented time from all manner of Charges," etc. *William and Mary College Quarterly*, v. 219.

sent to study mathematics with an expert named Hunter, "a Scotchman also and quite a recluse, who kept a small school in a retired place in Calvert County, Maryland." Much teaching was also done by private tutors. In the Mason household there were three Scotchmen in succession, of whom "the two last were especially engaged [in Scotland] to come to America (as was the practice in those times with families who had means) by my father to live in his house and educate the children. . . . The tutoress of my sisters was a Mrs. Newman. She remained in the family for some time."[1]

Sometimes the schoolmaster or private tutor was an indented white servant who had come out as a redemptioner, or even as a convict. Among the criminals there might be persons of rank, as Sir Charles Burton, a Lincolnshire baronet, who was transported to America in 1722 for "stealing a cornelian ring set in gold;" or scholars, like Henry Justice, Esq., of the Middle Temple, Barrister, who in 1736 was convicted of stealing from the library of Trinity College, Cambridge, "a Field's Bible with cuts, and Common-prayer, value £25, Newcastle's Horsemanship, value £10, several other books of great value, several Tracts cut out of books, etc." For this larceny, although Mr. Justice begged hard to be allowed to stay in England for the sake of his clients, "with several of whom he had great concerns," he was nevertheless sent to America for seven years, under penalty of death if he were to return within that time.[2] From such examples we see that, while the convict ships may not have brought many Eugene Arams, they certainly brought men more likely to find employment in teaching than in manual labour. Jonathan Boucher, rector at Annapolis in 1768, declares that "not a ship arrives with either redemptioners or convicts, in which schoolmasters are not as regularly advertised for sale as weavers, tailors, or any other

Convicts as tutors

[1] Miss Rowland's *Life of George Mason*, i. 97.

[2] Butler's "British Convicts Shipped to American Colonies," *American Historical Review*, ii. 27.

trade; with little other difference that I can hear of, except perhaps that the former do not usually fetch so good a price as the latter."[1]

Sometimes, as we have seen in the case of Augustine Washington and his son Lawrence, the young Virginians were sent to school in England. Oftener, perhaps, the education begun at the country school or with private tutors was "finished" (as the phrase goes) at one of the English universities. Oxford[2] seems to have been the favourite Alma Mater, doubtless for the same reason that caused Cambridge to be chiefly represented among the founders of New England; Oxford was ultra-royalist in sentiment, while Cambridge was deeply tinged with Puritanism.

Virginians at Oxford

[1] The worthy pastor even goes so far as to exclaim, with a groan, that two thirds of the schoolmasters in Maryland were convicts working out a term of penal servitude! Boucher's *Thirteen Sermons*, p. 182. But in such declamatory statements it is never safe to depend upon numbers and figures. In the present case we may conclude that the number of such schoolmasters was noticeable; we are not justified in going further.

[2] From the excellent papers by W. G. Stanard, on "Virginians at Oxford," *William and Mary College Quarterly*, ii. 22, 149, I have culled a few items which may be of interest: —

John Lee, *armiger* (son of 1st Richard, see above, p. 16), educated at Queens, B. A. 1662, burgess.

Rowland Jones, *cler.*, Merton, matric. 1663, pastor Bruton Parish.

Ralph Wormeley, *armiger*, of Rosegill (see above, p. 222), Oriel, matric. 1665, secretary of state, etc.

Emanuel Jones, *cler.*, Oriel, B. A. 1692, pastor Petsworth Parish.

Bartholomew Yates, *cler.*, Brasenose, B. A. 1698, Prof. Divinity W. & M.

Mann Page, *armiger*, St. John's, matric. 1709, member of council.

William Dawson, *plebs.*, Queens, matric. 1720, M. A. 1728, D. D. 1747, Prof. Moral Phil. W. & M. 1729, Pres. W. & M. 1743–52.

Henry Fitzhugh, *gent.*, Christ Church, matric. 1722, burgess.

Christopher Robinson, *gent.*, Oriel, matric. 1724, studied at Middle Temple.

Christopher Robinson, *gent.*, Oriel, matric. 1721, M. A. 1729, Fellow of Oriel.

Musgrave Dawson, *plebs.*, Queens, B. A. 1747, pastor Raleigh Parish.

Lewis Burwell, *armiger*, Balliol, matric. 1765.

This difference would readily establish habits and associations among the early Virginians which would be followed.

It was not in all cases necessary to go to England to obtain a thorough education. James Madison's tutors were the parish minister and an excellent Scotch schoolmaster; he was graduated at Princeton College in 1772, and never crossed the Atlantic; yet for the range,

James Madison

HOME OF THE WASHINGTON FAMILY

depth, and minuteness of his knowledge of ancient and modern history and of constitutional law, he has been rivalled by no other English-speaking statesman save Edmund Burke. Such an instance, however, chiefly shows how much more depends upon the individual than upon any institutions. There are no rules by which you can explain the occurrence of a heaven sent genius.

On the whole, the facilities for education, whether primary or advanced, were very imperfect in the Old Dominion. This becomes especially noticeable from the contrast with

New England, which inevitably suggests itself. It is no doubt customary with historical writers to make too much of this contrast. The people of colonial New England were not all well-educated, nor were all their country schools better than old field schools. The farmer's boy, who was taught for two winter months by a man and two summer months by a woman, seldom learned more in the district school than how to read, write, and cipher. For Greek and Latin, if he would go to college, he had usually to obtain the services of the minister or some other college-bred man in the village. There was often a disposition on the part of the town meetings to shirk the appropriation of a sum of money for school purposes, and many Massachusetts towns were fined for such remissness.[1] This was especially true of the early part of the eighteenth century, when the isolated and sequestered life of two generations had lowered the high level of education which the grandfathers had brought across the ocean. In those dark days of New England, there might now and then be found in rural communities men of substance who signed deeds and contracts with their mark.

Contrast with New England in respect of educational advantages

After making all allowances, however, the contrast between the New England colonies and the Old Dominion remains undeniable, and it is full of interest. The contrast is primarily based upon the fact that New England was settled by a migration of organized congregations, analogous to that of the ancient

Causes of the difference

[1] Weeden, *Economic and Social History of New England*, i. 282, 412, 419; ii. 861. For neglecting to "set up school" for the year, a town would be presented by the grand jury of the county, and would then try to make excuses. "In February, 1744, the usual routine was repeated. The farmers were summoned 'to know what the Town's Mind is for doing about a School for the insuing year.' The school of the previous year having cost £55 old tenor, which may have been equivalent to 55 Spanish dollars, and it being necessary to raise this sum by a general taxation, the Town's Mind was for doing nothing; and not until the following July did it consent to have a school opened." Bliss, *Colonial Times on Buzzard's Bay*, p. 118.

Greek city-communities; whereas the settlement of Virginia was effected by a migration of individuals and families. These circumstances were closely connected with the Puritan doctrine of the relations between church and state, and furthermore, as I have elsewhere shown,[1] the Puritan theory of life made it imperatively necessary, in New England as in Scotland, to set a high value upon education. The compactness of New England life, which was favoured by the agri-

SCHOOLHOUSE AT TUCKAHOE, WHERE THOMAS JEFFERSON WENT TO SCHOOL

cultural system of small farms owned by independent yeomen, made it easy to maintain efficient schools. In Virginia, on the other hand, the agricultural conditions interposed grave obstacles to such a result. There was no such pervasive

[1] In my *Beginnings of New England*, pp. 148–153.

organization as in New England, where the different grades of school, from lowest to highest, coöperated in sustaining each other. There were heroic friends of education in Virginia. James Blair and the faithful scholars who worked with him conferred a priceless boon upon the commonwealth; but the vitality of William and Mary College often languished for lack of sustenance that should have been afforded by lower schools, and it was impossible for it to exercise such a widespread seminal influence as Yale and Harvard, sending their graduates into every town and village as ministers, lawyers, and doctors, schoolmasters and editors, merchants and country squires.

Among the founders of New England were an extraordinary number of clergymen noted for their learning, such as Hooker and Shepard, Cotton and Williams, Eliot and the Mathers; together with such cultivated laymen as Winthrop and Bradford, familiar with much of the best that was written in the world, and to whom the pen was an easy and natural instrument for expressing their thoughts. The character originally impressed upon New England by such men was maintained by the powerful influence of the colleges and schools, so that there was always more attention devoted to scholarship and to writing than in any of the other colonies. Communities of Europeans, thrust into a wilderness and severed from Europe by the ocean, were naturally in danger of losing their higher culture and lapsing into the crudeness of frontier life. All the American colonies were deeply affected by this situation. While there were many and great advantages in the freedom from sundry Old World trammels, yet in some respects the influence of the wilderness was barbarizing. It was due to the circumstances above mentioned that the New England colonies were more successful than the others in resisting this influence, and avoiding a breach of continuity in the higher spiritual life of the community. This is strikingly illustrated by the history of American literature. Among men of letters and science born and educated in America before the Revolution, there were three whose fame is more than national, whose names belong among the great of all times and countries. Of these, Jonathan Edwards was a native of Connecticut, Benjamin Franklin and Count Rumford were natives of Massachusetts. In such men we can trace the continuity between the intellectual life of England in the seventeenth century and that of America in the nineteenth. In Virginia, if we except political writers, we find

Illustrations from history of American intellect

BYRD ARMS

no names so high as these. But there is one political book which must not be excepted, because it is a book for all time. "The Federalist" is one of the world's philosophical and literary masterpieces, and of its three authors James Madison took by far the deepest and most important part in creating it.[1]

[1] Of the numbers in *The Federalist*, 51 were written by Hamilton, 29 by Madison, and 5 by Jay. But the frame of government which the book was written to explain and defend was not at all the work of Hamilton, whose part in the proceedings of the Federal Convention was almost *nil*. It was very largely the work of Madison, and while

Among books of a second order, — books which do not rank among classics, — there are some which deserve and have won a reputation that is more than local. Of such books, Hutchinson's "History of Massachusetts Bay" is a good example. In the colonial times historical literature was of better quality than other kinds of writing; and Virginia produced three historical writers of decided merit. With Robert Beverley the reader has already made some acquaintance through the extracts cited in these pages. His "History of Virginia," published in London in 1705, is a little book full of interesting details concerning the country and the life of its red and white inhabitants. The author's love of nature is charming, and his style so simple, direct, and sprightly that there is not a dull page in the book. It was written during a visit to London, where Beverley happened to see the proof-sheets of Oldmixon's forthcoming "British Empire in America," and was disgusted with the silly blunders that swarmed on every page. He wrote his little book as an antidote, and did it so well that many coming generations will read it with pleasure.

Virginia's historians; Robert Beverley

A book of more pretension and of decided merit is the "History of Virginia" by Rev. William Stith, who was president of William and Mary College from 1752 to his death in 1755. The book, which was published at Williamsburg in 1747, was but the first volume of a work which, had it been completed on a similar scale, would have filled six or eight. It covers only the earliest period, ending with the downfall of the Virginia Company in 1624; and among its merits is the good use to which the author put the minutes of the Company's proceedings made at the instance of Nicholas Ferrar.[1] Stith's work is accurate and scholarly, and his narrative is dignified and often graphic. His account of James I. is pithy: "He had, in truth, all the

William Stith

The Federalist shows Hamilton's marvellous flexibility of intelligence, it is Madison who is master and Hamilton who is his expounder.

[1] See above, vol. i. p. 209.

THE

HISTORY

OF THE

First DISCOVERY

AND

SETTLEMENT

OF

VIRGINIA:

BEING

An ESSAY towards a General HISTORY of this COLONY.

By WILLIAM STITH. *A. M.*
Rector of *Henrico* Parish, and one of the Governors of *William* and *Mary* COLLEGE.

---

*Tantæ molis erat *** condere gentem.* Virg.

WILLIAMSBURG:
Printed by WILLIAM PARKS, M,DCC,XLVII.

MD

TITLE OF STITH'S HISTORY

forms of wisdom, — forever erring very learnedly, with a wise saw or Latin sentence in his mouth; for he had been bred up under Buchanan, one of the brightest geniuses and most accomplished scholars of that age, who had given him Greek and Latin in great waste and profusion, but it was not in his power to give him good sense. That is the gift of God and nature alone, and is not to be taught; and Greek and Latin without it only cumber and overload a weak head, and often render the fool more abundantly foolish. I must, therefore, confess that I have ever had . . . a most contemptible opinion of this monarch; which has, perhaps, been much heightened and increased by my long studying and conning over the materials of this history. For he appears in his dealings with the Company to have acted with such mean arts and fraud . . . as highly misbecome majesty."[1] From the refined simplicity of this straightforward style it was a sad descent to the cumbrous and stilted Johnsonese of the next generation, which too many Americans even now mistake for fine writing.

William Byrd

Contemporary with Beverley and Stith was William Byrd, one of the most eminent men of affairs in Old Virginia, and eminent also — probably without knowing it — as a man of letters. His father came to Virginia a few years before Bacon's rebellion, and bought the famous estate of Westover, on the James River and in Charles City County, with the mansion, which is still in the possession of his family, and is considered one of the finest old houses in Virginia. From his uncle Colonel Byrd inherited a vast estate which included the present site of Richmond. He sympathized strongly with his neighbour, Nathaniel Bacon, and held a command under him; but after the collapse of the rebellion he succeeded in making his peace with the raging Berkeley. He became one of the most important men in the colony, and was commissioned receiver-general of the royal revenues. On his death, in 1704, his son succeeded him in this office. The son had studied law in the Middle

[1] Stith, *History of Virginia*, preface, vi., vii.

Temple, and for proficiency in science was made a fellow of the Royal Society. He was for many years a member of the colonial council, and at length its president. He lived in much splendour on his estate of Westover, and we have seen what a library he accumulated there. A professional man of letters he was not, and perhaps his strong literary tastes might never have led to literary production but for sundry interesting personal experiences which he deemed it worth while to put on record. In 1727 he was one of the commissioners for determining the boundary between Virginia and North Carolina. In the journeys connected with that work he selected the sites where the towns of Richmond and Petersburg were afterwards built; and he wrote a narrative of his proceedings so full of keen observations on the people

INSTRUMENTS USED BY BYRD AND MAYO IN RUNNING THE DIVIDING LINE

and times as to make it an extremely valuable contribution to history.[1] Among early American writers Byrd is excep-

[1] Byrd's *History of the Dividing Line*, with his *Journey to the Land of Eden*, and *A Progress to the Mines*, remained in MS. for more than a century. They were published at Petersburg in 1841, under the title of *Westover Manuscripts*. A better edition, edited by T. H. Wynne, was published in 1866 under the title of *Byrd Manuscripts*.

tional for animation of style. There is a quaintness of phrase about him that is quite irrepressible. After a dry season he visits a couple of mills, and "had the grief to find them both stand as still for the want of water as a dead woman's tongue for want of breath. It had rained so little for many weeks above the falls that the Naiads had hardly water enough left to wash their faces." He suggests, of course with a twinkle in his eye, that the early settlers of Virginia ought to have formed matrimonial alliances with the Indians: "Morals and all considered, I can't think the Indians were much greater heathens than the first adventurers, who, had they been good Christians, would have had the charity to take this only method of converting the natives to Christianity. For after all that can be said, a sprightly lover is the most prevailing missionary that can be sent among these, or any other infidels. Besides, the poor Indians would have had less reason to complain that the English took away their land, if they had received it by way of portion with their daughters. . . . Nor would the shade of the skin have been any reproach at this day; for if a Moor may be washed white in three generations, surely an Indian might have been blanched in two."[1] With such moralizing was this amiable writer wont to relieve the tedium of historical discourse. We shall again have occasion to quote him in the course of our narrative.

Among other works by writers reared before the Revolution, the well-known "Notes on Virginia," by Thomas Jefferson, deserves high praise as an essay in descriptive sociology. Of American poetry before the nineteenth century, scarcely a line worth preserving came from any quarter. In 1777 James McClurg, an eminent physician, afterward a member of the Federal Convention, wrote his "Belles of Williamsburg," a specimen of pleasant society verse; but it had not such vogue as its author's "Essay on the Human Bile," which was translated into several European languages. Science throve better than poetry, and was well represented in Virginia by John Clayton,

Science; John Clayton

[1] *Byrd MSS.* i. 5.

who came thither from England in 1705, being then in his twentieth year, and dwelt there until his death in 1773, on the eve of the famous day which saw the mixing of tea with ice-water in Boston harbour. Clayton was attorney-general of Virginia, and for fifty years clerk of Gloucester County. His name has an honourable place in the history of botany; he was member of learned societies in nearly all the countries of Europe; and in 1739 his "Flora of Virginia" was edited and published by Linnæus and Gronovius.

In Old Virginia, as in all the other colonies, the scientific study and practice of medicine had scarcely made a beginning. Those were everywhere the days of "kill or cure" treatment, when there was small hope for patients who had not enough vitality to withstand both drugs and disease. In the light of the progress achieved since the mighty work of Bichat (1798–1801), the two preceding centuries seem a period of stagnation. Strong plasters, jalap, and bleeding were the universal remedies. Mr. Bruce gives us the items of a bill rendered by Dr. Haddon, of York, about 1660, for performing an amputation. "They included one highly flavoured and two ordinary cordials, three ointments for the wound, an ointment precipitate, the operation of letting blood, a purge *per diem*, two purges electuaries, external applications, a cordial and two astringent powders, phlebotomy, a defensive and a large cloth." On another occasion the same doctor prescribed "a purging glister, a caphalick and a cordial electuary, oil of spirits and sweet almonds, a purging and a cordial bolus, purging pills, ursecatory, and oxymell. His charge for six visits after dark was a hogshead of tobacco weighing 400 pounds."[1] Of the many thousand victims of these heroic methods, the most illustrious was George Washington, who, but for medical treatment, might probably have lived a dozen or fifteen years into the nineteenth century. When Washington in full vigour found that he had caught a very bad cold he sent for the doctors, and meanwhile had

Physicians

Washington's last illness

[1] Bruce, *Economic History*, ii. 234.

half a pint of blood taken from him by one of his overseers. Of the three physicians in attendance, one was his dear friend, the good Scotchman, Dr. James Craik, "who from forty years' experience," said Washington, "is better qualified than a dozen of them put together." His colleague, Dr. Elisha Dick, said, "Do not bleed the General; he needs all his strength." But tradition prevailed over common sense, and three copious bleedings followed, in the last of which a quart of blood was taken. The third attendant, Dr. Gustavus Brown, afterward expressed bitter regret that Dr. Dick's advice was not followed. Besides this wholesale bleeding, the patient was dosed with calomel and tartar emetic and scarified with blisters and poultices; or, as honest Tobias Lear said, in a letter written the next day announcing the fatal result, "every medical assistance was offered, but without the desired effect." [1]

The physician in Old Virginia was very much the same as elsewhere, but the parson was a very different character from the grave ministers and dominies of Boston and New York. He belonged to the class of wine-bibbing, card-playing, fox-hunting parsons, of which there were so many examples in the mother country after the reaction against Puritanism had set in. The religious tone of the English church during the first half of the eighteenth century was very low, and it was customary to send out to Virginia and Maryland the poorest specimens of clergymen that the mother country afforded. Men unfit for any appointment at home were thought good enough for the colonies. The royal governor, as vicegerent of the sovereign, was head of the colonial church, while ecclesiastical affairs were superintended by a commissary appointed by the

Virginia parsons

[1] See the history of the case, in Washington's *Writings*, ed. W. C. Ford, xiv. 255–260. According to Mr. Paul Ford, "there can scarcely be a doubt that the treatment of his last illness by the doctors was little short of murder." *The True George Washington*, p. 58. The question is suggested, if Washington had lived a dozen years longer, would there have been a second war with England?

BRUTON PARISH CHURCH, WILLIAMSBURG

Bishop of London. The first commissary, Dr. Blair, as we have seen, was president of the college, and in his successors those two offices were usually united. Several attempts were made to substitute a bishop for the commissary, but the only result of the attempts was to alienate people's sympathies from the church, while the conduct of the clergy was such as to destroy their respect for it. Bishop Meade has queer stories to tell of some of these parsons. One of them was for years the president of a jockey club. Another fought a duel within sight of his own church. A third, who was evidently a muscular Christian, got into a rough-and-tumble fight with his vestrymen and floored them ; and then justified himself to his congregation next Sunday in a sermon from a text of Nehemiah, "And I contended with them, and cursed them, and smote certain of them, and plucked off their hair." In 1711 a bequest of £100 was made to the vestry of Christ Church parish in Middlesex, providing that the interest should be paid to the minister for preaching four sermons each year against "the four reigning vices, — viz.: atheism and irreligion, swearing and cursing, fornication and adultery, and drunkenness." Later in the century the living was held for eighteen years, and the sermons were preached, by a minister who was notoriously guilty of all the vices mentioned. He used to be seen in the tavern porch, reeling to and fro with a bowl of toddy in his hand, while he called to some passer-by to come in and have a drink. When this exemplary man of God was dying in delirium, his last words were halloos to the hounds. In 1726 a thoughtful and worthy minister named Lang wrote to the Bishop of London about the scandalous behaviour of the clergy, of whom the sober part were "slothful and negligent," while the rest were debauched and "bent on all manner of vices." [1] This testimony against the clergy, it will be observed, comes from clergymen. Yet it seems clear that the cases cited must have been extreme ones, — cases of the sort that make a deep impression and are long remembered. A few such instances would suffice to bring down condemnation upon the whole establishment; and not unjustly, for a church in which such things could for a moment be tolerated must needs have been in a degraded condition. This state of things afforded an excellent field for the labours of Baptist and Presbyterian revivalist preachers, and to such good purpose did they work that by the time of the Revolution it was found that more than half of the people in Virginia were Dissenters. At that time the Episcopal clergy were not unnaturally inclined to the Tory side, and this last ounce was all that was needed to break down the establishment and cast upon it irredeemable discredit. The downfall of the Episcopal church in Virginia and its resurrection under more wholesome conditions make an interesting chapter of history.

In imputing to his tipsy parson the "vice" of atheism, Bishop Meade warns us that he does not mean a denial of the existence of God, but merely irreligion, or "living without

[1] Meade's *Old Churches*, i. 18, 361, 385.

God in the world." In 1724 the Bishop of London was officially informed that there were no "infidels" in Virginia, negroes and Indians excepted. A few years later, "when the first infidel book was imported, . . . it produced such an

ST. LUKE'S CHURCH, NEWPORT PARISH, NEAR SMITHFIELD

excitement that the governor and commissary communicated on the subject with the authorities in England." In those days freethinkers, if prudent, kept their thoughts to themselves. All over Christendom the atmosphere was still murky with intolerance, and men's conceptions of the universe were only beginning to emerge from the barbaric stage. Virginia was no exception to the general rule.

Freethinking

In respect also of superstition and crime the Old Dominion seems to have differed but little from other parts of English America. Belief in witchcraft lasted into the eighteenth century, and the statute book reveals an abiding dread of what rebellious slaves might do; but there were no epidemics of savage terror, as at Salem in 1692, or in the negro panic of 1741 in New York. Of violent crime there was surely much less than in the England of Jack Sheppard and Jonathan Wild, but probably more than in the colonies north of Delaware Bay; and its perpetrators seem to have been chiefly white freedmen and "outlying negroes."[1] Duelling seems to have been infrequent before the Revolution.[2] Murder, rape, arson, and violent robbery were punished with death; while pillory, stocks, whipping-post, and ducking-stool were kept in readiness for minor offenders. The infliction of the death penalty in a cruel or shocking manner was not common. Negroes were occasionally burned at the stake, as in other colonies, north and south; and an instance is on record in which negro murderers were beheaded and quartered after hanging.[3] No

Superstition and crime

[1] It is difficult to obtain exact data. My impression is derived from study of the statutes and from general reading.

[2] It is authoritatively stated in the *Virginia Magazine*, i. 347, that from the time of the Company down to the time of the Revolution, "there is no record of any duel in Virginia." In the thirteen volumes of Hening I find no allusion to duelling; for the mention of "challenges to fight" in such a passage as vol. vi. p. 80, clearly refers to chance affrays with fisticuffs at the gaming table, and not to duels. Yet in 1731 Rodolphus Malbone, for challenging Solomon White, a magistrate, "with sword and pistol," was bound over in £50 to keep the peace: see *Virginia Magazine*, iii. 89.

[3] *Virginia Magazine*, i. 128. A woman named Eve was burned in Orange County in 1746 for petty treason, *i. e.* murdering her master. Id. iii. 308. For poisoning the master's family a man and woman were burned at Charleston, S. C., in 1769. Id. iv. 341. For petty treason a negro woman named Phillis was burned at the stake in Cambridge, Mass., Sept. 18, 1755: see *Boston Evening Post*, Sept. 22, 1755; Paige's *History of Cambridge*, p. 217. For riotous murder in the city of New York 21 negroes were executed in 1712, several of whom were burned and one was broken on the wheel; and again in 1741, in the panic over an imaginary plot, 13 negroes were burned at the stake:

white persons were ever burned at the stake by any of the colonies.[1]

In the early days of Virginia there was not much practice of law except by the county magistrates in their work of maintaining the king's peace. The legal profession was at first held in somewhat low repute, being sometimes recruited by white freedmen whose careers of rascality as attorneys in England had suddenly ended in penal servitude. But after the middle of the seventeenth century the profession grew rapidly in importance and improved in character. During the eighteenth century the development in legal learning and acumen, and in weight of judicial authority, was remarkable. The profession was graced by such eminent names as Pendleton, Wythe, and Henry, until in John Marshall the Old Dominion gave to the world a name second to none among the great judges of English race and speech.

Lawyers

One cause of this splendid development of legal talent was doubtless the necessarily close connection between legal and

see *Acts of Assembly*, *New York*, ann. 1712; *Documents Relating to Colonial History of New York*, vol. vi. ann. 1741. There may have been other cases. These here cited were especially notable.

[1] Prof. M. C. Tyler (*History of American Literature*, i. 90) quotes a statement of Burk (*History of Virginia*, Petersburg, 1805, vol. ii. appendix, p. xxx.) to the effect that in Princess Anne County a woman was once burned for witchcraft. But Burk makes the statement on hearsay, and I have no doubt he refers to Grace Sherwood, who between 1698 and 1708 brought divers and sundry actions for slander against persons who had called her a witch, but could not get a verdict in her favour! She was searched for witch marks and imprisoned. It is a long way from this sort of thing to getting burned at the stake! Mrs. Sherwood made her will in 1733, and it was admitted to probate in 1741. See *William and Mary College Quarterly*, i. 69; ii. 58; iii. 96, 190, 242; iv. 18.—There is a widespread popular belief that the victims of the witchcraft delusion in Salem were burned; scarcely a fortnight passes without some allusions to this "burning" in the newspapers. Of the twenty victims at Salem, nineteen were hanged, one was pressed to death; not one was burned. See Upham's *History of Witchcraft and Salem Village*, Boston, 1867, 2 vols.

political activity. The Virginia planter meant that his government should be one of laws. With his extensive estates to superintend and country interests to look after, his position was in many respects like that of the country squire in England. In his House of Burgesses the planter had a parliament; and in the royal governor, who was liable to subordinate local to imperial interests, there was an abiding source of antagonism and distrust, requiring him to keep his faculties perpetually alert to remember all the legal maxims by which the liberties of England had been guarded since the days of Glanvil and Bracton. On the whole, it was a noble type of rural gentry that the Old Dominion had to show. Manly simplicity, love of home and family, breezy activity, disinterested public spirit, thorough wholesomeness and integrity, — such were the features of the society whose consummate flower was George Washington.

A government of laws

This chapter must not close without a brief mention of the social features of Maryland, but a brief mention is all that is needed for my purpose, since the portraiture just given of Leah will answer in most respects for her younger sister Rachel. The English colonists in Maryland were of the same excellent class as the Cavaliers who were the strength of Virginia. Though tidewater Virginia at the beginning of the eighteenth century contained but few people who did not belong to the Church of England, on the other hand, in Maryland, not more than one sixth of the white population belonged to that church, while one twelfth were Roman Catholics, and three fourths were Puritans. But these differences in religion did not run parallel with differences in birth, refinement, or wealth. Naturally, from the circumstances under which the colony was founded, some of the best human material was always to be found among the Catholics; and they wielded an influence disproportionately greater than their numbers.

Some characteristics of Maryland

For the first three generations tobacco played as important a part in Maryland as in Virginia. Nearly all the people became planters. Cheap labour was supplied at first by indented white servants and afterwards by negro slaves, who never came, however, to number more than from one fourth to one third of the whole population. There was the same isolation, the same absence of towns, the same rudeness of roads and preference for water-ways, as in Virginia. The facilities for education were somewhat poorer; there was no university or college, no public schools until 1728, no newspaper until 1745.

But early in the eighteenth century there came about an important modification of industries, which was in large part due to the rapid growth of Maryland's neighbour, Pennsylvania. In the latter colony a great deal of wheat was raised, and the export of flour became very profitable. This wheat culture extended into Maryland, where wheat soon became a vigorous rival of tobacco. In 1729 the town of Baltimore was founded, and at once rose to importance as a point for exporting flour. Moreover, as Pennsylvania exported various kinds of farm produce, besides large quantities of valuable furs, and as she had no seacoast and no convenient maritime outlet save Philadelphia, her export trade soon came to exceed the capacities of that outlet, and a considerable part of it went through Baltimore, which thus had a large and active rural district dependent upon it, and grew so fast that by 1770 it had become the fourth city in English America, with a population of nearly 20,000. The growth of Annapolis was further stimulated by these circumstances; and this development of town life, with the introduction of a wealthy class of merchants and the continual intercommunication with Pennsylvania, went far toward assimilating Maryland with the middle colonies while it diminished to some extent her points of resemblance to the Old Dominion.

CHAPTER XV

THE CAROLINA FRONTIER

"St. Augustine, a Spanish garrison, being planted to the southward of us about a hundred leagues, makes Carolina a frontier to all the English settlements on the Main." These memorable words, from the report of the governor and council at Charleston to the lords proprietors of Carolina in London, in the year 1708, have a deeper historic significance than was realized by the men who wrote them. In a twofold sense Carolina was a frontier country. It was not only the border region where English and Spanish America marched upon each other, but it served for some time as a kind of backwoods for Virginia. Until recently one of the most important factors in American history has been the existence of a perpetually advancing frontier, where new territory has often had to be won by hard fighting against its barbarian occupants, where the life has been at once more romantic and more sordid than on the civilized seaboard, and where democracy has assumed its most distinctively American features. The cessation of these circumstances will probably be one of the foremost among the causes which are going to make America in the twentieth century different from America in the nineteenth. Now for the full development of this peculiar frontier life two conditions were requisite, — first, the struggle with the wilderness; secondly, isolation from the currents of European thought with which the commercial seaboard was kept in contact. These conditions were first realized in North Carolina, and there was originated the type of backwoods life which a century later prevailed among

The Spanish frontier

The wilderness frontier

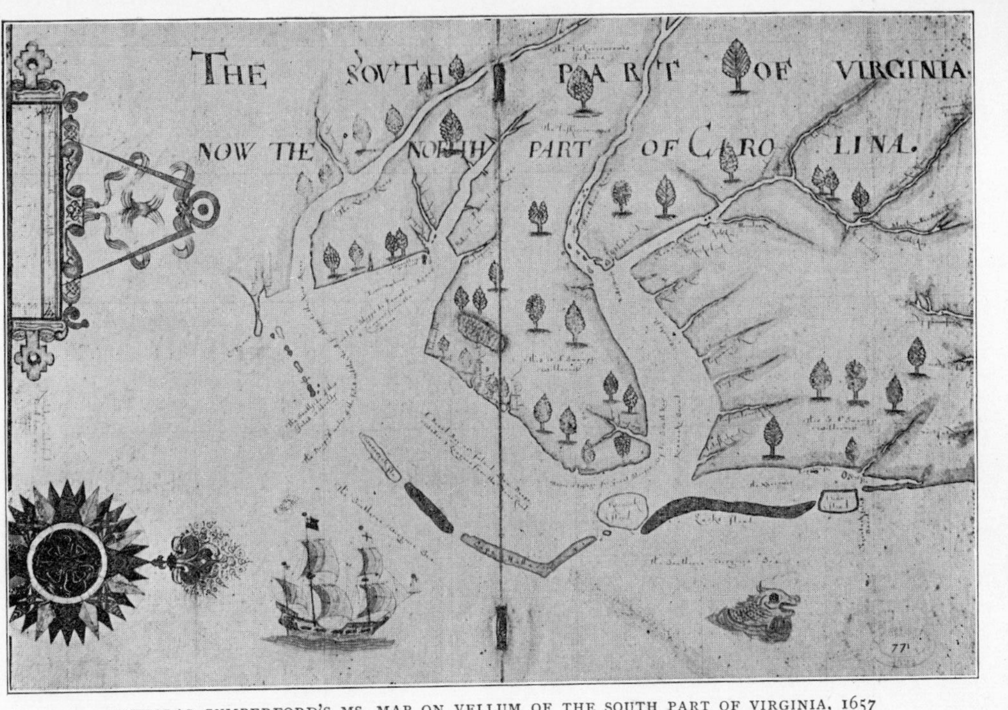

NICHOLAS CUMBERFORD'S MS. MAP ON VELLUM OF THE SOUTH PART OF VIRGINIA, 1657

the settlers of Tennessee and Kentucky. That was the one point where the backwoods may be said to have started at the coast; and in this light we shall have to consider it. On the other hand, South Carolina, with the Georgia colony for its buffer, is to be considered more in the light of a frontier against the Spaniard. We shall have furthermore to contemplate the whole Carolina coast as preëminently the frontier upon which were wrecked the last remnants of the piracy and buccaneering that had grown out of the mighty Elizabethan world-struggle between England and Spain. Without some mention of all these points, our outline sketch of the complicated drama begun by Drake and Raleigh would be incomplete.

The region long vaguely known as Carolina, or at least a portion of it, had formed part of Sir Walter Raleigh's Virginia; but the Spaniards had never ceased to regard it as part of Florida. In defiance of their claims, Jean Ribaut planted his first ill-fated Huguenot colony at Port Royal in 1562, and built a fort which he called Charlesfort, after Charles IX. of France. Whether the name "Carolina" was applied to the territory at that early time is doubtful,[1] but we find it used in England, in the time of Charles I., when the first Lord Baltimore was entertaining a plan for a new colony south of Virginia. The name finally served to commemorate Charles II., who in 1663 granted the territory to eight "lords proprietors," gentlemen who had done him inestimable services. To the most eminent, George Monk, Duke of Albemarle, he owed his restoration to the throne; the support of Edward Hyde, Earl of Clarendon, had been invaluable; the others were Anthony Ashley Cooper, afterwards Earl of Shaftesbury, Lord Craven, Lord Berkeley, and his brother, Sir William Berkeley, governor of Virginia, Sir George Carteret, and Sir John Colleton. All these names appear to-day on the map, — Albemarle Sound, Hyde, Craven, and Carteret counties in North Carolina; Clarendon and Colleton counties, Berkeley parish, and

The grant of Carolina

[1] Winsor, *Narr. and Crit. Hist.* v. 286.

the Ashley and Cooper rivers, in South Carolina, while in Charleston we have the name of the king.

Shaftesbury and Locke

These gentlemen contemplated founding a colony which should emulate the success of Virginia. The most actively engaged in the enterprise was the one whom we know best by his title of Shaftesbury, and it was thus that the founding of Carolina became connected for a moment with one of the greatest names in the history of England. A charming story is that of the residence of John Locke in the Ashley family, as physician, private tutor, and general adviser and guardian angel; how he once saved his lordship's life by most daring and skilful surgery, how he taught Greek to the young Ashley, how he took the boy at the age of seventeen to Haddon Hall and made a happy match for him with pretty Lady Dorothy Manners aged twenty, how he

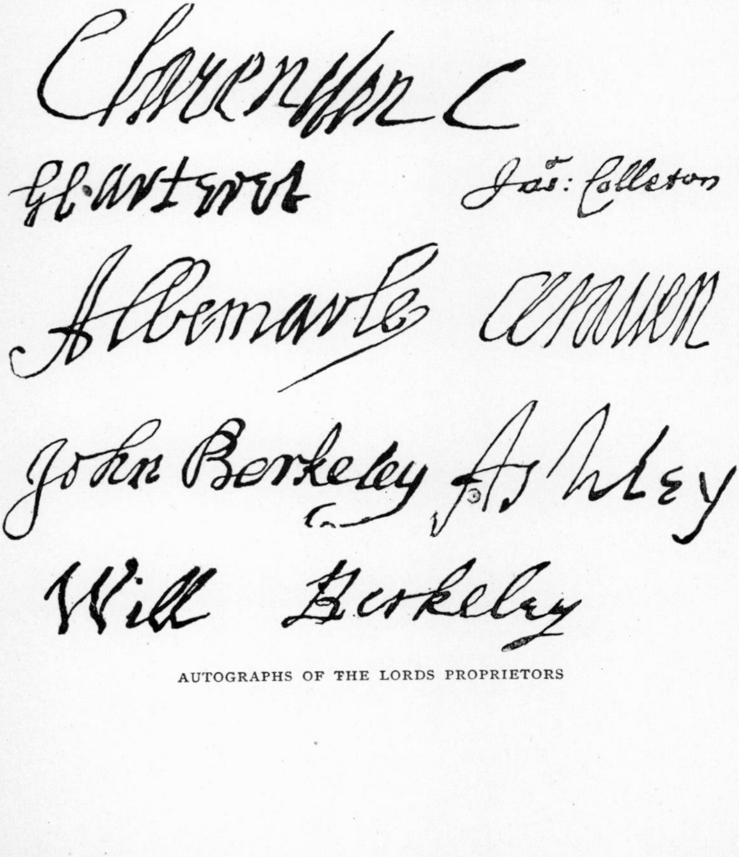

AUTOGRAPHS OF THE LORDS PROPRIETORS

afterward assisted at the birth of the grandson destined to become even more famous in literature than the grandfather in political history, — all this is pleasantly told by the grandson. "My father was too young and inexperienced to choose a wife for himself, and my grandfather too much in business to choose one for him. The affair was nice; for, though my grandfather required not a great fortune, he insisted on good blood, good person and constitution, and, above all, good education and a character as remote as possible from that of court or town-bred lady. All this was thrown upon Mr. Locke, who being . . . so good a judge of men, my grandfather doubted not of his equal judgment in women. He departed from him, entrusted and sworn, as Abraham's head servant that ruled over all that he had, and went into a far country (the north of England) to seek for his son a wife, whom he as successfully found."[1]

In the summer of 1669, while the great philosopher was engaged upon this match-making expedition, he varied the proceedings by drawing up a constitution for Carolina, the original draft of which, a small neatly written volume of 75 pages bound in vellum, is still preserved among the Shaftesbury papers. This constitution diverges widely in some respects from such a document as would have expressed Locke's own ideas of the right sort of government. The scheme which it set forth was in the main Ashley's, with such modifications as were necessary to secure the approval of the other proprietors. It is not worth our while to recount its complicated provisions, inasmuch as it was never anything but a dead letter, and civil government sprouted up as spontaneously in Carolina as if neither statesman nor philosopher had ever given thought to the subject. One provision, however, expressed an idea of which Locke was one of the foremost representatives, and herein Ashley agreed with him; it was the idea of complete liberty of conscience in matters of religion. It was provided that any seven or more persons who could agree among themselves

The Fundamental Constitutions

[1] Fox-Bourne's *Life of John Locke*, i. 203.

upon any sort of notion about God or any plan for worshipping him might set up a church and be guaranteed against all interference or molestation. An ideal so noble as this was never quite realized in the history of any of the colo-

FIRST EARL OF SHAFTESBURY

nies; but there can be little doubt that the publication of Locke's "Fundamental Constitutions" in 1670, in 1682, and 1698 had much influence in directing toward Carolina the stream of Huguenot emigration from France, which was an event of the first importance.[1]

[1] The Fundamental Constitutions are printed in Locke's *Works*, London, 1824, ix. 175–199. An excellent analysis of them is given by Professor Bassett, "The Constitutional Beginnings of North Carolina,"

In its general character the government created by the Fundamental Constitutions was a palatinate modelled after that of Durham. The difference between Carolina and Maryland consisted chiefly in the fact that the palatinate privileges were granted to eight co-proprietors instead of a single proprietor. Those privileges were quasi-royal, but they were limited by giving to the popular assembly the control over all money bills. This limitation, however, was partly offset by giving to the higher officers regular salaries payable from quit-rents or the

The Carolina Palatinate

EDWARD HYDE, EARL OF CLARENDON

sales of public lands. These salaries went far toward making such officers independent of the legislature, and thus led to much complaint and dissatisfaction. Before the Revolution

J. H. U. Studies, xii. 97–169; see, also, Whitney, "Government of the Colony of South Carolina," Id. xiii. 1–121.

questions concerning the salaried independence of high public officials had in several of the colonies come to be one of the most burning questions of the day.

The lords proprietors, as tenants-in-chief of the crown, were feudal sovereigns over Carolina. They could grant estates on any terms they pleased, and subinfeudation, which had been forbidden in England since 1290, was expressly permitted here. The eldest of the proprietors was called the Palatine; he presided at their meetings, and his vote with those of three associates was reckoned a majority. As the proprietors remained in England, it was arranged that each of them should be represented in Carolina by a deputy; and the Palatine's deputy, sometimes called Vice-Palatine, was to be governor of the colony. But any one of the proprietors coming into the colony, or the oldest of those coming, if there were more than one, was to take precedence over everybody and become at once Vice-Palatine.

The Palatine

By a curious provision of the charter, the lords proprietors could grant titles of nobility, provided they were unlike those used in England. Hence the outlandish titles, such as "landgrave" and "cacique," which occur in the Fundamental Constitutions. With the titles there was combined an artificial system of social gradations which is not worth recounting. As for the political status of the settlers, they were guaranteed in the possession of all the rights and privileges enjoyed by Englishmen in England.

Titles of nobility

The planting of two distinct colonies in Carolina was no part of the original scheme, but the early centres of colonization were so far apart and communication between them was so difficult that they could not well be united in a single community, although more than once there was a single governor over the whole of Carolina. Emigration from Virginia had begun as early as 1653, when Roger Greene with a hundred men made a small settlement in the Chowan precinct, on the north shore of Albemarle Sound.[1] In 1662 George

[1] Hening, i. 380.

Durant[1] followed, and began a settlement in the Perquimans precinct, just east of Chowan. In 1664 Governor Berkeley, of Virginia, — himself one of the eight lords proprietors, — severed this newly settled region from Virginia, and appointed William Drummond as its governor. Such were the beginnings of Albemarle, the colony which in time was to develop into North Carolina.

The Albemarle colony

Meanwhile in 1660 a party from New England made a settlement at the mouth of Cape Fear River; or perhaps we ought rather to call it a visit. It lasted no longer than Thorfinn Karlsefni's visit to Vinland,[2] for the settlers had all departed by 1663. There is a tradition that they were sorely harassed by the natives, in revenge for their sending sundry Indian lads and girls aboard ship, to be taken to Boston and "educated," *i. e.* sold for slaves.[3] This is not improbable. At all events, these New Englanders went off in a mood not altogether amiable, leaving affixed to a post, at the mouth of the river, a "scandalous writing . . . the contents whereof tended not only to the disparagement of the land . . . but also to the great discouragement of all such as should hereafter come into those parts to settle."[4]

The visit of New Englanders

But this emphatic warning did not frighten away Sir John Yeamans, who arrived at Cape Fear early in October, 1663, and ascended the river for more than a hundred and fifty miles. Sir John was the son of a gallant Cavalier who had lost life and estate in the king's service, and he had come out to Barbadoes to repair his fortunes. His report of the Cape Fear country was so favourable that by the end of May, 1665, we find him there again, with several hundred settlers from Barbadoes, to make the beginnings of the new colony of Clarendon, of which the

The Clarendon colony

[1] He is commonly called a Quaker, but the tradition is ill supported. See Weeks, *Southern Quakers and Slavery*, p. 33.

[2] See my *Discovery of America*, i. 167–169.

[3] Hawks, *History of North Carolina*, ii. 72.

[4] Lawson, *A Description of North Carolina*, London, 1718, p. 73.

lords proprietors had appointed him governor. In the same year the colony of Albemarle elected its first assembly.

In 1667 William Sayle, a Puritan from Bermuda, explored the coast, and reported the value of the Bahama Islands for offensive and defensive purposes in case of war with Spain. These islands were accordingly appropriated and annexed to Carolina, as the Bermudas had once been annexed to Virginia. It was decided to make a settlement at Port Royal; the venerable Sayle, whose years were more than three-score-and-ten, was appointed governor; and on March 17, 1670, the first colonists arrived on

The Ashley River colony

WILLIAM, FIRST EARL OF CRAVEN

the Carolina coast. On further inspection Port Royal seemed too much exposed to the attacks of Spaniards from St. Augustine, and accordingly the ships pursued their way northward till they reached and entered the spacious bay formed by the junction of two noble rivers since known as Ashley and Cooper. They proceeded up the Ashley as far as an easily defensible highland at Albemarle Point, where they began building a village which they called Charles

Town. Their cautiousness was soon justified. Spain and England were then at peace, but no sooner were the Spaniards notified of these proceedings than a warship started from St. Augustine and came as far as Stono Inlet, where it learned the strength of the English position and concluded to retreat.[1] The next year Governor Sayle died, and was succeeded by Sir John Yeamans, who came in 1672, bringing from Barbadoes the first negro slaves ever seen in Carolina. In 1674 Yeamans was superseded by Joseph West, under whom the first assembly was elected.

Founding of Charleston, 1670

Thus there were three small communities started on the coast of Carolina: 1. Albemarle, on the Virginia border, constituted in 1664; 2. Clarendon, on the Cape Fear River, in 1665; 3. The Ashley River colony, in 1670.

For a moment we must follow the fortunes of Albemarle, where in 1667 Drummond was succeeded in the governorship by Samuel Stephens. Two years later there was passed a statute which enacted that no subject could be sued within five years for any cause of action that might have arisen outside of the colony; that all debts contracted outside of the colony were *ipso facto* outlawed; and that all new settlers should be exempted from taxes for one year.[2] Moreover, all "transient persons," not intending to remain in the colony, were forbidden to trade with the Indians. It was furthermore provided that, since there were no clergymen in the colony to perform the ceremony of marriage, a declaration of mutual consent, before the governor and council and in the presence of a few acquaintances, should be deemed a binding contract.[3] These laws were of course intended to stimulate immigration, and the effect of the first two was soon plainly indicated in the indignant epithet, "Rogue's Harbour," bestowed by Virginia people upon the colony of Albemarle.[4]

First legislation in Albemarle

[1] Rivers, *Early History of South Carolina*, Charleston, 1856, p. 96.

[2] Williamson, *History of North Carolina*, Philadelphia, 1812, i. 120.

[3] Williamson, *op. cit.* i. 121.

[4] Moore's *History of North Carolina*, Raleigh, 1880, i. 18.

A Brief DESCRIPTION
OF
The Province
OF
CAROLINA
On the COASTS *of* FLOREDA.
AND
More perticularly of a *New-Plantation* begun by the *ENGLISH* at *Cape-Feare*, on that River now by them called *Charles-River*, the 29th. of *May*. 1664.

Wherein is set forth
The *Healthfulness* of the *Air*; the *Fertility* of the *Earth*, and *Waters*; and the great *Pleasure* and *Profit* will accrue to those that shall go thither to enjoy the same.

Also,
Directions and advice to such as shall go thither whether on their own accompts, or to serve under another.

Together with
A most accurate MAP of the whole *PROVINCE*.

London, Printed for *Robert Horne* in the first Court of *Gresham-Colledge* neer *Bishopsgate street*, 1666.

TITLE OF "A BRIEF DESCRIPTION, ETC., OF CAROLINA"

The desire of increasing the number of settlers, without regard to their quality, induced the lords proprietors to sanction these curiosities of legislation. But troubles, not of their own creating, were at hand in this little forest community. In 1673 the Fundamental Constitutions were promulgated by Governor Stephens, who soon afterward died. Under his temporary successor, George Carteret, president of the council, the troubles broke out, and it has been customary to ascribe them to the attempt to enforce the Fundamental Constitutions upon an unwilling community. It does not appear, however, that the official promulgation of this frame of government was followed by any serious attempts to enforce it.[1] The real source of the disturbances was undoubtedly the Navigation Act, — that mischievous statute with which the mother country was busily weaning from itself the affections of its colonies all along the American seaboard. Sundry unfounded rumours increased the bitter feeling. The king's grant of Virginia to Arlington and Culpeper in 1673 was part of the news of the day. It was reported that the proprietors of Carolina were going to divide up the province among themselves, and that Albemarle was to be the share of Sir William Berkeley, a man especially hated by the Virginians of small means, who were the larger part of the Albemarle population. Though these reports were baseless, they found many believers. But the Navigation Act and the attempts to break up the trade with Massachusetts were very real grievances. Ships from Boston and Salem brought down to Albemarle Sound all manner of articles needed by the planters, and took their pay in cattle and lumber, which they carried to the West Indies and exchanged for sugar, molasses, and rum. Often with this cargo they returned to Albemarle and exchanged it for tobacco, which they carried home and sent off to Europe at a good round profit, in supreme defiance of the

Troubles caused by the Navigation Act

The trade with New England

[1] I am glad to find this opinion corroborated by Professor Bassett in his able paper above cited, *J. H. U. Studies*, xii. 109.

George Monk, Duke of Albemarle

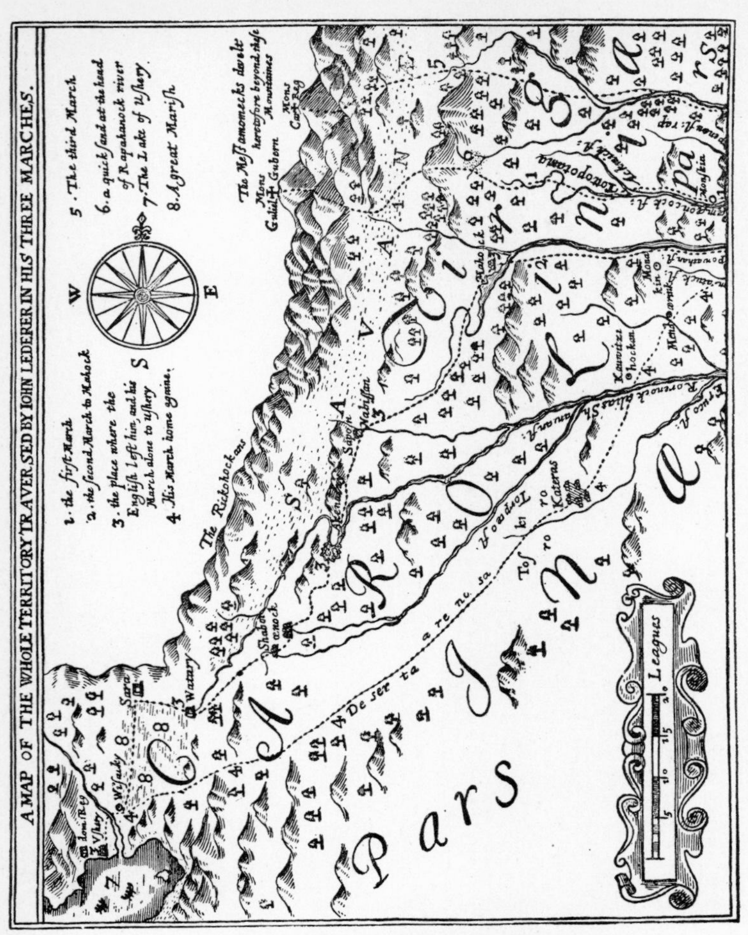

LEDERER'S MAP OF CAROLINA, 1670

statutes. It was said that the new colony was enriching Yankee merchants much faster than the lords proprietors.[1] In truth the trade was profitable to merchants and planters alike, and by the summer of 1676 sundry attempts to break it up had brought the little colony into quite a rebellious

[1] Hawks, *History of North Carolina*, ii. 470.

frame of mind. We have seen how Bacon looked forward to possible help from Carolina against Sir William Berkeley. Bacon spoke of the desirableness of the people electing their own governors.[1] New England furnished examples of such elected governors who were in full sympathy with the people. The men of Albemarle were likely to make trouble for governors appointed in England to carry out an unpopular policy.

When Carteret resigned his position in 1676, two men, who were supposed to represent the popular party, had lately gone over to England. One of them, by name Eastchurch, had been speaker of the assembly; and so anxious were the lords proprietors to have their intentions carried out without irritating the people, that in the autumn of 1676 they appointed him governor of Albemarle. The other was a person named Miller, who had been illegally carried to Virginia and tried by Governor Berkeley for making a seditious speech in Carolina. In England he found it profitable to pose as a martyr. The proprietors made him secretary of Albemarle, and the king's commissioners of customs made him collector of the revenues of that colony. Early in 1677 the new governor and secretary sailed for America, and made a stop at the little island of Nevis, famous in later years as the birthplace of Alexander Hamilton. For Eastchurch it proved to be an isle of Calypso. He fell in love with a fair Creole and staid to press his suit, while he appointed Miller president of the council, and sent him on in that capacity to govern Albemarle.

Eastchurch and Miller

That little commonwealth of less than 3000 souls had in the mean time been enjoying the sweets of uncurbed liberty, when there was no king in Israel, and every man did what was right in his own eyes. Miller, as a martyr to free speech, was cordially welcomed, but as proprietary governor and king's collector he found his popularity quickly waning. He tried to suppress the trade with Massachusetts, and thus arrayed against himself the Yankee skippers, aided by a "party within," at the head of which was the wealthy George Durant,

[1] See above, p. 73 of the present volume.

the earliest settler of Perquimans. The train was well laid for an insurrection when a demagogue arrived with the match to fire it. This man was John Culpeper, surveyor-general of Carolina, whose seditious conduct on the Ashley River had lately made it necessary for him to flee northward to escape the hangman. Culpeper's proposal to resist the enforcement of the odious Navigation Act brought him many followers. In December, 1677, a Yankee schooner, heavily armed and bearing a seductive cargo of rum and molasses, appeared in Pasquotank River. Her skipper, whose name was Gillam, had scarcely set foot on land when he was arrested by the governor and held to bail in £1000. The astute Yankee, with an air of innocent surprise, meekly promised to weigh anchor at once and not return. Hereupon a thirsty mob, maddening with the thought of losing so much rum, beset Gillam with entreaties to stay. Governor Miller was a man in whom bravery prevailed over prudence, and, hearing at this moment that Durant was on the schooner, he straightway boarded her, pistol in hand, and arrested that influential personage on a charge of treason. This rash act was the signal for an explosion. Culpeper's mob arrested the governor and council, and locked them up. Then they took possession of the public records, convened the assembly, appointed new justices, made Culpeper governor, and, seizing upon £3000 of customs revenue collected by Miller for the king, they applied it to the support of this revolutionary government.

The Culpeper usurpation, 1677–79

For two years these adventurers exercised full sway over Albemarle. During this time Governor Eastchurch arrived from the island of Nevis, bringing with him the fair Creole as his bride. He met with a cold reception, and lost no time in finding shelter in Virginia, where he drank a friendly glass with Governor Chicheley, and asked for military aid against the usurping Culpeper. The request was granted, but before the troops were ready the unfortunate Eastchurch succumbed to chagrin, or perhaps to malaria, and his Creole bride was left a widow.

Culpeper, however, remained in some dread of what Virginia might do. He had issued a manifesto, accusing Miller of tyranny and peculation and seeking to justify himself; but he thought it wise to play a still bolder part. He went to England in the hope of persuading the lords proprietors to sanction what he had done, and to confirm him in the governorship. In London he was surprised at meeting the deposed Miller, who had broken jail and arrived there before him. The twain forthwith told their eloquent but conflicting tales of woe, and Culpeper's tongue proved the more persuasive with the lords proprietors. He seemed on the point of returning in triumph to Carolina, when suddenly the king's officers arrested him for robbing the custom-house of £3000. This led to his trial for treason, in the summer of 1680, before the King's Bench, under the statute of Henry VIII. anent "treason committed abroad;" the same statute under which it was sought, on a fine April morning ninety-five years later, to arrest Samuel Adams and John Hancock. The Earl of Shaftesbury ably defended Culpeper, and he was acquitted but not restored to power.[1] He returned to Carolina, a sadder if not a wiser man; and in his old capacity of surveyor, it is said, laid out the plan of the city of Charleston on its present site. The original Charles Town, as already mentioned, was begun at Albemarle Point on Ashley River, in 1670. Another settlement was made two years later at Oyster Point, on the extremity of the peninsula enclosed between the two rivers. This new situation had greater advantages for a seaport, and its cooler breezes were appreciated by sojourners in that fiery climate. It grew at the expense of the older settlement, until in 1680 it had a population of 2500 souls, and took over the name of Charles Town, while Albemarle Point was abandoned. So the autumn of 1680 had work at Oyster Point for a surveyor like Culpeper.

How Culpeper fared in London

Charleston moved to a new site

[1] Dr. Hawks, in his *History of North Carolina*, ii. 463–483, gives a detailed and very entertaining account of the Culpeper rebellion, to which I am indebted for several particulars.

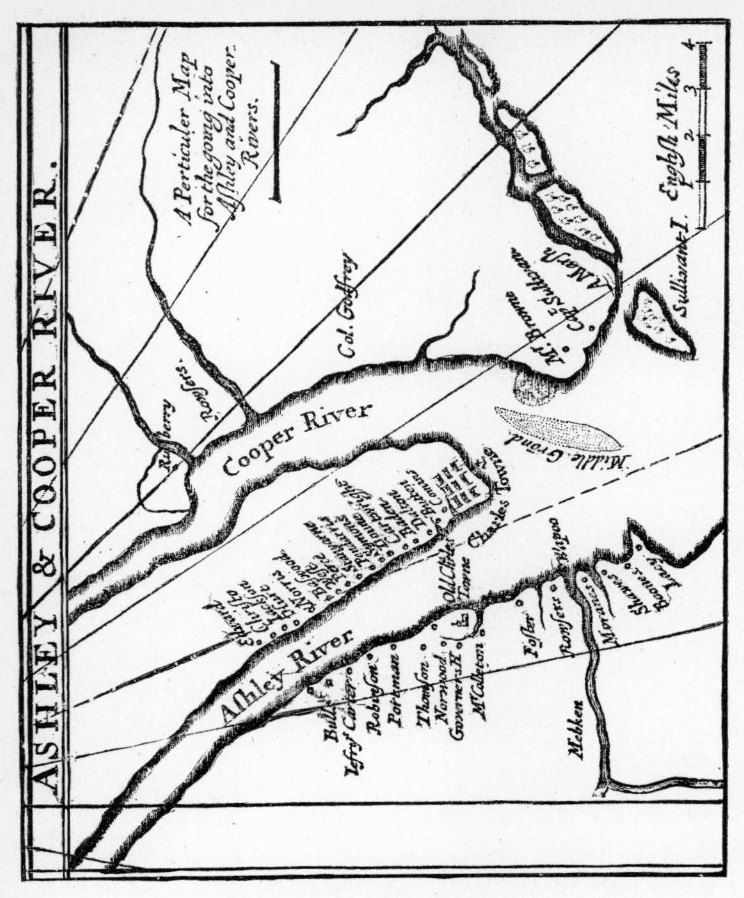

COOPER AND ASHLEY RIVERS

The governor who succeeded this usurper in the Albemarle colony was a new lord proprietor, by name Seth Sothel, to whom the Earl of Clarendon had sold out his rights and interests. On his way to America, early in 1680, Sothel was captured by Algerine pirates and carried off into slavery. Not until 1683 did Sothel obtain his freedom and arrive at his destination. In five years of misrule

Seth Sothel

over Albemarle he proved himself one of the dirtiest knaves that ever held office in America. A few specimens of his conduct may be cited. On the arrival of two ships from Barbadoes on legitimate business, Sothel seized them as pirates and threw their captains into jail, where one of them died of ill-treatment. The dying man made a will in which he named one of the most respected men in the colony, Thomas Pollock, as his executor; but Sothel refused to let the will go to probate, and seized the dead man's effects; the executor then threatened to carry the story of all this to England, whereupon the governor lodged him in jail and kept him there. George Durant called such proceedings unlawful, whereupon Sothel straightway imprisoned him and confiscated his whole estate. If he saw anything that pleased his fancy, be it a cow or a negro or a pewter dish, he just took it without ceremony, and if the owner objected he locked him up. From criminals he took tips and saved them from the gallows. The people of Albemarle endured this tyranny until 1688, — that year when over all English lands the sky was so black with political thunder-clouds. One day certain leading colonists laid hands upon Seth Sothel, and prepared to send him to England to be tried for a long list of felonies. Then this model for governors and lords proprietors, suddenly realizing the dismal prospect before him, with Tyburn looming up in the distance, begged with frantic sobs and tears that he might be tried by the assembly, and not be sent to England; for he felt sure that the assembly would hardly dare take the responsibility of hanging him. In this he calculated correctly; he was banished from the colony for one year, and declared forever incapable of holding the governorship.[1]

Banishment of Sothel

The prudence of the assembly was well considered. The lords proprietors in England, ill informed as to the affairs of their colony, wearied with the everlasting series of complaints, and unwilling to believe that one of their associates could be such a scoundrel, were inclined to scold the colo-

[1] Hawks, *op. cit.* ii. 489.

nists for their treatment of Sothel. As for that worthy, his full career was not yet run. Scenes of turbulence were awaiting him in the little settlement between the Ashley and Cooper rivers. Joseph West had ruled there with a strong hand from 1674 to 1683, and the colony prospered during that time, but disagreements arose between West and the proprietors which ended in his removal. The next seven years were a period of anarchy. After five changes of governors in quick succession, the office was given to James Colleton, brother of Colleton the lord proprietor, but the situation was not improved. The troubles arose partly from the practice of kidnapping Indians for slaves, which invited bloody reprisals; partly from the demand that quit-rents be paid in coin, which was very scarce in Carolina; partly from the low character of many of the settlers and their dealings with pirates; partly from the unwillingness of the English settlers to admit the Huguenot immigrants to a share in the franchise; and partly from the fitful and arbitrary manner in which the lords proprietors tried from beyond sea to cure the complicated evils. The muddle was aggravated by Spanish hostility. In 1683 a few Scotch families were brought by Lord Cardross to Port Royal, where they made the beginnings of a settlement. Those were the cruel days of Claverhouse in Scotland, and a scheme was entertained for bringing 10,000 sturdy Covenanters to Carolina; but it came to nothing. Cardross got into difficulties with the people at Charleston, and went back to Scotland in disgust. In 1686, in time of peace, a Spanish force pounced upon Port Royal, murdered some of the Scotchmen, flogged others within an inch of their lives, carried off what booty they could find, and left the place a smoking ruin. Dire was the indignation of the Charleston men at these "bloody insolencies." Two stout ships with 400 men were just ready to sail against St. Augustine, when the newly appointed Governor Colleton arrived upon the scene and forbade their sailing. His mandate was obeyed with growls and curses. The

Troubles in the southern colony

The Scotch at Port Royal, 1683–86

lords proprietors upheld him. "No man," as they reasonably said, "can think that the dependencies of England can have power to make war upon the king's allies without his knowledge or consent."[1] It was an inauspicious beginning for Colleton. The old troubles continued, along with others growing out of the Navigation Act. The wrangling between governor and assembly grew so hot that in 1689 the proprietors instructed Colleton to summon no more parliaments in Carolina without express orders from them. The effect of such an order was probably not foreseen by those well-meaning gentlemen. It was a curious feature in the Ashley River colony that the acts of its assembly expired at the end of twenty-three months unless renewed. This term had so nearly elapsed when the order arrived that "in 1690 not one statute law was in force in the colony!"[2]

A state without laws

This heroic medicine did not cure the malady. Things grew worse in the spring of 1690, when Colleton proclaimed martial law. The air was thick with sedition when Sothel arrived in Charleston. As a lord proprietor he had the right to act as governor over Colleton's head. Several of the leading colonists begged him to call a parliament, and forthwith the exemplary Sothel posed as "the people's friend." He summoned a parliament which banished Colleton and enacted sundry laws. A queer spectacle it was, the victim of one popular revolution becoming the ringleader of another, the banished playing the part of banisher! But the lords proprietors had become aware of Sothel's misdeeds; they annulled the acts of his parliament, deposed him, and ordered him to return to England to answer the charges against him. Sothel did not relish this. His term of banishment from Albemarle had expired, and he believed it to be a safer hiding-place than London. Where he skulked or how he died is unknown. All we know is that his will was admitted

Reappearance of Sothel

His death

[1] Rivers, *Early History of South Carolina*, p. 145.

[2] Id. p. 153.

MORDEN'S MAP OF CAROLINA, 1687

to probate February 5, 1694; and that his tombstone, which came from England, was never paid for![1]

Since the founding of the Ashley River colony it had fared ill with the Clarendon colony on Cape Fear River, which under favouring circumstances might perhaps have developed into a Middle Carolina. There were not people enough, and there was not trade enough for so many settlements. So Clarendon dwindled until 1690, when it was abandoned. This left a wide interval of

Clarendon Colony abandoned

[1] *Records of General Court of Albemarle*, 1697; Hawks, *op. cit.* ii. 491.

forest and stream between Albemarle and the Ashley River colony, or North Carolina and South Carolina, as they were beginning to be called. The formal separation of Carolina into two provinces did not take place until 1729, but the two colonies were from the outset, as we have seen, distinct and independent growths; and by 1690 the epithets North and South were commonly used.

Just at this time, however, the two were united under one governor. Colonel Philip Ludwell, of Virginia, who had ably supported Berkeley against Bacon, and had afterward married Berkeley's widow, was Sothel's successor in Albemarle in 1689, and he was appointed to succeed him at Charleston in 1691. The proprietors wished

Philip Ludwell

to bring all Carolina under one government, and the Albemarle people were requested to send their representatives to the assembly at Charleston, but distance made such a scheme impracticable. The northern colony, however, was often governed by a deputy appointed at Charleston. The troubles were not yet over. Ludwell was an upright and able man, but the disagreements between the settlers and the lords proprietors were more than he could cope with, and in 1692 he was superseded.

It is not worth while to recount the names of all the men who served as governors in the two Carolinas. In the world of history there is a certain amount of meaningless mediocrity which a general survey like the present may well pass by without notice. The brief administration of John Archdale, in 1695, marks a kind of era. Archdale was a Quaker, a man of broad intelligence and character at once strong and gentle. He had become one of the lords proprietors, and in that capacity came out to Carolina, where for one year he ruled the whole province

John Archdale

with such authority as no one had wielded before ; for while he was backed up by the proprietors, he conciliated the assemblies. In the matter of the Indians and the quit-rents much was done, and the veto power of the proprietors was curtailed. After a year Archdale felt able to go home, leaving his friend Joseph Blake, a nephew of the great admiral, as governor in Charleston. Under Blake still further progress was made by admitting to full political rights and privileges the Huguenot immigrants, who had come to be in some respects the most important element in the population of South Carolina. But after Blake's death, in 1700, it grew stormy again. The new governor, James Moore, came out to make money, and to that end he renewed the vile practice of kidnapping Indians. This presently made it necessary to gather troops and defeat the angry red men. Quarrels with the assembly were chronic. When the war of the Spanish Succession broke out, Moore invaded Florida, but accomplished nothing except the creation of a heavy public debt. In 1703 he was superseded by Sir Nathaniel Johnson, a precious bigot, who undertook to force through the assembly a law excluding from it all Dissenters. This was effected by trickery ; the act was passed by a majority of one, in a house from which several members were absent. After the fraud was discovered, the assembly by a large majority voted to repeal the act, but the governor refused to sign the repeal. The Dissenters were perhaps three fourths of the population. They made complaint to the lords proprietors, but a majority of that body sustained the governor. Then a successful appeal was made to the House of Lords, and the proprietors suddenly found themselves threatened with the

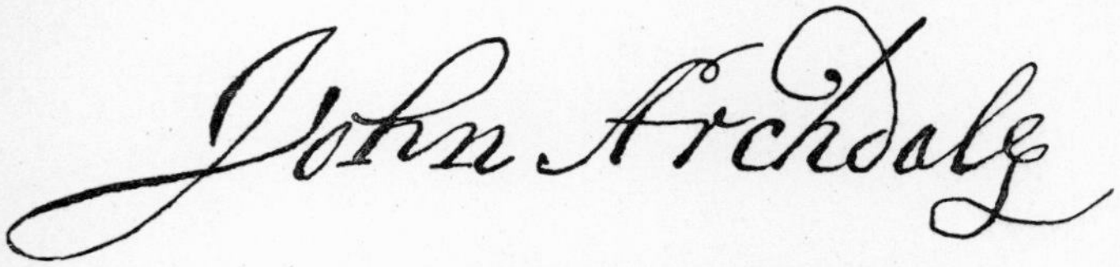

Joseph Blake

Sir Nathaniel Johnson and the Dissenters

loss of their charter. The result was a great victory for the South Carolina assembly, which at its next session restored Dissenters to their full privileges.

Like many another bigot, Governor Johnson was a good fighter. In August, 1706, Charleston was attacked by a

SIR NATHANIEL JOHNSON

French and Spanish squadron. A visitation of yellow fever, with half a dozen deaths daily in a population of 3000, had frightened many people away from the town. On a broiling Saturday afternoon five columns of smoke floating lazily up over Sullivan's Island announced that five warships were descried in the offing. They were French privateers with Spanish reinforcements from Cuba and St. Augustine. When the signal was reported to the governor at his country house, the militia were called together from all quarters and the

Unsuccessful attempt of a French and Spanish fleet upon Charleston

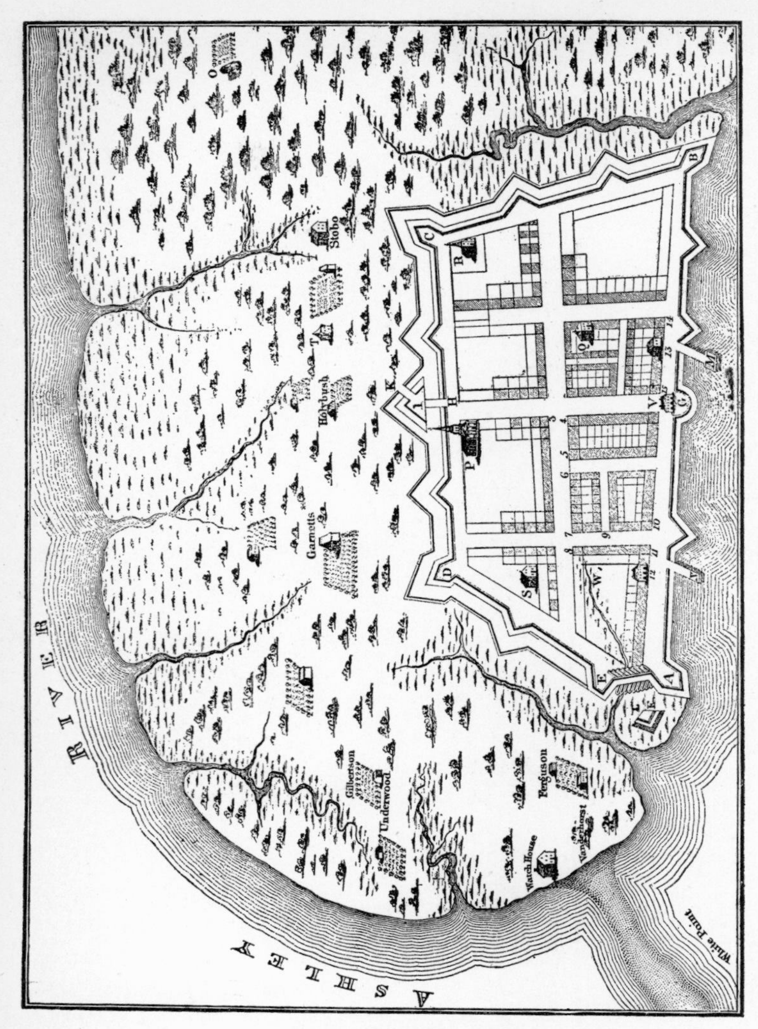

PLAN OF CHARLESTON, 1704

THE KEY: A, Granville bastion. B, Craven bastion. C, Carteret bastion. D, Colleton bastion. E, Ashley bastion. F, Blake's bastion. G, Half-moon. H, Drawbridge. I, Johnson's covered half-moon. K, Drawbridge. L, Palisades. M, Lieut.-Col. Rhett's bridge. N, Smith's bridge. O, Minister's house. P, English Church. Q, French Church. R, Independent Church. S, Anabaptist Church. T, Quaker meeting-house. V, Court of guard. W, First rice patch in Carolina. — Owners of houses as follows: 1, Pasquero and Garrett. 2, Landsack. 3, Jno. Crosskeys. 4, Chevelier. 5, Geo. Logan. 6, Poinsett. 7, Elicott. 8, Starling. 9, M. Boone. 10, Tradds. 11, Nat. Law. 12, Landgrave Smith. 13, Col. Rhett. 14, Ben: Skenking. 15, Sindery.

ships in the harbour were quickly made ready for action. The evening air was vocal with alarm guns. But the enemy approached with such excessive caution that Johnson had ample time for preparation. It was not until Wednesday that the affair matured. Then the French commander sent a flag of truce ashore and demanded, in the name of Louis XIV., the surrender of the town and its inhabitants; the governor, he said, might have an hour to consider his answer. Johnson replied that he did not need a minute, and told the Frenchman to go to the devil. The enemy then landed 150 men on the north shore of the harbour, at Haddrell's Beacon, but the militia soon drove them into the water, with the loss of a dozen killed and more than thirty prisoners. Many more were drowned in swimming to their boats. Another detachment on the south shore was similarly discomfited. On Thursday Colonel William Rhett, with six small craft heavily armed and a fire-ship, bore down upon the enemy's fleet. But instead of waiting to fight, the French commander hastily stood out to sea. This conduct, as well as his whole delay, may be explained by the fact that an important part of his force had not come up. The best of the French ships, carrying beside her marine force some 200 regular infantry, did not arrive until Friday, when, in ignorance of the repulse of her consorts, she entered Sewee Bay and landed her soldiers. It was rushing into the lion's jaws. The soldiers were promptly attacked and put to flight with the loss of one third of their number, while at the same time Colonel Rhett blockaded the bay and took the French ship with all on board. Thus the ill-concerted attack ended in ignominious defeat, with the loss of the best ship and 300 men out of 800.

After the halcyon days of Archdale there was quiet in North Carolina until 1704, when Governor Johnson sent a deputy, Robert Daniel, to rule there and set up the Church of England, while making it hot for Dissenters. As nearly all the Albemarle people came within the latter category, there was trouble at once. It was allayed for a moment by the same proceedings in England which gave victory to the Dissenters of South Carolina. The Quakers of Albemarle succeeded in getting Johnson to appoint a new deputy, Thomas Carey, in whom they had confidence. But their confidence proved to have been misplaced. A recent act of Queen Anne's Parliament had prescribed certain test oaths for all public officials, without making any reservation in behalf of the conscientious scruples of Quakers. Carey, as deputy governor of North Carolina, undertook to administer these test oaths, and at

Thomas Carey and the Quakers in North Carolina

LADY JOHNSON

once disgusted the Quakers, who sent John Porter to England to plead with the lords proprietors. This Porter, who was himself a Quaker, had a persuasive tongue. Acts of Parliament had not usually been heeded by the colonies; it was by no means clear that they were even intended to apply to the colonies without some

Porter's mission to England

declaratory clause to that effect, or without being supplemented by a royal order in council. The lords proprietors virtually admitted that the Queen Anne test oath act did not apply to the colonies, when in response to Porter's petition they removed Carey from office. At the same time they suspended Governor Johnson's authority over North Carolina. This action left that colony without a head, and there ought to have been no delay in appointing a new governor, but there was delay. On Porter's return William Glover was chosen president of the council, which made him temporary governor. Glover belonged to the Church of England, but was believed to be opposed to the test oaths. We can fancy, then, the wrath of the Quakers when he insisted upon administering the oaths, precisely as the deposed Carey had done! The remedy was an instance of political homœopathy, or treatment with a hair of the dog that bit you. The angry Porter at once turned to Carey and entered into an alliance with him from which dire evils were to grow. Porter contrived to assemble various resident deputies of the lords proprietors, and persuaded them to depose Glover and reinstate Carey; but Glover refused to be bound by these irregular proceedings. He continued to act as governor and issued writs for the election of an assembly; Carey did likewise, and anarchy reigned supreme. Several of the principal colonists fled to Virginia for safety. In 1710, after a delay of more than three years, the proprietors sent out Edward Hyde, a kinsman of the queen's grandfather, the first Earl of Clarendon, to govern North Carolina. His commission needed the signature of the governor-in-chief at Charleston, but that dignitary happened to die just before Hyde's arrival, so that further delay was entailed in completing his commission. Early in 1711, before receiving it, he issued writs for an election. Carey made strenuous efforts to secure the election of a majority of his friends and adherents to the Commons House of Assembly, or House of Commons, as it came to be called. Failing in this attempt he maintained

Alliance between Porter and Carey

Edward Hyde

that the election was illegal because Hyde had not received his vouchers. The assembly retorted by summoning Carey to render an account of all the public moneys which he had used, and presently it issued orders for his arrest. Thus driven to bay, Carey set up a rival government and tried to arrest Hyde, who appealed to Virginia for military aid. Virginia's response was prompt and effective. The discomfited Carey fled to the wilderness between the heads of Albemarle and Pamlico sounds. After a while he ventured into Virginia, intending to take passage there for England; but he was arrested and sent to England to be tried for treason. For lack of accessible evidence he seems to have been released without trial, and thereupon he made his way to the West Indies, where history loses sight of him. With his disappearance from North Carolina tranquillity seemed for the moment restored; but more terrible scenes were at hand.

Carey's rebellion

In spite of all the turmoil the little colony had received new settlers, and had begun to expand until North Carolina was no longer synonymous with Albemarle. In the first decade of the eighteenth century, numbers of Huguenots settled in the neighbourhood of Bath, where the Taw River widens into an arm of Pamlico Sound; and parties of Swiss, with many Germans from the Rhenish Palatinate, under the lead of Baron de Graffenried, founded the town of New Berne, where the Trent River flows into the Neuse. The increase of population in Albemarle, moreover, had carried the frontier from the Chowan to the Roanoke. All this entailed some real and still more prospective displacement of native tribes, and some kind of mild remonstrance, after the well-known Indian fashion, was to be expected. It was believed by many persons at the time that Carey, on the occasion of his flight to the wilderness between the Roanoke and Taw rivers, solicited aid from the Indians, and that his Quaker friend, John Porter, had gone as emissary to the Tuscaroras, "promising great rewards to incite

Expansion of the northern colony; arrival of Graffenried

Improbable charges against Carey and Porter

them to cut off all the inhabitants of that part of Carolina that adhered to Mr. Hyde."[1] But a charge of such frightful character needs strong evidence to make it credible, and in this case there is little but hearsay and the vague beliefs of men hostile to Carey and Porter, in a season of fierce political excitement. No such infernal wickedness is needed to account for the Indian outbreak. The ordinary incidents connected with the advance of the white man's frontier into the red man's country are quite sufficient to explain it. But, without feeling it necessary to accuse Carey and Porter of having urged the Indians to murder their fellow-countrymen, we must still admit that the civil discord into which they had plunged the colony had so weakened it as to offer the watchful red men an excellent opportunity.

Carolina Indians; Algonquin tribes

The Indians of North Carolina at the time which we are treating belonged to three ethnic families. Along the coast, northward from Cape Lookout to the Virginia line, the Corees, Pamlicos, Mattamuskeets, Pasquotanks, and Chowanocs all belonged to the Algonquin family, and they could muster in all about 400 warriors. The coast territory occupied by these tribes was continuous with that which had once been controlled by the Powhatan Confederacy to the northward. The Corees, in Carteret Precinct, were the southernmost of these Algonquin tribes. The Cape Fear Indians, on the coast southwest of Carteret, belonged to the great Sioux or Dakota family. From the meridian of 77° 30′ westward to the Blue Ridge, and from the Santee River on the south to the Potomac on the north, the country was occupied by Sioux tribes, of which the names most familiarly known are the Waxhaws, Cataw-

Sioux tribes

[1] Spotswood's *Official Letters* (Va. Hist. Soc. Coll.), Richmond, 1882, i. 106. Several other passages in Spotswood's letters of the summer and autumn of 1711 express a similar belief. The opinion of Spotswood is adopted in Hawks, *History of North Carolina*, ii. 522–533, who is followed by Moore, *History of North Carolina*, i. 35. I am glad to find that my opinion of the inadequacy of the evidence is shared by so great an authority as Professor Rivers, in Winsor, *Narr. and Crit. Hist.* v. 298.

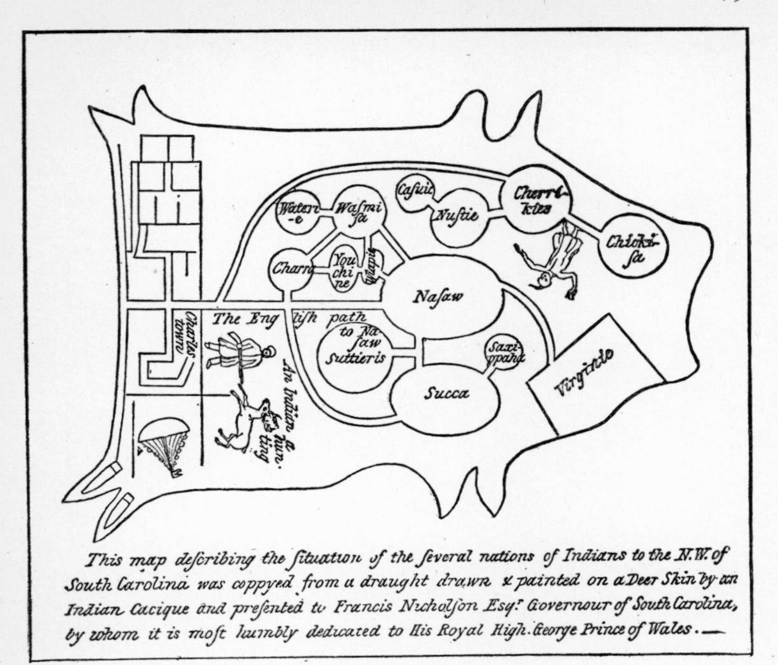

INDIAN MAP OF SOUTH CAROLINA ABOUT 1730

bas, Waterees, Saponis and Tutelos, Monacans and Manahoacs.[1] Now deep into this Sioux country, in North Carolina, there ran a powerful wedge of alien stock. The thick end of the wedge covered the precincts of Bath and Craven, with part of New Hanover; and from its centre, at the mouth of Trent River, it ran northwestward more than a hundred miles, a little beyond the site of Raleigh, with an average width of less than thirty miles. This wedge of population consisted of the Tuscaroras, a large tribe of the dreaded Iroquois family, able to send forth at least 1200 warriors. Another tribe of Iroquois then dwelt in

Iroquois tribes

[1] See the learned essay by James Mooney, *The Siouan Tribes of the East* (Bureau of Ethnology, Bulletin 22), Washington, 1894. Until recent years it was not known that there were ever any Sioux in the Atlantic region. The Catawbas, etc., were supposed to be Muskogi.

Bertie Precinct, between the Chowan and Roanoke rivers. It was known as the Meherrins, and was really the remnant of the fierce Susquehannocks, from whom Bacon had delivered Virginia in 1676. Its fighting numbers can hardly have been much over a hundred. Just north of the Meherrins was another small Iroquois tribe called Nottoways. To frame our picture, although it takes us away from the scene of action, we should add that the whole Alpine region west of the Sioux country, from the Peaks of Otter as far southwest as Lookout and Chickamauga mountains, belonged to the great Iroquois tribe of Cherokees; while to the south of Santee River, from Florida to the Mississippi River, we encounter a fourth ethnic family, the Muskogi, represented by such tribes as Choctaws and Chickasaws, the Creek Confederacy, the Yamassees, and others.

Muskogi tribes

Between the Tuscaroras and the numerous Sioux tribes by which they were partly surrounded there was incessant and murderous hostility. On the other hand, there was amity and alliance, at least for the moment, between the Tuscaroras and the Algonquin coast tribes whose lands the palefaces were invading. The first murders of white settlers occurred in Bertie Precinct at the hands of Meherrins, and seem to have been isolated cases. But a general conspiracy of Iroquois and Algonquin tribes was not long in forming, and the day before the new moon, September 22, 1711, was appointed for a wholesale massacre.

Algonquin-Iroquois conspiracy

A few days before the appointed time the Baron de Graffenried started in his pinnace from New Berne to explore the Neuse River. His only companions were a negro servant and John Lawson, a Scotchman who for a dozen years had been surveyor-general of the colony. Lawson was the author of an extremely valuable and fascinating book on Carolina and its native races, — a book which one cannot read without loving the writer and mourning his melancholy fate.[1] No man in the colony was

Capture of Graffenried and Lawson

[1] Lawson, *A New Voyage to Carolina, containing the Exact Descrip-*

A NEW

VOYAGE

TO

CAROLINA;

CONTAINING THE

Exact Deſcription and *Natural Hiſtory*

OF THAT

COUNTRY:

Together with the *Preſent State* thereof.

AND

A JOURNAL

Of a Thouſand Miles, Travel'd thro' ſeveral Nations of *INDIANS*.

Giving a particular Account of their Cuſtoms, Manners, *&c.*

By JOHN LAWSON, Gent. Surveyor-General of *North-Carolina*.

LONDON:

Printed in the Year 1709.

TITLE OF LAWSON'S BOOK

better known by the Indians, who had frequently observed and carefully noted the fact that his appearance in the woods with his surveying instruments was apt to be followed by some fresh encroachment upon their lands. Lawson and Graffenried had advanced but little way into the Tuscarora wilderness when they were surrounded by a host of Indians and taken prisoners. The Indians were very curious to learn why they had come up the river; perhaps it might indicate that the people at New Berne had some suspicion of the intended massacre and had sent them forward as scouts. If any such dread beset the minds of the red men, it was probably soon allayed; for it is clear that, had there been any suspicion, Graffenried and Lawson would not thus have ventured out of all reach of support. The barbarians were two or three days in making up their minds what to do. Then they took poor Lawson, and thrust into his skin all over, from head to foot, sharp splinters of lightwood, almost dripping with its own turpentine, and set him afire.[1] The negro was also put to death with fiendish torments, but Graffenried was kept a prisoner, perhaps in order to be burned on some festal occasion.

Lawson's horrible death

Before the news of this dreadful affair could reach New Berne, the blow had fallen, not only there, but also at Bath and on the Roanoke River. Some hundreds of settlers were massacred,—at New Berne 130 within two hours from the signal. No circumstance of horror was wanting. Men were gashed and scorched, children torn in pieces, women impaled on stakes. The slaughter went on for three days. A war-chief called by the white men Handcock seems to have been the leading spirit in this

The massacre, Sept. 22–24, 1711

tion and Natural History of that Country: together with the Present State thereof. And a Journal of a Thousand Miles travelled through several Nations of Indians, giving a particular Account of Their Customs, Manners, etc. London, 1709, small quarto, 258 pages.

[1] For this and other atrocities see the letter of November 2, 1711, from Major Christopher Gale to his sister, printed in Nichols's *Illustrations of the Literary History of the Eighteenth Century*, iv. 489–492.

concerted attack, but as usual in Indian warfare the concert was incomplete.[1] An outlying detachment of Tuscaroras in Bertie Precinct, whose head war-chief was called Tom Blunt, took no part in the massacre and remained on good terms with the whites. Perhaps

Aid from Virginia and South Carolina

TOMB OF COLONEL WILLIAM BYRD AT WESTOVER

Blunt's attitude may have been affected by nearness to Virginia and its able governor, Alexander Spotswood, who was

[1] In Professor Rivers's version of the story there was either no general conspiracy or only a sudden one conceived after the murder of Lawson. He suggests that "being fearful of the consequences" of that act, the Indians "were hurried into the design of a widespread massacre," etc. *Early History of South Carolina*, p. 253. It may be so. Questions relating to concert between Indian tribes are apt to be hard to settle. I think, however, that in this case the simultaneity of attack at distant points is in favour of the generally accepted view of a conspiracy arranged before Lawson's death.

certainly instrumental in keeping the Nottoways and Meherrins quiet. Through Blunt's intervention, Spotswood secured the release of Graffenried, after five weeks of captivity, and it was not the fault of this valiant governor that Virginia troops did not march against Handcock; for his House of Burgesses, after advising such a measure, behaved like a "whimsical multitude," and refused to vote the necessary funds.[1] Important aid, however, was obtained from South Carolina, which had for the moment a more complaisant assembly, and in Charles Craven a wise and able governor. Advantage was taken of the deadly hatred which the Sioux and Muskogi tribes bore to the Iroquois. With a small body of white men, supported by large numbers of Muskogi Creeks and Yamassees, and of Sioux Catawbas, Colonel John Barnwell made a long and arduous winter march through more than 250 miles of virgin forest to the Neuse River, where he encountered the Tuscaroras, and in an obstinate battle defeated them with the loss of 400 warriors. Then Handcock, retiring behind a stockade, sought and obtained terms from Barnwell; a treaty was made, and the South Carolina forces went home.

Barnwell defeats the Tuscaroras, Jan. 28, 1712

They had scarcely departed when the faithless red men renewed their bloody work, and in March the distracted colony was again obliged to ask for succour. Summer added to the other horrors the scourge of yellow fever, which carried off some hundreds of victims, among them Governor Hyde. In December a force of 50 white men and 1000 Indians from South Carolina, under Colonel James Moore, arrived on the scene, and in March, 1713, Handcock was

[1] Spotswood to the Lords of Trade and to Lord Dartmouth, December 28, 1711, *Official Letters*, i. 129–138. This was one of the early instances of the extreme difficulty of obtaining money from "whimsical" legislatures for the common defence, which in later years led Parliament to the attempt to cure the evil by means of the Stamp Act. Even in what he did accomplish on the border, Spotswood had to depend upon voluntary contributions, just as money was raised by Franklin in 1758 for the expedition against Fort Duquesne, and by Robert Morris in the great crisis of Washington's Trenton-Princeton campaign.

William Earle of Craven
Lord viscount Craven Barron of
Hampstead Marshall Palatine

To Thomas Smith Esq[r]
Governo[r] of the Province of
Carolina:

Whereas it is agreed by y[e] Lords Prop[rs] of
the Said Province that the Palatine Should
name the Govern[r] I out of the trust and
Confydence I have of the wisdome Prudence
Integrety & loyallty of you Thomas Smith
doe hereby nominate Constitute & apoint you
the Said Thomas Smith to be Governor and
Comander in Cheife in Carolina with full
power [illegible]
Such Jurisdictions & powers as by virtue of
the Rules of Governm[t] & Instructions given by
my Selfe & y[e] Rest of the Lords prop[rs] of y[e] Said
Province a Governo[r] is to Doe & Exercise, and
you are to follow Such Instructions as are
herew[th] sent you or that you shall hereafter
from time to time receive from my Selfe
& the Rest of the Lords propr[s] of the Said
Province & thus to Continue Dureing my
pleasure Given under my hand & Seale this
twenty Ninth day of November in y[e]
yeare of our Lord one thousand Six hundred
Ninty & three.

Craven Palatine

Read in Councill y[e] 15th day of March 169[3/4] [illegible]
The above is a true Copy of y[e] hono[ble]
Tho[s] Smith Commission Examined and
attested wth y[e] publique Seale of this
Province this 26th of April 1694
[illegible] Secr[y]

CRAVEN'S INSTRUCTIONS

driven to cover on the site of the present town of Snow Hill, in Greene County. His palisaded fort was stormed with great slaughter, and that was the end of the Indian power in eastern North Carolina. The remnant of defeated Tuscaroras withdrew to the upper waters of the Roanoke, and thence migrated northward to central New York, where they were admitted into the great confederacy of their kinsmen, the Iroquois of the Long House. Thus did the celebrated Five Nations become the Six Nations.

Crushing defeat of the Tuscaroras; migration to New York

After Hyde's death the government was ably administered by one of the leading colonists, Thomas Pollock, as president of the council. In 1714 Charles Eden came out as governor. Under the stress of war the colony had begun to issue paper money, a curse from which it was destined long to suffer. But some other evils were remedied. Liberty of conscience was secured to Dissenters, and in the matter of test oaths the Quaker's affirmation was accepted as an equivalent. Eden was a very popular governor and managed affairs with ability until his death in 1722. His name is preserved in that of the town of Edenton, in Chowan County, which was in his time the seat of government.

Charles Eden

We must now turn to South Carolina, where we have seen Governor Craven using the Yamassee and Catawba warriors as allies to be sent against the Tuscaroras. The year 1713, which witnessed the crushing defeat of the Tuscaroras, was the year of the treaty of Utrecht, which ended the long war of the Spanish Succession. Throughout that war the powerful tribe of Yamassees had been steadfast friends of the English. From time to time they made incursions into Florida and brought away many a Spanish captive to be burned alive, until government checked their cruelty by offering a ransom for Spanish prisoners delivered in safety at Charleston; the prisoners were then sent home on payment of the amount of their ransom by the government at St. Augustine.

The Yamassees and the Spaniards

The Yamassee country was the last quarter from which

the South Carolinians would have expected hostilities to come. But after 1713, in spite of treaty obligations, the St. Augustine government bent all its energies to stirring up all the frontier tribes to a concerted attack upon the English. Bribes in the shape of gaudy coats, steel hatchets, and fire-arms were distributed among the chiefs ; the solemn palavers, the banquets of boiled dog, the exchanges of wampum belts,

ORIGINAL BROAD SEAL OF SOUTH CAROLINA

the puffing of red clay pipes, the beastly orgies of fire-water, may be left to our imagination, for we have no such minute chroniclers here as the Jesuits of Canada. The outcome of it all was a grand conspiracy of Yamassees, Creeks, Catawbas, and Cherokees, with other less important tribes, comprising perhaps 7000 or 8000 warriors, against the colony of South Carolina. But, as in all such plans for concerted action among Indians, the concert was very imperfect. Hostilities began in April, 1715, with the massacre of ninety persons at Pocotaligo, and lasted until February, 1716, by which time 400 Christians had lost their lives ; while the red men were thoroughly vanquished, and the shattered remnant of the Yamassees sought shelter in Florida.

Alliance of Indian tribes against the South Carolinians

The Indian war

Governor Craven, who had conducted this war with great ability and courage, was a man of high character, and when he returned to England in 1717 his departure was mourned. His successor, Robert Johnson, was son of Sir Nathaniel

Johnson, who had formerly been governor. The younger Johnson, an able and popular official, was the last governor of South Carolina under the lords proprietors. His romantic experiences in dealing with pirates will be recounted in my next chapter. The chain of events which brought about a political revolution in 1719 admits of brief description. The Indian war had laden South Carolina with debt, and it was felt that the lords proprietors ought to contribute something toward relieving the distress of a colony which had yielded them a princely income. But the lords proprietors did not take this view of the case. As a means of discharging the public debt, the assembly laid a revenue tariff upon imports, but the lords proprietors vetoed it. The assembly proposed to raise money by selling Yamassee lands to settlers, but the lords proprietors laid claim to the conquered territory for their own use and behoof. Thus the situation was fast becoming unendurable.

Robert Johnson

In December, 1718, war broke out again between Spain and England. The Spaniards planned an expedition against Charleston, and Johnson asked the assembly for money. They proposed to raise it by collecting revenue under the tariff act, in disregard of the veto. Nicholas Trott, the chief justice, declared that this would not do; the courts would uphold delinquents who

The revolution of 1719 in South Carolina

should refuse to pay. The assembly denied the right of the proprietors to veto their acts. The members consulted their constituents and were sustained by them. Finally the assembly resolved itself into a revolutionary convention, deposed the lords proprietors, and offered the governorship to

Johnson as royal governor. On his refusal to take part in such proceedings, the convention chose for provisional royal governor Colonel James Moore, the hero of the Tuscarora war. Johnson's only reliance, in such an emergency, was the militia; but the militia deserted him and went over to the convention, and thus, in December, 1719, the popular revolution was complete. When the news reached London,

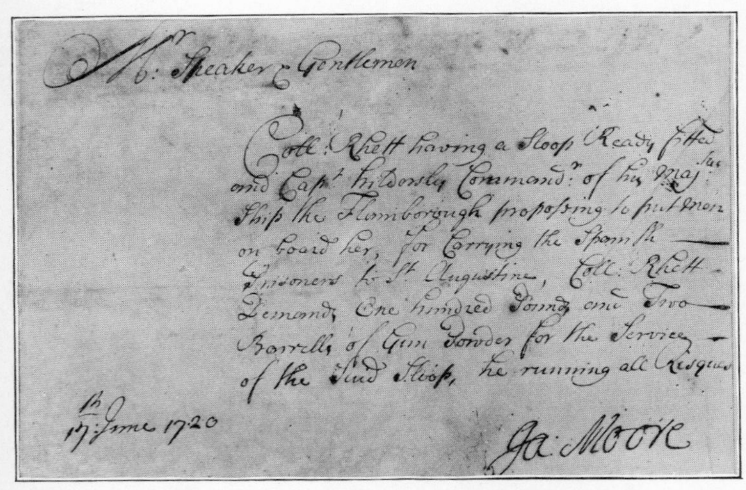

Mr: Speaker & Gentlemen

Coll: Rhett having a Sloop Ready fitted and Capt. Hildesley Command.r of his Majesties Ship the Flamborough proposing to put men on board her, for Carrying the Spanish Prisoners to St. Augustine, Coll: Rhett Demands One hundred Pounds and Two Barrells of Gun Powder for the Service of the Said Sloop, he running all Resques

17th June 1720

Ja: Moore

COLONEL JAMES MOORE'S ORDER FOR SUPPLIES

the course of the assembly was approved by the crown, the proprietary charter was declared to be forfeited, and our old friend Sir Francis Nicholson was sent out to South Carolina as royal governor.

Three years later there was renewal of civil discord in North Carolina, after the death of Governor Eden and the arrival of his successor, George Burrington, a vulgar ruffian who had served a term in prison for an infamous assault upon an old woman. Five years of turmoil, with changes of governors, followed. In 1728 Parliament requested the king to buy Carolina, and appropriated money for the purpose. The proprietors were

End of the proprietary government

Henry Somerset, Duke of Beaufort, and his brother, Lord Charles Somerset; Lord Craven; Lord Carteret; John Cotton; the heirs of Sir John Colleton; James and Henry Bertie; Mary Dawson and Elizabeth Moore. Lord Carteret would not sell his share. All the others consented to sell for a modest sum total scarcely amounting to £50,000; and so in 1729 the many-headed palatinate founded by Charles II. came to an end, and in its place were the two royal provinces of North and South Carolina.

The careers of the two southern colonies whose beginnings we have thus sketched were very different, and between their respective social characteristics the contrasts were so great that it is impossible to make general statements applicable alike to the two. In one respect the contrast was different from that which one would observe in comparing Virginia with New England. In New England a marked concentration of social life in towns and villages co-existed with complete democracy, while in Virginia the isolated life upon great plantations was connected with an aristocratic structure of society. But between the two Carolinas the contrast was just the reverse of this. Of all the southern colonies, North Carolina was the one in which society was the most scattered, and town life the least developed, while it was also the one in which the general aspect of society was the least aristocratic. On the other hand, in South Carolina there was a peculiarly strong concentration of social life into a single focus in Charleston; and in connection with this we find a type of society in some respects more essentially aristocratic than in Virginia. We shall find it worth our while to dwell for a moment upon some of the immediate causes of these differences.

Contrasts between the two Carolinas

The history of North America affords an interesting illustration of the way in which the character of a community may be determined for good or ill by geographical circumstances. There have been historians and philosophers unable to see anything except such

Effect of geographical conditions

PLAN OF CHARLESTON, 1732

physical conditions at work in determining the course of human affairs. With such views I have small sympathy,[1] but it would be idle to deny that physical conditions are very important, and the study of them is highly instructive. But for the peculiar physical conformation of its coast, North

[1] See my *Outlines of Cosmic Philosophy*, ii. 200.

Carolina, rather than Virginia, would doubtless have been the first American state. It was upon Roanoke Island that the earliest attempts were made, but Ralph Lane in 1585 already came to the conclusion that the Chesapeake region would afford better opportunities. First and foremost, the harbourage was spoiled by the prevalent sandbars. Then huge pine barrens near the coast hindered the first efforts of the planter, and extensive malarial swamps imperilled his life.[1] The first attempts at cultivation increased the danger, which was of a kind that would yield only to modern methods of drainage. It was only by the coast that the conditions were thus forbidding. No American state has greater natural advantages than North Carolina. For diversity of eligible soils, for salubrity of climate, for variety of flora and fauna, she is unsurpassed; while for beauty and grandeur of scenery she may well claim to be first among the states east of the Rocky Mountains.[2] John Lawson describes North Carolina with enthusiasm as "a delicious country, being placed in that girdle of the world which affords wine, oil, fruit, grain, and silk, with other rich commodities, besides a sweet air, moderate climate, and fertile soil. These are the blessings, under Heaven's protection, that spin out the thread of life to its utmost extent, and crown our days with the sweets of health and plenty, which, when joined with content, render the possessors the happiest race of men upon earth."[3] The good Lawson, who was somewhat inclined to see things in rose-colour, praised even the gentleness of the Indians, who (as we have seen) returned the compliment after their manner, by roasting him alive. But, with all this beauty and

Interior of North Carolina contrasted with the coast

[1] Dr. Hugh Williamson, in his *History of North Carolina*, Philadelphia, 1812, ii. 173–211, gives a very interesting account of these malarial swamps, their geological causes, and their effects upon the people.

[2] For a sprightly account of the Alpine region of North Carolina and its inhabitants, see Zeigler and Grosscup, *The Heart of the Alleghanies*, Raleigh, 1883.

[3] Lawson's *New Voyage to Carolina*, London, 1718, p. 79.

richness of the interior country, the obstacles presented at the coast turned the first great wave of English colonization into Virginia; and thereafter the settlement of North Carolina was determined largely, and by no means to its advantage, by the social conditions of the older colony.

In its early days North Carolina was simply a portion of Virginia's frontier; and to this wild frontier the shiftless people who could not make a place for themselves in Virginia society, including many of the "mean whites," flocked in large numbers. In their new home they soon acquired the reputation of being very lawless in temper, holding it to be the chief end of man to resist all constituted authority, and above all things to pay no taxes. In some respects, as in the administration of justice, one might have witnessed such scenes as continued for generations to characterize American frontier life. The courts sat oftentimes in taverns, where the tedium of business was relieved by glasses of grog, while the judge's decisions were not put on record, but were simply shouted by the crier from the inn door or at the nearest market-place. It was not until 1703 that a clergyman was settled in the colony, though there were Quaker meetings before that time. As late as 1729 Colonel Byrd writes of Edenton, the seat of government: "I believe this is the only metropolis in the Christian or Mohammedan world where there is neither church, chapel, mosque, synagogue, or any other place of public worship, of any sect or religion whatsoever." In this country "they pay no tribute, either to God or to Cæsar." [1]

Unkempt life

According to Colonel Byrd, these people were chargeable with laziness, but more especially the men, who let their wives work for them. The men, he says, "make their wives rise out of their beds early in the morning, at the same time that they lie and snore till the sun has run one third of his course and dispersed all the unwholesome damps. Then, after stretching and yawning for half an hour, they light their pipes, and under the pro-

A genre picture by Colonel Byrd

[1] *Byrd MSS.* i. 59, 65.

tection of a cloud of smoke venture out into the open air; though, if it happens to be never so little cold, they quickly return shivering into the chimney corner. When the weather is mild, they stand leaning with both their arms upon the cornfield fence, and gravely consider whether they had best go and take a small heat at the hoe, but generally find reasons to put it off until another time. Thus they loiter away their lives, like Solomon's sluggard, with their arms across, and at the winding up of the year scarcely have bread to eat." [1] Every one has met with the type of man here described. In Massachusetts to-day you may find sporadic examples of him in decaying mountain villages, left high and dry by the railroads that follow the winding valleys; or now and then you may find him clustered in some tiny hamlet of crazy shanties nestling in a secluded area of what Mr. Ricardo would have called "the worst land under cultivation," and bearing some such pithy local name as "Hardscrabble" or "Satan's Kingdom." Such men do not make the strength of Massachusetts, or of any commonwealth. They did not make the strength of North Carolina, and it should not be forgotten that Byrd's testimony is that of an unfriendly or at least a satirical observer. Nevertheless there is strong reason for believing that his portrait is one for which the old Albemarle colony could have furnished many sitters. Such people were sure to be drawn thither by the legislation which made the colony an Alsatia for insolvent debtors.

The industries of North Carolina in the early times were purely agricultural. There were no manufactures. The simplest and commonest articles of daily use were imported from the northern colonies or from England. Agriculture was conducted more wastefully and with less intelligence than in any of the other colonies. In the northern counties tobacco was almost exclusively cultivated. In the Cape Fear region there were flourishing rice-fields. A great deal of excellent timber was cut; in particular the yellow pine of North Car-

[1] *Byrd MSS.* i. 55.

VIRGO TRIUMPHANS:

OR,

VIRGINIA

richly and truly valued; more especially the South part thereof: *viz.*
The fertile CAROLANA, and no lesse excellent Isle of ROANOAK, of Latitude from
31 to 37 Degr. relating the meanes of
raising infinite profits to the Adventurers and Planters:
Humbly presented as the Auspice of a beginning Yeare,
To the Parliament of ENGLAND,
And Councell of STATE.

By EDVVARD WILLIAMS, Gent.

LONDON, Printed by *Thomas Harper*, for *John Stephenson*,
and are to be sold at his Shop on Ludgate-Hill, at the Signe
of the Sunne, 1650.

TITLE OF WILLIAMS'S "VIRGO TRIUMPHANS"

olina was then, as now, famous for its hardness and durability. Tar and turpentine were also produced in large quantities. All this furnished the basis for a flourishing foreign commerce; but the people did not take kindly to the sea, and the carrying trade was monopolized by New Englanders. The fisheries, which were of considerable value, were altogether neglected. All business or traffic about the coast was carried on under perilous conditions; for pirates were always hovering about, secure in the sympathy of many of the people, like the brigands of southern Italy in recent times.

Industries

In the absence of manufactures, and with commerce so little developed, there was no town life. Byrd describes Edenton as containing forty or fifty houses, small and cheaply built: "a citizen here is counted extravagant if he has ambition enough to aspire to a brick chimney."[1] As late as 1776 New Berne and Wilmington were villages of five or six hundred inhabitants each. Not only were there no towns, but there were very few large plantations with stately manor-houses like those of Virginia. A great part of the country was covered with its primeval forest, in which thousands of hogs, branded with their owners' marks, wandered and rooted until the time came for hunting them out and slaughtering them. Where rude clearings had been made in the wilderness there were small, ill-kept farms. Nearly all the people were small farmers, whose work was done chiefly by black slaves or by white servants. The treatment of the slaves is said to have been usually mild, as in Virginia. The white servants fared better, and the general state of society was so low that when their time of service was ended they had here a good chance of rising to a position of equality with their masters. The country swarmed with ruffians of all sorts, who fled thither from South Carolina and Virginia; life and property were insecure, and lynch law was not unfrequently administered. The small planters were apt to be hard drinkers, and among

Absence of towns

[1] *Byrd MSS.* i. 59.

their social amusements were scrimmages, in which noses were sometimes broken and eyes gouged out. There was a great deal of gambling. But, except at elections and other meetings for political purposes, people saw very little of each other. The isolation of homesteads, which prevailed over the South, reached its maximum in North Carolina. It is not strange, then, that the colony was a century old before it could boast of a printing-press, or that there were

BIRTHPLACE OF SIR WALTER RALEIGH AT HAYES IN DEVONSHIRE

no schools until shortly before the war for Independence. A mail from Virginia came some eight or ten times in a year, but it only reached a few towns on the coast, and down to the time of the Revolution the interior of the country had no mails at all.

All these consequences clearly followed from the character of the emigration by which North Carolina was first peopled, and that character was determined by its geographical position as a wilderness frontier to such a commonwealth as Virginia. In the character of this emigration we find the reasons for the comparatively democratic state of society. As there were so few large plantations and

A frontier democracy

wealthy planters, while nearly all the white people were small landowners, and as the highest class was thus so much lower in dignity than the corresponding class in Virginia, it became just so much the easier for the "mean whites" to rise far enough to become a part of it. North Carolina, therefore, was not simply an Alsatia for debtors and criminals, but it afforded a home for the better portion of Virginia's poor people. We can thus see how there would come about a natural segregation of Virginia's white freedmen into four classes: 1. The most enterprising and thrifty would succeed in maintaining a respectable existence in Virginia; 2. A much larger class, less thrifty and enterprising, would find it easier to make a place for themselves in the ruder society of North Carolina; 3. A lower stratum would consist of persons without enterprise or thrift who remained in Virginia to recruit the ranks of "white trash;" 4. The lowest stratum would comprise the outlaws who fled into North Carolina to escape the hangman. Of the third class the eighteenth century seems to have witnessed a gradual exodus from Virginia, so that in 1773 it was possible for the traveller, John Ferdinand Smyth, to declare that there were fewer cases of poverty in proportion to the population than anywhere else "in the universe." The statement of Bishop Meade in 1857, which was quoted in the preceding chapter,[1] shows that the class of "mean whites" had not even then become extinct in Virginia; but it is clear that the slow but steady exodus had been such as greatly to diminish its numbers and its importance as a social feature. Some of these freedmen went northward into Pennsylvania,[2] but most of them sought the western and southern frontiers, and at first the southern frontier was a far more eligible retreat than the western. Of this outward movement of white freedmen the governor of Virginia wrote in 1717: "The Inhabitants of our frontiers are generally composed of such as have been transported hither as Servants, and being

Segregation and dispersal of Virginia's poor whites

[1] See above, p. 171 of the present volume.

[2] *William and Mary College Quarterly*, ii. 146.

John Locke

my concluding chapter, where it forms the most important part of the story of the westward advance of Virginia. For the present it may suffice to point out that in North Carolina they had come, before the Revolutionary War, to be the strongest element in the population of the colony. Under the influence of these various and excellent streams of immigration, the character of the colony was gradually but effectively altered. Industry and thrift came to prevail in the wilderness, and various earnest Puritanic types of religion flourished side by side on friendly terms.

The Scotch-Irish immigration

As society in North Carolina became more and more orderly and civilized, the old mean white element, or at least the more intractable part of it, was gradually pushed out to the westward. This stream that had started from Old Virginia flowed for a while southwestward into the South Carolina back-country. But the southerly movement was gradually turned more and more to the westward.

Displacement and further dispersal of poor whites

Always clinging to the half-savage frontier, these poor white people made their way from North Carolina westward through Tennessee, and their descendants may still be found here and there in Arkansas, southern Missouri, and what is sometimes known as the Egyptian extremity of Illinois. From the South Carolina back-country, through Georgia, they were scattered here and there among the states on the Gulf of Mexico. Taken at its worst, this type of American citizen is portrayed in Martin Chuzzlewit's unwelcome visitor, the redoubtable Hannibal Chollop. Specimens of him might have been found among the border ruffians led by the savage Quantrell in 1863 to the cruel massacre at Lawrence, and among the desperadoes whose dark deeds used forty years ago to give such cities as Memphis an unenviable prominence in the pages of the "Police Gazette." But in the average specimens of the type one would find not criminality of disposition so much as shiftlessness. Of the stunted, gaunt, and cadaverous "sandhillers" of South Carolina and

Georgia, a keen observer says that "they are incapable of applying themselves steadily to any labour, and their habits are very much like those of the old Indians."[1] The "clay-eaters," who are said to sustain life on crude whiskey and aluminous earth, are doubtless of similar type, as well as the "conches," "crackers," and "corn-crackers" of various Southern states. All these seem to represent a degraded variety or strain of the English race. Concerning the origin of this degraded strain, detailed documentary evidence is not easy to get; but the facts of its distribution furnish data for valid inferences such as the naturalist entertains concerning the origin and migrations of some species of animal or plant.

"Crackers," etc.

There is, *first*, the importation of degraded English humanity in large numbers to the two oldest colonies in which there is a demand for wholesale cheap labour; *secondly*, the substitution of black cheap labour for white; *thirdly*, the tendency of the degraded white humanity to seek the frontier, as described by Spotswood, or else to lodge in sequestered nooks outside of the main currents of progress. These data are sufficient in general to explain the origin and distribution of the "crackers," but a word of qualification is needed. It is not to be supposed that the ancestors of all the persons designated as "crackers" were once white freedmen in Virginia and Maryland; it is more probable that this class furnished a nucleus about which various wrecks of decayed and broken-down humanity from many quarters were gradually gathered. Nor are we bound to suppose that every community of ignorant, semi-civilized white people in the Southern states is descended from those white freedmen. Prolonged isolation from the currents of thought and feeling that sway the great world will account for almost any extent of ignorance and backwardness; and there are few geographical situations east of the Mississippi River more conducive to isolation than the southwestern portion of the great Appalachian highlands. All these circumstances

[1] Olmsted's *Slave States*, p. 507.

should be borne in mind in dealing with what, from whatever point of view, is one of the interesting problems of American history.

Settlers of South Carolina

The settlement of South Carolina took place under different circumstances from those of the sister colony, and the resulting state of society was very different. In the earliest days there were many settlers of a rough and turbulent character, which their peculiar dealings with pirates, to be recounted in the following chapter, did not tend to improve. But the Huguenots, in whose

BRUTON PARISH CHURCH, FROM THE REAR

veins flowed some of the sturdiest blood of France, soon came in great numbers. From the acquaintanceship of the Berkeleys, the Ashleys, the Hydes, and others, there came a certain number of Cavaliers; but at the end of the seventeenth century the impulse which had carried thousands of Cavaliers to Virginia had quite died out, and on the whole the general complexion of South Carolina, as regarded religion and politics, was strongly Puritan.

In one respect there is a resemblance by no means superficial between the settlement of South Carolina and that of Massachusetts. Most of the South Carolina settlers had left their homes in Europe for reasons connected with religion; and emigrants who quit their homes for such reasons

CAROLINA COMPANY MEDAL

are likely to show a higher average of intelligence and energy than the great mass of their fellow-countrymen who stay at home. Calvinism was the prevailing form of theology in South Carolina, though there were some Lutherans, and perhaps one fifth of the people may have belonged to the Church of England, which was established by the proprietary charter, and remained the state church until 1776. We have seen how much disturbance was caused by the attempts of the High Churchmen early in the eighteenth century to enforce conformity on the part of the Dissenters; but such attempts were soon abandoned as hopeless, and a policy of toleration prevailed. Though the Church of England was supported by public taxation, yet the clergymen were not appointed to office, but were elected by their congregations like the Dissenting clergymen. Their education was in general very good, and their character lofty; and in all respects the tone of the church in South Carolina was far higher than in Virginia. At the outbreak of the Revolution the elected Episcopal clergy of South Carolina were generally found on the side

Churchmen and Dissenters

of the Whigs; a significant contrast to the appointed Episcopal clergy of Virginia, whose Toryism was carried so far as to ruin the reputation of their church. But the most interesting feature connected with the establishment of the English church was the introduction of the parish system of local self-government in very much the same form in which it existed in England. The vestries in South Carolina discharged many of the functions which in New England were performed by the town meeting, — the superintendence of the poor, the maintenance of roads, the election of representatives to the Commons House of Assembly, and the assessment of the local taxes.

The vestries

In one fundamental respect the political constitution of South Carolina was more democratic than that of Virginia. The vestrymen were elected yearly by all the taxpayers of the parish. In this they were analogous to the selectmen of New England. Parish government in Virginia was in the hands of a close vestry; in South Carolina it was administered by an open vestry. Moreover, while in Virginia the unit of representation in the legislature was the county, in South Carolina it was the parish. Now the South Carolina parish was of purely English origin, not of French origin like the parishes of Louisiana. The Louisiana parish is analogous to a county, that of South Carolina was nearly equivalent to a township.[1] Although the colony had such a large proportion of French settlers, and of such marked ability and character, the development of its governmental institutions was as thoroughly English as if no Frenchman had ever set foot upon its soil. The approximation to the New England township is interesting. The freemen of South Carolina, with their open vestry, possessed what the smaller landed proprietors of Virginia in Bacon's rebellion strove for in vain.

The South Carolina parish

In this connection it is worth while to observe that, from the first decade of the eighteenth century, a strong interest

[1] Cf. Ramage, "Local Government and Free Schools in South Carolina," *Johns Hopkins Univ. Studies*, vol. i.

in popular education was felt in South Carolina. The same obstacles to schools in the rural districts that we have already observed in Virginia prevented the growth of anything like the public school system of New England. But of private free schools in the colony of South Carolina there were quite a number, and their quality was very good. The first was established in Charleston in 1712, and it not only taught the three *Rs*, along with bookkeeping, but it had classes in Greek and Latin. Private donations were encouraged by a provision that every giver of £20 "could nominate a scholar to be taught free for five years." The commissioners of the school also appointed twelve scholars. Free schools were afterward erected by private bequests and subscriptions at Dorchester, Beaufort, Ninety-Six, and in many other places. A noteworthy instance was afforded by St. Thomas parish, where "James Childs bequeathed £600 toward erecting a free school, and the parishioners, by local subscription, increased the amount to £2800."[1] In such beginnings there lay the possibilities of a more healthy development than can be secured by the prevalent semi-socialist method of supporting schools by public taxation;[2] but the influences of negro slavery were adverse to any such development.

Free schools

The economic circumstance which chiefly determined the complexion of society in South Carolina was the cultivation of rice and indigo. The value of the former crop was discovered in 1693, when a ship from Madagascar, accidentally stopping at Charleston, had on board a little bag of rice, which was planted with very notable success. Rice was not long in becoming the great staple of the colony. By 1740 it yielded more than £200,000 yearly. Indigo was next in importance. Much corn was raised, and

Rice and indigo

[1] Ramage, *op. cit.*

[2] The remarks of Herbert Spencer on state education, in his *Social Statics*, revised ed., London, 1892, pp. 153–184, deserve most careful consideration by all who are interested in the welfare of their fellow-creatures.

cattle in large numbers were exported to the West Indies. Some attention was paid to silk, flax, and hemp, tobacco, olives, and oranges. Some cotton was raised, but that crop did not attain paramount importance until after the invention of the gin and the development of great factories in England.

Rice and indigo absorbed the principal attention of the colony, as tobacco absorbed the attention of Virginia. Manufactures did not thrive. Every article, great or small, whether a mere luxury or an article of prime necessity, that had to be manufactured, was imported, and paid for with rice or indigo. This created a very prosperous trade in Charleston. The planters did not deal directly with the shipmasters, as in Virginia, but sold their crops to the merchants in Charleston, whence they were shipped, sometimes in British, sometimes in New England vessels, to all parts of the world.

Now the cultivation of rice and the cultivation of indigo are both very unhealthy occupations. The work in the swamps is deadly to white men. But after 1713 negroes were brought to South Carolina in such great numbers that an athletic man could be had for £40 or less. Every such negro could raise in a single year much more indigo or rice than would repay the cost of his purchase, so that it was actually more profitable to work him to death than to take care of him. Assuming, then, that human nature in South Carolina was neither better nor worse than in other parts of the civilized world, we need not be surprised when told that the relations between master and slave were noticeably different from what they were in Virginia, Maryland, and North Carolina. The negroes of the southern colony were reputed to be more brutal and unmanageable than those to the northward, and for this there is a twofold explanation. In the first place, slaves newly brought from Africa, half-savage heathen, were less tractable than African slaves who had lived many years under kindly treatment among white people, and far less tractable than slaves of the next generation born in America. Such newcomers as had been tribal chiefs or elders in their native country were noted as especially insolent and insubordinate.[1] In many respects the negro has proved quickly amenable to the softening influences of civilized life, and to the teachings of Christianity, however imperfectly apprehended. In the second place, the type of Virginia slavery was old-fashioned and patriarchal, while South Carolina slavery was of the modern and commercial type. The slaves on a Virginia plantation were like members of a great family, while in a South Carolina rice swamp their position was much more analogous to that of a gang of navvies. This circumstance was closely connected with a peculiarity of South Carolina life, in which it afforded a striking contrast to the slave states north of it. Except in the immediate neighbourhood of Charleston, few if any planters lived on their estates. The reason for this was doubtless the desire to escape the intense heat and unwholesome air of the newly tilled lowlands. The latitude of South Carolina is that of Morocco, and it was natural for settlers coming from the cool or chilly climates of France and England to seek such relief as the breezes of Charleston harbour could afford.[2] As a rule, the planters had houses in Charleston and dwelt there the year round, making occasional visits to their plantations, but leaving them in the mean while to be managed by overseers. Thus the slaves, while set to much harder labour than in Virginia, were in the main left subject to the uncurbed tyranny of underlings, which is apt to be a very harsh kind of tyranny. The diminutions in their numbers, whether due to hardship or to whatever cause, were repaired by fresh importations from Africa, so that there was much less improvement in

Some characteristics of South Carolina slavery

[1] Bruce, *Economic History of Virginia*, ii. 108.

[2] Americans are apt to forget how much nearer the equator the familiar points in this country are than familiar points in Europe. Although every family has an atlas, many persons are surprised when their attention is called to the facts that Great Britain is in the latitude of Hudson Bay, that Paris and Vienna are further north than Quebec, that Montreal is nearly opposite to Venice, Boston to Rome, Charleston to Tripoli, etc.

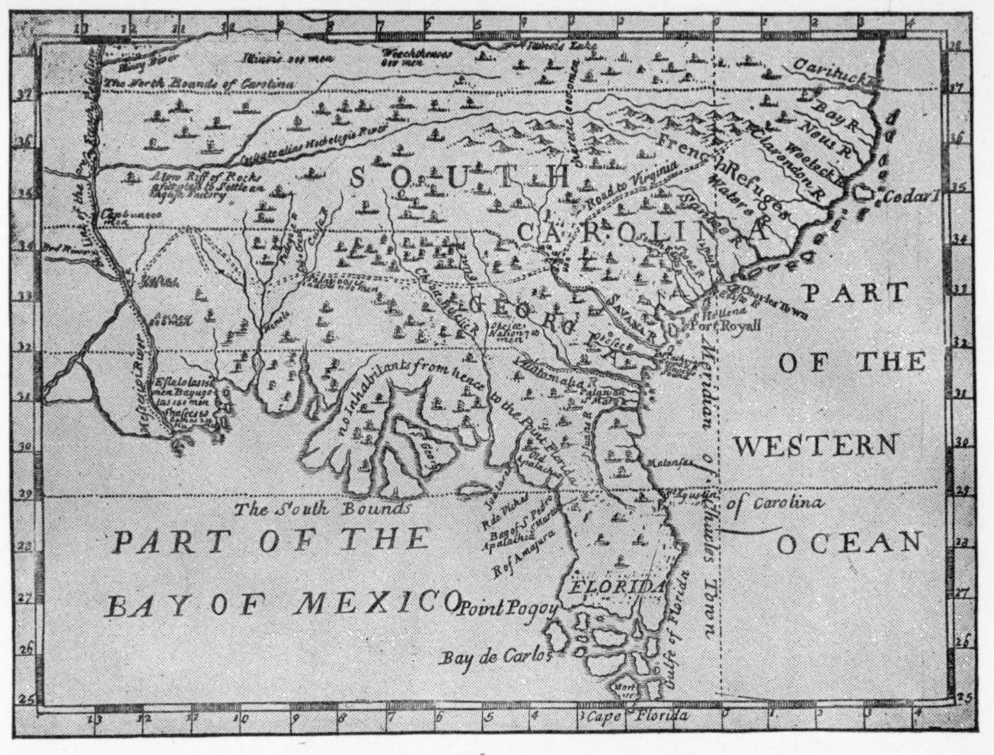

MAP OF SOUTH CAROLINA AND GEORGIA, 1733

their quality than under the milder patriarchal system. The dog that is used to kicks is prone to snarl and bite, and the slaves of South Carolina were an object of dread to their masters, all the more so because of their overwhelming numbers. Nothing can indicate more forcibly the social difference between the two Carolinas than the different ratios of their black to their white population. About 1760 the inhabitants of North Carolina were reckoned at 200,000, of whom one fourth were slaves; those of South Carolina at 150,000, of whom nearly or quite three fourths were slaves. In the former case the typical picture is that of a few black men raising tobacco and corn on the small plantation where the master lives; in the latter case it is that of an immense gang toiling in a rice swamp under the lash of an overseer. Care should always be taken not to exaggerate such contrasts, but after making all allowances the nature of the difference is here, I think, correctly indicated.

In 1740, while war was going on between Spain and England, there was a brief but startling insurrection of slaves in South Carolina. It was suspected that Spanish emissaries were concerned in it. However that may have been, the occasion of such a war might well seem to the negroes to furnish a good opportunity. Under the lead of a fellow named Cato the insurgents gathered near Stono Inlet and began an indiscriminate massacre of men, women, and children. The alarm was quickly given and the affair was soon brought to an end, though not until too many lives had been lost. The news arrived in Wilton while the people were attending church. It was the custom of the planters to carry rifles and pistols, and very little time was lost before Captain Bee led forth a well-equipped body of militia in quest of the rebels. They were overtaken in a large field, all in hilarious disorder, celebrating their bloody achievement with potations of rum; in which plight they were soon dispersed with slaughter, and their ringleaders were summarily hanged.[1]

Negro insurrection of 1740

[1] Simms' *History of South Carolina*, p. 106; Williams, *History of the Negro Race in America*, i. 299.

The habit of carrying fire-arms to church was part of a general system of patrol which grew out of the dread in which the planters lived. The chief business of the patrol was to visit all the plantations within its district at least once a fortnight and search the negro quarters for concealed weapons or stolen goods.[1] The patrolmen also hunted fugitives, and were authorized to flog stray negroes wherever found. The ordinary death penalty for the black man was hanging. Burning at the stake was not unknown, but, as I have already mentioned, there is one instance of such an execution in Massachusetts, and there are several in New York, so that it cannot be cited as illustrating any peculiarity of the South Carolina type of slavery. The most hideous instance of cruelty recorded of South Carolina is that of a slave who for the murder of an overseer was left to starve in a cage suspended to the bough of a tree, where insects swarmed over his naked flesh and birds had picked his eyes out before the mercy of death overtook him.[2] That such atrocities must have been condemned by public opinion is shown by the act of 1740, prescribing a fine of £700 current money for the wilful murder of a slave by his master or any other white man; £350 for killing him in a sudden heat of passion, or by undue correction; and £100 for inflicting mutilation or cruel punishment.[3]

Cruelties

The circumstance that most of the great planters had houses in Charleston went along with the brisk foreign trade to make it a very important town, according to the American standards of those days. In 1776, with its population of

[1] Whitney, "Government of the Colony of South Carolina," *Johns Hopkins Univ. Studies*, xiii. 95; *Statutes of South Carolina*, iii. 395–399, 456–461, 568–573.

[2] The story is told by St. John de Crèvecœur, in his *Letters from an American Farmer*, Philadelphia, 1793, pp. 178–180. Crèvecœur was on his way to dine with a planter when he encountered the shocking spectacle. He succeeded in passing a shell of water through the bars of the cage to the lips of the poor wretch, who thanked him and begged to be killed; but the Frenchman had no means at hand.

[3] *Statutes of South Carolina*, vii. 410, 411.

15,000 souls, it ranked as the fifth city of the United States.

Life in Charleston

Charleston had a theatre, while concerts, balls, and dinner parties gave animation to its social life. It was a general custom with the planters to send their children to Europe for an education, and it was said that a knowledge of the world thus acquired gave to society in South Carolina a somewhat less provincial aspect than it wore in other parts of English America.[1] The sharpest contrast, however, was with its next neighbour. As South Carolina may have been in some respects the most cosmopolitan of the colonies south of Pennsylvania, so on the other hand North Carolina was certainly the most sequestered and provincial. As I observed at the beginning of this chapter, for the development of the frontier or backwoods phase of American life two conditions were requisite: first, the struggle with the wilderness; secondly, isolation from European influences. This combination of conditions was not realized in the case of the first settlers of Virginia and Maryland, of the Puritans in New England, or the Dutch in New Netherland, or the Quakers in Pennsylvania. In all these cases there was more or less struggle with the wilderness, but the contact with European influences was never broken. With North Carolina it was different; the direct trade with England was from the outset much less than that of the other colonies. For a time its chief seaport was Norfolk in Virginia; European ideas reached it chiefly through slow overland journeys; and it was practically a part of Virginia's backwoods. On the other hand, South Carolina, focussing all its activities in the

Contrast between the two Carolinas

[1] "La plupart des riches habitans de la Caroline du Sud, ayant été élevés en Europe, en ont apporté plus de gout, et des connaissances plus analogues à nos mœurs, que les habitans des provinces du Nord, ce qui doit leur donner généralement sur ceux-ci de l'avantage en société. Les femmes semblent aussi plus animées que dans le Nord, prennent plus de part à la conversation, sont davantage dans la société. . . . Elles sont jolies, agréables, piquantes; mais . . . les hommes et les femmes vieillissent promptement dan ce climat." La Rochefoucauld-Liancourt, *Voyage dans les États-Unis*, Paris, 1799, iv. 13.

single seaport of Charleston, was eminently accessible to European influences. Its life was not that of a wilderness frontier, like its northern neighbour. But its military position, with reference to the whole Atlantic seaboard, was that of an English march or frontier against the Spaniards in Florida and the West Indies.

The contrast above indicated applies only to lowland South Carolina, the only part with which the earlier decades of the eighteenth century are concerned. At that time the highlands of both Carolinas remained in the possession of the Cherokees, so that they have nothing to do with my comparison. At a later time that whole highland region became a wilderness frontier, the scene of the civilized white man's backwoods life. All the way, indeed, from Pennsylvania to Georgia, along the Appalachian chain, there was a strong similarity of conditions and of life, in marked contrast with the divergencies along the coast region, in stepping from Pennsylvania into Maryland, thence into Virginia, and so on ; but that life along the coast which approached most nearly to the life of the interior wilderness was to be seen about Albemarle and Pamlico sounds.

The mention of Georgia serves to introduce the statement that, with the growth of civilization on the South Carolina coast, the need for a buffer against the Spaniards began to be more and more strongly felt. We have seen how the vexatious Yamassee war of 1715 was brought on by Spanish intrigues. After the overthrow of the Yamassees the troubles did not entirely cease. For some years the Indians continued to be a source of annoyance, and in their misdeeds the secret hand of Spain was discernible. The multitude of slaves, too, in regions accessible to Spanish influence, greatly increased the danger.

The Spanish frontier

In 1732 the state of affairs on the South Carolina frontier attracted the attention of a gallant English soldier whose name deserves a very high place among the heroes of early American history. James Oglethorpe, an officer who in youth had served with distinction under Prince Eugene against the Turks,[1] conceived the plan of freeing the insolvent debtors who crowded English prisons by carrying them over to America and establishing a colony which might serve as a strong military outpost against the Spaniards. The scheme was an opportune one, as the South Sea Bubble and other wild projects had ruined hundreds of English families. The land between the Savannah and Altamaha rivers, with the strip starting between their two main sources and running westward to the Pacific Ocean,[2] was made over to a board of trustees, and was named Georgia, in honour of the king, George II. The charter created a kind of proprietary government, but with powers less plenary and extensive than had been granted to the proprietors of Maryland, Carolina, and Pennsylvania. Oglethorpe was appointed governor; German Protestants and Highlanders from Scotland were brought over in large numbers; and a few people from New England joined in the enterprise, and founded the town of Sunbury. All laws were to be made by the trustees, and the settlers were at first to have no representative assembly and no voice in making the government. But this despotic arrangement was merely temporary and provisional; it was intended that after the lapse of one-and-twenty years the colony should be

James Oglethorpe

[1] Boswell has a characteristic anecdote of Oglethorpe, who was very high-spirited, but extremely sensible. When a lad of nineteen or so, he was dining one day with a certain Prince of Würtemberg and others, when the insolent prince fillipped a few drops of wine into his face. "Here was a nice dilemma. To have challenged him instantly might have fixed a quarrelsome character upon the young soldier; to have taken no notice of it might have been considered as cowardice. Oglethorpe, therefore, keeping his eye upon the prince and smiling, . . . said, 'That's a good joke, but we do it much better in England,' and threw a whole glass of wine in the prince's face. An old general, who sat by, said, 'Il a bien fait, mon prince, vous l'avez commencé;' and thus all ended in good humour." *Life of Johnson*, ed. Birkbeck Hill, ii. 180.

[2] See the charter, in Jones's *History of Georgia*, i. 90.

held to have come of age, and should choose its own government. Military drill was to be rigidly enforced. Slave-labour was absolutely prohibited, as was also the sale of intoxicating liquors; so that Maine cannot rightfully claim the doubtful honour of having been the first American commonwealth to try the experiment of a "Maine Law." Such were the beginnings of Georgia, and in the Spanish war of 1739 it quite justified the foresight of its founder. The valour of the Highlanders and the admirable generalship of Oglethorpe were an efficient bulwark for the older colonies. In 1742 the Spaniards were at last decisively

Beginnings of Georgia

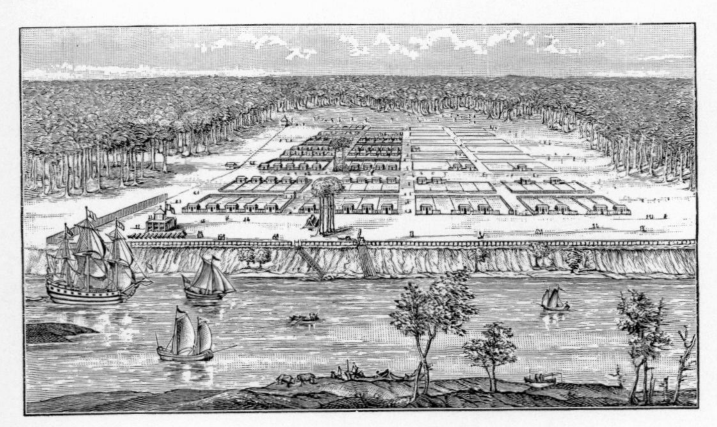

SAVANNAH IN 1741

defeated at Frederica, and from that time forth until the Revolution the frontier was more quiet. But proprietary government in Georgia fared no better than in the Carolinas. In 1752, one year before the coming of age, the government by trustees was abandoned. Georgia was made a crown colony, and a representative government was introduced simultaneously with negro slavery and Jamaica rum.

The social condition of colonial Georgia does not present many distinctive or striking features. In 1770 the population numbered about 50,000, of which perhaps one half were slaves. There was no town life. Rice and indigo were the principal crops, and there was a large export of lumber. Near Savannah there were a few extensive plantations, with fine houses, after the Virginia pattern; but most of the estates were small, and their owners poor. The Church of England was supported by the government, but the clergy had little influence. The condition of the slaves differed but slightly, if at all, from their condition in South Carolina. There were a good many "mean whites," and there was, perhaps, more crime and lawlessness than in the older colonies. The roads were mere Indian trails, and there were neither schools, nor mails, nor any kind of literature. Colonial Georgia, in short, with many of the characteristics of a "wild West," stood in relation to South Carolina somewhat as North Carolina to Virginia. It was essentially a frontier community, though the activity of Savannah as a seaport somewhat qualified the situation.

Cavaliers and Puritans once more

A comparative survey of Old Virginia's neighbours shows how extremely loose and inaccurate is the common habit of alluding to the old Cavalier society of England as if it were characteristic of the southern states in general. Equally loose and ignorant is the habit of alluding to Puritanism as if it were peculiar to England. In point of fact the Cavalier society was reproduced nowhere save on Chesapeake Bay. On the other hand, the English or Independent phase of Puritanism was by no means confined to the New England colonies. Three fourths of the people of Maryland were Puritans; English Puritanism, with the closely kindred French Calvinism, swayed South Carolina; and in our concluding chapter we shall see how the Scotch or Presbyterian phase of Puritanism extended throughout the whole length of the Appalachian region, from Pennsylvania to Georgia, and has exercised in the southwest an influence always great and often predominant. In the South to-day there is much more Puritanism surviving than in New England.

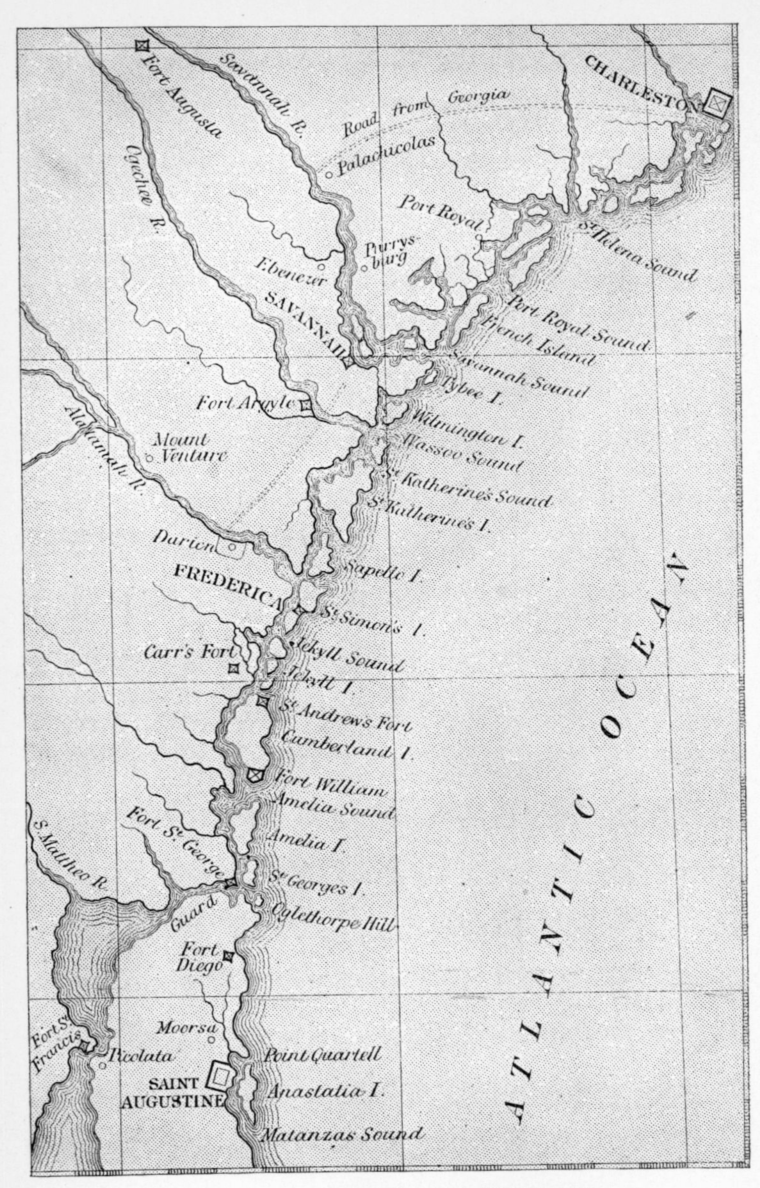

GEORGIA, COAST SETTLEMENTS BEFORE 1743

But before we join in the westward progress from tide-water to the peaks of the Blue Ridge and the Great Smoky range, we must look back upon the ocean for a moment and see how it came to be infested with buccaneers and pirates, and what effects they wrought upon our coasts.

CHAPTER XVI

THE GOLDEN AGE OF PIRATES

At no other time in the world's history has the business of piracy thriven so greatly as in the seventeenth century and the first part of the eighteenth. Its golden age may be said to have extended from about 1650 to about 1720. In ancient times the seafaring was too limited in its area to admit of such wholesale operations as went on after the broad Atlantic had become a highway between the Old World and the New. No doubt those Cretan and Cilician pirates who were suppressed by the great Pompey were terrible fellows. After the destruction of Carthage they controlled the Mediterranean from the coast of Judæa to the Pillars of Hercules, and captured the cargoes of Egyptian grain till at times Rome seemed threatened with famine. Roman commanders one after another went down before them, until at length, in the year B. C. 67, Pompey was appointed dictator over the Mediterranean and all its coasts for fifty miles inland. The dimensions of his task are indicated by the fact that in the course of that year he captured 3000 vessels, hanged or crucified 10,000 pirates, and made prisoners of 20,000 more, whom he hustled off to hard labour in places far from the sound of surf. Nevertheless those ancient pirates worked on a much smaller scale than the buccaneers of America. In the Indian Ocean and adjacent stretches of the Pacific there has always been much piracy until the recent days when French and English ships have patrolled those waters. The fame of the Chinese and Malays as sea robbers is well established. So too with those vile

Pompey and the pirates

Piracy on the Indian Ocean and Mediterranean Sea

communities north of Sahara which we used to call the Barbary States, their eminence in crime is unsurpassed. From the fifteenth century to the first years of the nineteenth, piracy was one of their chief sources of revenue; their ships were a terror to the coasts of Europe, and for devilish atrocity scarcely any human annals are so black as those of Morocco and Algiers. But as these Mussulman pirates and those of eastern Asia were as busily at work in the seventeenth century as at any other time, their case does not impair my statement that the age of the buccaneers was the Golden Age of piracy. The deeds done in American waters greatly swelled, if they did not more than double, the volume of maritime robbery already existing.

If we look into mediæval history for examples to compare with those already cited, we may observe that the Scandinavian Vikings, such men as sailed with Rolf and Guthorm and Swegen Forkbeard, are sometimes spoken of as pirates. If such a classification of them were correct, we should be obliged to assign the Golden Age of piracy to the ninth and tenth centuries, for surely all other slayings and plunderings done by seafaring men shrink into insignificance beside the operations of those mighty warriors of the North. But it is neither a just nor a correct use of language that would count as pirates a race of men who simply made war like all their contemporaries, only more effectively. The warfare of the Vikings was that of barbarous heathen, but it was not criminal unless it is a crime to be born a barbarian. The moral difference between killing the enemy in battle and murdering your neighbour is plain enough. If there is any word which implies thorough and downright criminality, it is pirate. In the old English law the pirate was declared an enemy to the human race, with whom no faith need be kept. "As therefore," says Blackstone, "he has renounced all the benefits of society and government, and has reduced himself afresh to the savage state of nature by declaring war against all mankind, all mankind must de-

The Vikings were not pirates in the strict sense

Blackstone on the crime of piracy

clare war against him, and every community hath a right by the rule of self-defence to inflict that punishment upon him which every individual would in a state of nature have been otherwise entitled to do for any invasion of his person or property."[1] Pirates taken at sea were commonly hung from the yard-arm without the formality of a trial, and on land neither church nor shrine could serve them as sanctuary. It was also well understood that they were not included in the benefit of a general declaration of pardon or amnesty.

The pirate thus elaborately outlawed was anybody who participated in violent robbery on the high seas, or in criminal plunder along their coasts. The details of such crimes were apt to be full of cruelty. The capture of a merchant ship with more or less bloodshed was usually involved, and such bloodshed was wholesale murder. If provisions were less than ample, the survivors were thrown overboard, or set ashore on some lonely island and left to starve, and this often happened. Murders from sheer wantonness were not uncommon, and the sack of a coast town or village was attended with nameless horrors. On the whole we cannot wonder that public opinion should have branded the skippers and crews who did such things as the very worst of criminals. One can see that in old trials for piracy, as in trials for witchcraft, the dread and detestation were often so great as to outweigh the ordinary English presumption that an accused person must have the benefit of the doubt until proved guilty. Desire to extirpate the crime became a stronger feeling than reluctance to punish the innocent. The slightest suspicion of complicity with pirates brought with it extreme peril.

Character of piracy

When we thus recall what the crime of piracy really was, we cannot fail to see how reprehensible is the language sometimes applied, by writers who should know better, to the noble sailors who in the days of Queen Elizabeth saved England from the Spanish Inquisition.[2] Had it not been

[1] Blackstone's *Commentaries*, bk. iv. chap. 5.

[2] See above, vol. i. p. 26.

for the group of devoted men among whom Sir Francis Drake was foremost, there was imminent danger three hundred years ago that human freedom might perish from off the face of the earth. The name of Drake is one that should never be uttered without reverence, especially by Americans, since it is clear that but for him our history would not have begun in the days of Elizabeth's successor. His character was far loftier than that of Nelson, the only other sea warrior whose achievements have equalled his. His performances never transgressed the bounds of legitimate warfare as it was conducted in the sixteenth century. Among his contemporaries he was exceptionally humane, for he would not permit the wanton destruction of life or property. To use language which even remotely alludes to such a man as a pirate is to show sad confusion of ideas. As for Elizabeth's other great captains, — such as Raleigh, Cavendish, Hawkins, Gilbert, Grenville, Frobisher, Winter, and the Howards, — few of them rose to the moral stature of Drake, but they were very far above the level of freebooters. It seems ridiculous that it should be necessary to say so. Their business was warfare, not robbery.

To call the Elizabethan sea kings "pirates" is silly and outrageous

It is nevertheless undeniable that naval warfare in the days of Elizabeth stood on a lower moral plane than naval warfare in the days of Victoria, and things were done without hesitation then that would not be tolerated now. Wars are ugly things at best, but civilized people have learned how to worry through them without inflicting quite so much misery as formerly. Three centuries ago not only were the usages more harsh than now, but the methods of conducting maritime warfare contained a feature out of which, under favouring circumstances, piracy afterward grew. There can be no doubt that the seventeenth century was the golden age of pirates because it came immediately after the age of Elizabeth. The circumstances of the struggle of the Netherlands and England against the greatest military power in the world made

Features of maritime warfare out of which piracy could grow

it necessary for the former to rely largely, and the latter almost exclusively, upon naval operations. Dutch ships on the Indian Ocean and English ships off the American coasts effectually cut the Spaniard's sinews of war. Now in that age ocean navigation was still in its infancy, and the work of creating great and permanent navies was only beginning. Government was glad to have individuals join in the work of building and equipping ships of war, and it was accordingly natural that individuals should expect to reimburse themselves for the heavy risk and expense by taking a share in the spoils of victory. In this way privateering came into existence, and it played a much more extensive part in maritime warfare than it now does. The navy was but incompletely nationalized. Into expeditions that were strictly military in purpose there entered some of the elements of a commercial speculation, and as we read them with our modern ideas we detect the smack of buccaneering.

Privateering

To this it should be added that fighting between hostile states occurred much more frequently than now without a formal declaration of war. There were times in the thirteenth and fourteenth centuries when the hatred between the commercial rivals, Venice and Genoa, was so fierce that whenever their ships happened to meet on the Mediterranean they went to fighting at sight, yet those bloody scrimmages did not always lead to war. In the youth of Christopher Columbus it was seldom that Christian and Turkish ships met without bloodshed, on the assumption that war was the normal state of things between Crescent and Cross. So when the Dutch were contending against Philip II. the English often helped their heroic cousins by capturing Spanish ships long before war was declared between Philip and Elizabeth. Such laxity of international usage made it easy to cross the line which demarcates privateering from piracy.

Fighting without declaring war

It should also be remembered that the ships of neutral nations had no such protection as now. The utmost that is now permitted the belligerent ship is to search the neutral ship for weapons or other materials of war bound for an enemy's port, and to confiscate such materials without further injury to person or property. In the sixteenth century it was allowable to confiscate the neutral ship bound for an enemy's port, sell her cargo for prize money, and hold her crew and passengers for ransom. The milder doctrine that any kind of goods might be seized, but not the ship and her people, had been propounded but was not yet generally accepted.

Lack of protection for neutral ships

All the circumstances here mentioned were favourable to the growth of piracy. At the same time the temptations were unusually strong. There was a vague widespread belief that America was a land abounding in treasure, and there were facts enough to explain such a belief. Immense quantities of gold and silver were carried across the Atlantic in Spanish ships, to say nothing of other articles of value. This treasure was used to support a war which threatened English liberty, and therefore English cruisers were right in seizing it wherever they could. But it only needed that such cruising should fall into the hands of knaves and ruffians, and that it should be kept up after Spain and England were really at peace, for this semi-mediæval warfare to develop into a gigantic carnival of robbery and murder. And so it happened.

Spanish treasure

It was toward the end of the sixteenth century, in the course of the great Elizabethan war, that the West Indies witnessed the first appearance of the marauders known as "Brethren of the Coast." They were of various nationalities, chiefly French, English, and Dutch. They all regarded Spain as the world's great bully that must be teased. The Spaniards had won such a reputation for tyranny and cruelty that public opinion was not shocked when they were made to swallow a dose or two of their own medicine. After peace had been declared, any foreign adventurers coming to the West Indies were liable to be molested as intruders, and their ships sometimes had

Origin of buccaneering

to fight in self-defence. Wherefore the more unscrupulous rovers, expecting ill-treatment, used not to wait for it, but when they saw a good chance for robbing Spaniards they promptly seized it. This they called, in the witty phrase of a French captain, *se dédommager par avance*, or recouping one's self beforehand.

It was not all the people of Spanish America, however, that frowned upon foreigners. Among those who came were sundry small traders of the illicit sort. Like all semi-barbarous governments, the court of Spain pursued a highly protectionist policy. The colonists were not allowed to receive European goods from any but Spanish ports, and thus the Spanish exporters were enabled to charge exorbitant prices. Many of the colonists therefore welcomed smugglers who brought European wares to exchange for cargoes of sugar or hides. To suppress this traffic, the authorities at San Domingo patrolled the coasts with small cruisers known as *guardacostas*, and when they caught the intruders they pitched them overboard, or strung them up to the yard-arm, without the smallest ceremony. In revenge the intruders combined into fleets and made descents upon the coasts, burning houses, plundering towns, and committing all manner of outrages. Thus there grew up in the West Indies a chronic state of hostilities quite independent of Europe. It came to be understood among the intruders that, whether their countries were at peace or war with one another, all persons coming to the West Indies were friends and allies against that universal enemy, the Spaniard. Thus these rovers took the name of "Brethren of the Coast."

Illicit traffic

As the consequence of more than a century of frightful misrule the beautiful island of Hispaniola, or Hayti, had come to be in many parts deserted. Many good havens were unguarded, and everywhere there were immense herds of cattle and swine running wild. Some of the brethren, mostly Frenchmen, were thus led to settle in the island and do a thriving business in hides, tallow, smoked beef, and salted pork, which they bartered with their sailor brethren for things smuggled from Europe. They drove away the Spaniards who tried to disturb them, and amid perpetual fighting the island came to be more and more French. Presently, from 1625 to 1630, they took possession of the little islands of St. Christopher and Nevis, and built strong fortifications at Tortuga. About this time they began to be called "boucaniers" or "buccaneers." To cure meat by smoking was called by the Indians "boucanning" it. La Rochefort says of the Caribs that they used to eat their prisoners well boucanned. In the days before cattle came to the New World, Americus Vespucius saw boucanned human shoulders and thighs hanging in Indian cabins as one would hang a flitch of bacon. The buccaneers were named for the excellent boucanned beef and pork which they sold. For their brethren on shipboard another name was at first used. The English word "freebooter" became in French mouths "flibustier," in spelling which a silent *s* was inserted after the *u* by a false analogy, as so often happens. In recent times "flibustier" has come back into English as "filibuster," a name originally given to such United States adventurers as William Walker, making raids upon Spanish-American coasts in the interests of slavery. In the first use of the epithets, if you lived on shore and smoked beef you were a *boucanier;* but if you lived on ship and smuggled or stole wherewithal to buy the beef you were a *flibustier.* Naturally, however, since so many of these restless brethren passed back and forth from the one occupation to the other, the names came to be applied indiscriminately, and whether you called a scamp by the one or the other made no difference.

Buccaneers and "flibustiers"

Those "Brethren of the Coast" were recruited in every way that can be imagined. Cutthroats and rioters, spendthrifts and debtors, thieves and vagabonds, runaway apprentices, broken-down tradesmen, soldiers out of a job, escaped convicts, religious cranks, youths crossed in love, every sort of man that craved excitement or change of luck, came to swell the number of the buccaneers. Graceless sons of good families usually assumed some new

The kind of people that became buccaneers

ONE OF EXQUEMELING'S PRINTS

name. Yet not all were ashamed of their lawless occupation. Some gloried in it, and deemed themselves pinks of propriety in matters pertaining to religion. One day, when a certain sailor was behaving with unseemly levity in church while a priest was saying mass, his captain suddenly stepped up and rebuked him for his want of reverence, and then blew his brains out. It is told of a Frenchman from Languedoc that his career was determined by reading a book on the cruelties of the Spaniards in America, probably "The Destruction of the Indies," by Las Casas. This perusal inflamed him with such furious hatred of Spaniards that he conceived it to be his sacred mission to kill as many as he could. So he joined the buccaneers, and murdered with such exemplary diligence that he came to be known as Montbars the Exterminator. Another noted freebooter, Raveneau de Lussan, joined the fraternity "because he was in debt, and wished, as every honest man should do, to have wherewithal to satisfy his creditors." [1]

One of the early exploits of the brethren was performed by Pierre of Dieppe, surnamed "the Great." In a mere longboat, with a handful of men, he surprised and captured the Spanish vice-admiral's ship, heavily freighted with treasure, set her people ashore in Hispaniola, and took his prize to France. This exploit is said to have given quite an impetus to buccaneering. In 1655 the buccaneers had grown so powerful that they gave important aid to Cromwell's troops in conquering Jamaica. When any nation went to war with Spain, the buccaneers of that nationality would get from the government letters of marque, which made them privateers and entitled them to certain rights of belligerents. Their aid was so liable to be useful in time of need that the English and French governments connived at some of their performances. No civilized government could countenance their cruelties. One monster, called Olonnois, having captured a Spanish ship with a crew of ninety men, beheaded them all with a sabre in his own hands.

Deeds of Olonnois

[1] Burney, *History of the Buccaneers of America*, p. 52.

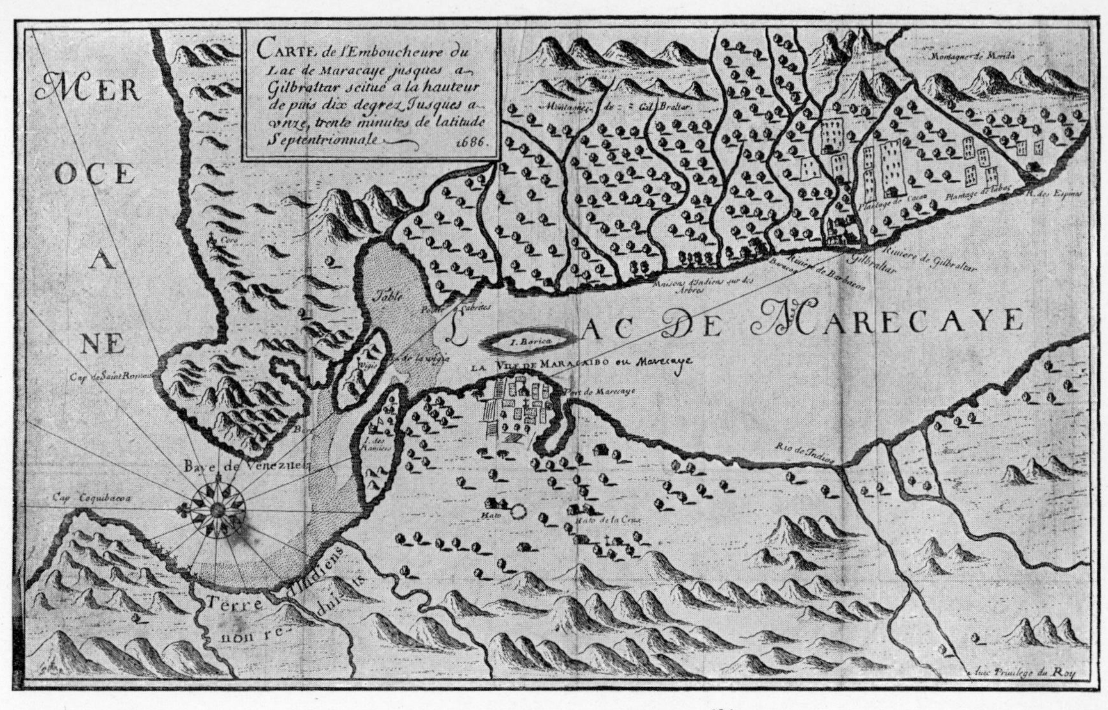

MAP OF THE GULF OF MARACAIBO, 1686

Four cases are on record in which he threw the whole crew overboard, and it is said that he sometimes tore out and devoured the bleeding hearts of his victims, after the Indian fashion. In concert with another wretch, Michel le Basque (whose name tells his origin), at the head of 650 men, he captured the towns of Gibraltar and Maracaibo, in the Gulf of Venezuela, and carried off a booty of nearly half a million crowns, equivalent to more than two million modern dollars. Prisoners were tortured to disclose hidden treasure. But this precious Olonnois was soon afterward paid in his own coin : he fell into the hands of a party of hungry Indians, who cooked and ate him.

Such incidents as these in Venezuela made many Spanish towns prefer to buy off the buccaneers, and thus a system of blackmail was established. It was for the buccaneer to decide for himself whether he deemed it more profitable to end all in one mad frolic of plunder and slaughter, or to accept a round sum and leave the town for the present unharmed. Operations on a grand scale began about 1664, under a leader named Mansvelt, who soon died and was succeeded by Henry Morgan, the most famous of the buccaneers and one of the vilest of the fraternity. This Welshman is said to have been of good family and well brought up. He made his way to Barbadoes as a redemptioner, and after serving out his term joined the pirates. He was a man of remarkable courage and resource. For cruelty no Apache could surpass him, and his perfidy equalled his cruelty. He paid so little heed to the maxims of honour among thieves that it is a wonder he should have retained his leadership through several expeditions.

Henry Morgan

One of Morgan's early exploits was the capture of Puerto del Principe, in Cuba. Then with 500 men he attacked Porto Bello, on the Isthmus of Darien. Having taken a convent, he forced the nuns to carry scaling ladders and plant them against the walls of the citadel, perhaps in the hope that Spaniards would not fire upon Spanish women ; but many of the poor nuns were killed. After the garrison

ENGRAVED TITLE OF EXQUEMELING'S BOOK — DUTCH EDITION OF 1678

had surrendered, Morgan set fire to the magazine and blew into fragments the fort with its defenders. The scenes that followed must have won Satan's approval. With greed unsatisfied by the enormous booty, the monster devised horrible tortures for the discovery of secret hoards that doubtless existed only in his fancy. Many victims died under the infliction.

Soon afterward Morgan met in the Caribbean Sea a powerful French pirate ship and invited her to join him. On the French captain's refusal, Morgan, with an air of supreme cordiality, invited him to come over to dinner with all his officers. No sooner had these guests arrived than they were seized and put in irons, while Morgan attacked their ship and captured it. Then came a strange retribution. Morgan put some of his own officers with 350 of his crew into the French ship; presently the officers got drunk, and through accident or carelessness the ship was blown up with all the English crew and the French prisoners. This story is told by a pious and literary Dutch buccaneer, the fraternity's best historian, by name Alexander Exquemeling, sometimes corrupted into Oexmelin. His well-written narrative was first published at Amsterdam in 1678, entitled *De Americaensche Zee-Roovers.* It has been translated into nearly all the languages of Europe, and ranks among the most popular books of the last two centuries.[1] The pious Exquemeling, in recounting the ex-

Alexander Exquemeling

[1] Exquemeling was sent to Tortuga in 1666, in one of the Dutch West India Company's ships, and on his arrival was sold for thirty crowns into three years' servitude. He says very neatly: "Je ne dis rien de ce qui a donné lieu à mon embarquement, suivi d'un si fâcheux esclavage, parce que cela seroit hors de propos, et ne pourroit estre qu'ennuyeux." He was cruelly treated. After gaining his freedom he joined the buccaneers, apparently because there was nothing else to do. He went home in 1674 in a Dutch ship, "remerciant Dieu de m'avoir retiré de cette miserable vie, estant la première occasion de la quitter que j'eusse rencontré depuis cinq années." Oexmelin, *Histoire des avanturiers*, Paris, 1686, i. 13; ii. 312. The English version of his book is entitled "History of the Bucaniers of America" (London, 1684). The

De

AMERICAENSCHE

ZEE-ROOVERS.

Behelsende een pertinente en waerachtige Beschrijving van alle de voornaemste Roveryen, en onmenschelijcke wreedheden, die de Engelse en Franse Rovers, tegens de Spanjaerden in America, gepleeght hebben.

Verdeelt in drie deelen:

Het Eerste Deel verhandelt hoe de Fransen op Hispanjola gekomen zijn, de aerdt van 't Landt, Inwoonders, en hun manier van leven aldaer.
Het Tweede Deel, de opkomst van de Rovers, hun regel en leven onder malkander, nevens verscheyde Roveryen aen de Spanjaerden gepleeght.
Het Derde 't verbranden van de Stadt *Panama*, door d'Engelsche en Franse Rovers gedaen, nevens het geen de Schrijver op sijn Reys voorgevallen is.

Hier achter is bygevoeght,

Een korte verhandeling van de Macht en Rijkdommen/ die de Koninck van Spanje/ Karel de Tweede, in America heeft/ nevens des selfs Inkomsten en Regering aldaer.

Als mede een kort begrijp van alle de voornaemste Plaetsen in het selve Gewest, onder Christen Potentaten behoorende.

Beschreven door A. O. Exquemelin.

Die self alle dese Roveryen, door noodt, bygewoont heeft.

Met schoone Figuren, Kaerten, en Conterfeytsels, alle na 't leven geteeckent, versien.

t'AMSTERDAM.
By JAN ten HOORN, Boeckverkoper/ over 't Oude Heeren Logement. Anno 1678.

PRINTED TITLE OF EXQUEMELING'S BOOK — DUTCH EDITION OF 1678

plosion of the captured ship, sees in it a special divine judgment upon Morgan for treachery to guests, a kind of philosophizing which is duly ridiculed by Voltaire in his "Candide."[1]

The loss of 350 men and a ship better than any of his own was a serious blow to Morgan, but it did not prevent him from capturing those unhappy towns, Maracaibo and Gibraltar, where he shut up a crowd of prisoners in a church and left them to die of starvation. His own escape from capture, however, was a narrow one. Three Spanish galleons arrived at the entrance to the Gulf of Venezuela and strongly garrisoned a castle that stood there, so that it began to look as if the day of reckoning for Morgan had come. But he made one of his vessels into a fire-ship and succeeded in burning two of the galleons. Then it became easy for his little fleet to surround and capture the third, after which a masterly series of stratagems enabled him to slip past the castle, richer by a million dollars than when he entered the Gulf, and ready for fresh deeds of wickedness.

Maracaibo and Gibraltar

The British government lamented these cruel aggressions upon people whose only offence was that of having been born Spaniards, and in 1670 a treaty was made between Spain and Great Britain for the express purpose of putting an end to buccaneering. This interesting treaty, which was con-

Spanish version is known as "Los Piratas." Not only do the titles thus differ, but each translator has added more or less material from other sources, in order to exalt the fame of the rascals of his own nation.

[1] "Le capitaine . . . du vaisseau submergé était un pirate hollandais; c'était celui-là même qui avait volé Candide. Les richesses immenses dont ce scélérat s'était emparé furent ensevelies avec lui dans la mer, et il n'y eut qu'un mouton de sauvé. Vous voyez, dit Candide à Martin, que le crime est puni quelquefois; ce coquin de patron hollandais a eu le sort qui'il méritait. Oui, dit Martin; mais fallait-il que les passagers qui était sur son vaisseau périssent aussi? Dieu a puni ce fripon, le diable a noyé les autres." Voltaire, *Œuvres*, Paris, 1785, tom. xliv. p. 294.

HISTOIRE
DES
AVANTURIERS
DES
BOUCANIERS
ET
DE LA CHAMBRE
DES COMPTES
établie
dans les
INDES
1686.

innocenter *pro peccatis*

A PARIS,
Chez JACQUES LE FEBVRE, au dernier pillier de la
Grand'Salle, vis-a-vis les Requestes du Palais.

ENGRAVED TITLE OF EXQUEMELING'S BOOK — FRENCH EDITION OF 1686

ceived in an unusually liberal and enlightened spirit, was called the treaty of America. As soon as the buccaneers heard of it, they resolved to make a defiant and startling exhibition of their power. Thirty-seven ships, carrying more than 2000 men of various nationalities, were collected off the friendly meat-curing coast of Hispaniola. Morgan was put in the chief command, and it was decided to capture Panama. On arriving at the isthmus they stormed the castle at the mouth of the river Chagres and put the garrison to the sword. Thus they gained an excellent base of operations. Leaving part of his force to guard castle and fleet, Morgan at the head of 1200 men made the difficult journey across the isthmus in nine days. Panama was not fortified, but a force of 2000 infantry and 400 horse confronted the buccaneers. In an obstinate battle, without quarter asked or given, the Spaniards lost 600 men and gave way. The city was then at the mercy of the victors. It contained about 7000 houses and some handsome churches, but Morgan set fire to it in several places, and after a couple of days nearly all these buildings were in ashes. By the light of those flames most hideous atrocities were to be seen, — such a carnival of cruelty and lust as would have disgraced the Middle Ages. After three bestial weeks the buccaneers departed with a long train of mules laden with booty, and several hundred prisoners, most of whom were held for ransom. Among these were many gentlewomen and children, whom Morgan treated savagely. He kept them half dead with hunger and thirst, and swore that if they failed to secure a ransom he would sell them for slaves in Jamaica. Exquemeling draws a pathetic picture of the poor ladies kneeling and imploring at Morgan's feet while their starving children moaned and cried; the only effect upon the ruffian was to make him ask them how much ransom they might hope to secure if these things were made known to their friends. When the party arrived at Chagres, there was a division of spoil, and the rascals were amazed to find how little there seemed to be to distribute. Morgan

Treaty of America, 1670

Sack of Panama

HISTOIRE
DES
AVANTURIERS
QUI SE SONT SIGNALEZ DANS LES INDES,
CONTENANT
CE QU'ILS ONT FAIT DE PLUS REMARQUABLE DEPUIS VINGT ANNÉES.

AVEC

La Vie, les Mœurs, les Coûtumes des Habitans de Saint Domingue & de la Tortuë, & une Description exacte de ces lieux;

Où l'on voit

L'établissement d'une Chambre des Comptes dans les Indes, & un Etat, tiré de cette Chambre, des Offices tant Ecclesiastiques que Seculieres ou le Roy d'Espagne pourvoit, les Revenus qu'il tire de l'Amerique, & ce que les plus grands Princes de l'Europe y possedent.

Le tout enrichi de Cartes Geographiques & de Figures en Taille-douce.

Par ALEXANDRE OLIVIER OEXMELIN.

TOME PREMIER.

A PARIS,
Chez JACQUES LE FEBVRE, au dernier pillier de la Grand' Salle, vis-à-vis les Requestes du Palais.

M. DC. LXXXVI.

AVEC PRIVILEGE DU ROY.

PRINTED TITLE OF EXQUEMELING'S BOOK — FRENCH EDITION OF 1686 was accused of loading far more than his rightful share upon his own vessels, whereupon, not wishing to argue the matter, he made up his mind to withdraw from the scene, "which he did," says our chronicler, "without calling any council or bidding any one adieu, but went secretly on board his own ship and put out to sea without giving notice, being followed only by three or four vessels of the whole fleet, who it is believed went shares with him in the greatest part of the spoil." All that can be said for him is that most of his comrades would gladly have done the same by him.

Morgan absconds

With Morgan's departure the pirate fleet was scattered, and plenty of strong language was used in reference to their tricksome commodore.[1] The arrival of a new English governor at Jamaica, with instructions to enforce the treaty of America, led to the hanging of quite a number of buccaneers; and a crew of 300 French pirates, shipwrecked on the coast of Porto Rico, were slaughtered by order of the Spanish governor. But such casualties produced little effect upon the swarming multitude of rovers, and within half a dozen years we find the governor of Jamaica conniving at them and sharing in their plunder. One pirate crew brought in a Spanish ship so richly freighted that there was £400 for every man after a round sum in hush-money had been handed to the governor. Then the pirates burned the ship and embarked in respectable company for England, "where," says Exquemeling, "some of them live in good reputation to this day."

Scotching the snake

But what shall we say when we find the devil turning monk, when we see the arch-pirate Morgan administering the king's justice upon his quondam comrades and sending them by scores to the gallows! It reads like a scene in comic opera, how this dirty fellow, after absconding with a lion's share of the Panama spoil and bringing it to Jamaica, suddenly put on airs of righteousness, wooed and won the fair daughter of one of the most eminent personages on the

[1] *Histoire des avanturiers*, ii. 216.

island, and was appointed a judge of the admiralty court. The finishing touch was put upon the farce when Charles II. decorated him with knighthood. It is not clear how he won the king's favour, but we know that Charles was not above taking tips. After this our

Morgan's metamorphosis

capacity for amazement is so far exhausted that we read with benumbed acquiescence how in 1682 Sir Henry Morgan was appointed deputy-governor of Jamaica.[1] But when we find

[1] Exquemeling says: "A l'heure que je parle il est élevé aux plus éminentes dignitez de la Jamaique; ce qui fait assez voir qu'un homme, tel qu'il soit, est toujours estimé & bien receu par tout, pourveu qu'il ait de l'argent." *Histoire des avanturiers*, ii. 214.

him handing over to the tender mercies of the Spaniards a whole crew of English buccaneers who had fallen into his clutches, we seem to recognize the old familiar touch, and cannot repress the suspicion that he sold them for hard cash! He remained in office three years, until James II. ascended the throne, when the Spanish government accused him of secret complicity with the pirates. On this charge he was removed from office and sent to England, where he was for some years imprisoned but never met the fate which he deserved.

Exquemeling expresses the opinion that, after the trick which Morgan played upon his comrades at Chagres, he must have thought it more prudent to be on the side of government than to stay with the buccaneers. He may also have foreseen that sooner or later the treaty of America was likely to interfere with the business of piracy. It is curious that, after all his caution, his downfall on a charge brought by Spain before the British government was due to the treaty of America. Although imperfectly enforced, that treaty seems to have marked the turning point in the history of buccaneering. The sack of Panama was the apogee of the golden age of pirates; the events that followed are incidents in a gradual but not slow decline. In 1684 the number of French buccaneers in the West Indies and on adjacent coasts was estimated at 3000, and of other nationalities there were perhaps as many more; but their operations were on a smaller and tamer scale than those of Olonnois and Morgan.

Decline of buccaneering

About this time the South Sea began to be the favourite field of work for some of the most famous buccaneers. In 1680 the first party crossed the isthmus and set sail on the Bay of Panama in a swarm of canoes, with which on the same day they captured a Spanish vessel of 30 tons. With this ship they captured another the next day, and so on till at the end of the week they were in possession of quite a fleet, comprising some ships of 400 tons. They cruised as far as the island of Juan Fernandez

Buccaneers of the South Sea

and beyond, capturing many ships and much treasure, but not doing much harm ashore. One of the officers, Basil Ringrose, an educated man, left a journal of this cruise, the original manuscript of which is in the British Museum. Other voyages followed until the buccaneers had visited such remote places as the Ladrone Islands, Easter Island, the coasts of Australia, and Tierra del Fuego. Among their

WILLIAM DAMPIER

commanders were men of far better type than those that have hitherto been mentioned; such were Ambrose Cowley, Edward Davis, the surgeon Lionel Wafer, and the celebrated William Dampier, whom we are more wont to remember as a great navigator and explorer than as a pirate. Cowley, Wafer, and Dampier have left charming narratives of their adventures, in which a mixture of scientific inquisitiveness with the love of barbaric independence is more conspicuous than mere greed. As Henry Morgan was a pirate of the worst type, so Edward Davis, discoverer of Easter Island, was of the best. He never would permit acts of cruelty or wanton bloodshed, and his loyalty and kindness to his comrades won their affection, so that his mellowing influence over rough natures was remarkable. In 1688 he took advantage of a royal proclamation of amnesty to quit buccaneering and go to England, where he was afterward counted as "respectable."

As we read the journals of those remote voyages it is easy to forget for a moment that the business is piracy. We seem to see the staunch ships, superbly handled by their expert sailors, blithely cleaving the blue waters under the Southern Cross; we breathe the cool salt breeze; we watch with interest the gray cliffs, the strange foliage, the birds and snakes and insects which arouse the curiosity of the mariners; we follow them to the Galapagos Islands, which first suggested to Darwin and afterward to Wallace the theory of natural selection; we note with pleasure their description of the uncouth natives of Australia; and we remember Thackeray when we encounter oysters so huge that Basil Ringrose has to cut them in quarters.[1] In the careless freedom of life on an unknown sea with each morrow bringing its new adventures, we forget what company we are in, till suddenly the victim ship heaves in sight, the brief chase ends in a deadly struggle, the Spanish colours go down before the black flag, a few bodies are buried in the depths, and a rich spoil is divided. It is vulgar robbery and murder after all, and there was a good deal of it in the South Sea. The coast of Peru, where there were the richest towns, suffered the most. The Lima Almanacs for 1685–87, comprising an official record of events for each year immediately preceding, mention the towns of Guayaquil, Santiago de Miraflores, and five others as plundered by the pirates. When Davis divided his booty at Juan Fernandez, there was enough to give every man a sum equivalent to $20,000. Very often a pirate got more gold and silver than he could handle or carry, but it was apt to slip away easily. Many of Davis's company quickly lost every dollar in gambling

Plunder of Peruvian towns

[1] Ringrose's *MS. Narrative*, British Museum, Sloane collection, No. 3820.

with their comrades. Our friend Raveneau de Lussan, who took to piracy in order to satisfy his creditors, tells his readers that his winnings at play, added to his share of booty, amounted to 30,000 pieces of eight, which would now be

equivalent to at least $120,000; so we may hope that he paid his debts like an honest man.

The event which did more than anything else to put an end to buccaneering was the accession of a Bourbon prince, Philip V., to the throne of Spain in 1701. It was then that his grandfather, Louis XIV., declared there were no longer any Pyrenees. Ever since the days of Ferdinand and Isabella, Spain and France had been enemies. Their relations now became so friendly that all the ports of Spanish America, whether in the West Indies or on the Pacific coast, were thrown open to French merchants. This made trade more profitable than piracy, and united the French and Spanish navies in protecting it. The English and Dutch fleets also put forth redoubled efforts, and during the next score of years the decline of the pirates was rapid.

Effects of the alliance between France and Spain

The first English settlements south of Virginia were made at the time when buccaneering was mighty and defiant. The colony of Sir John Yeamans, on Cape Fear River, was begun in 1665, and it was in 1670, the very year of the treaty of America, that Governor Sayle landed at Port Royal. The earliest settlers in Carolina, as we have seen, were not of such good quality as those who came a few years later. They furnished a convenient market for the pirates, who were apt to be open-handed customers, ready to pay good prices in Spanish gold, whether for clothes, weapons, and brandy brought from Europe, or for timber, tar, tobacco, rice, or corn raised in America. One of the Bahama Islands, called New Providence, had been settled by the English. Its remarkable facilities for anchorage and its convenient situation made it a favourite haunt of pirates, whose evil communications corrupted the good manners of the inhabitants. Rather than lose such customers they befriended them in every possible way, so that the island became notorious as one of the worst nests of desperadoes in the American waters. The malady was not long in spreading to the mainland. The Carolina coast, with its numerous sheltered harbours and inlets, afforded excellent lurking-places, whither one might retreat from pursuers, and where one might leisurely repair damages and make ready for further mischief. The pirates, therefore, long haunted that coast, and it was rather a help than a hindrance to them when settlements began to be made there. For now instead of a

Carolina and the Bahamas

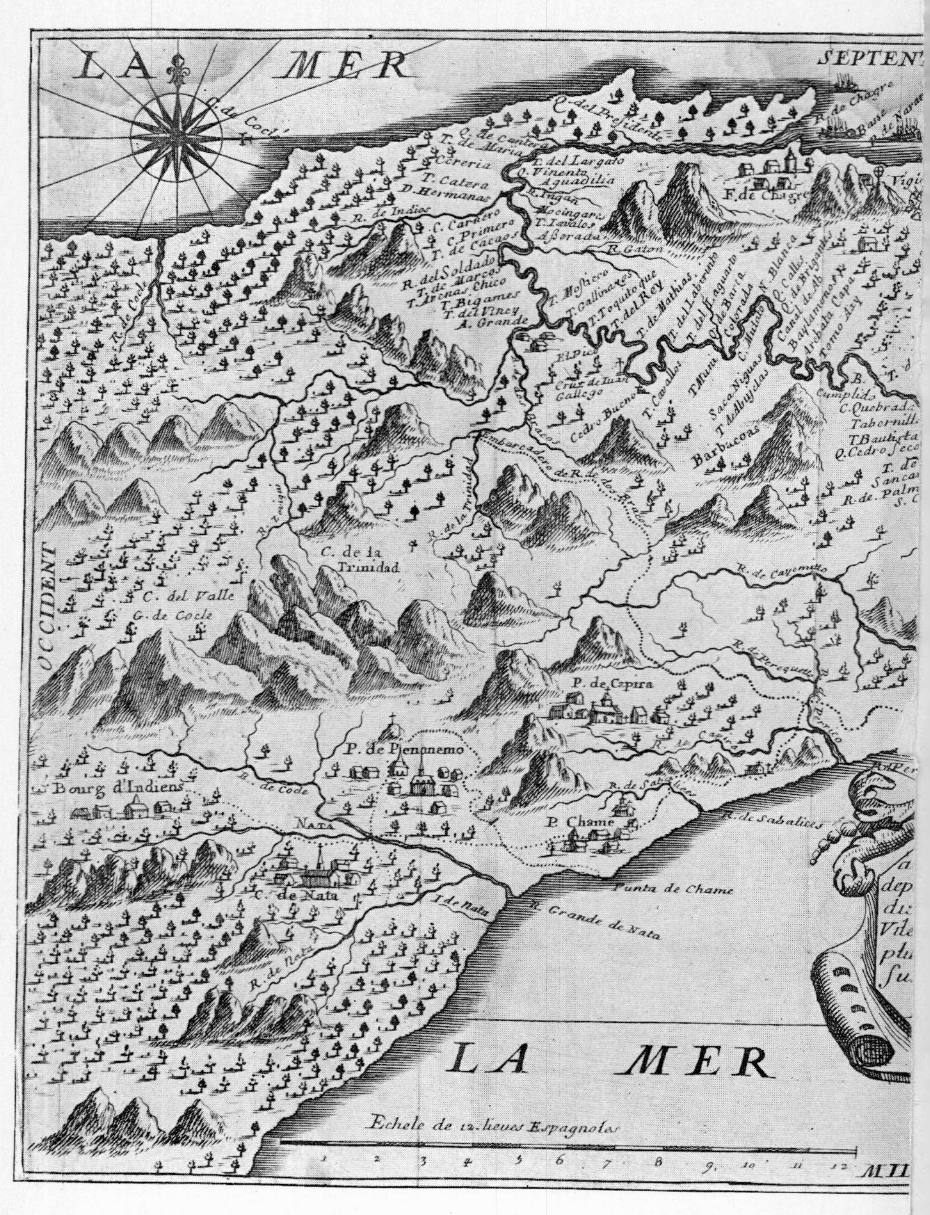

MAP OF THE ISTHMU

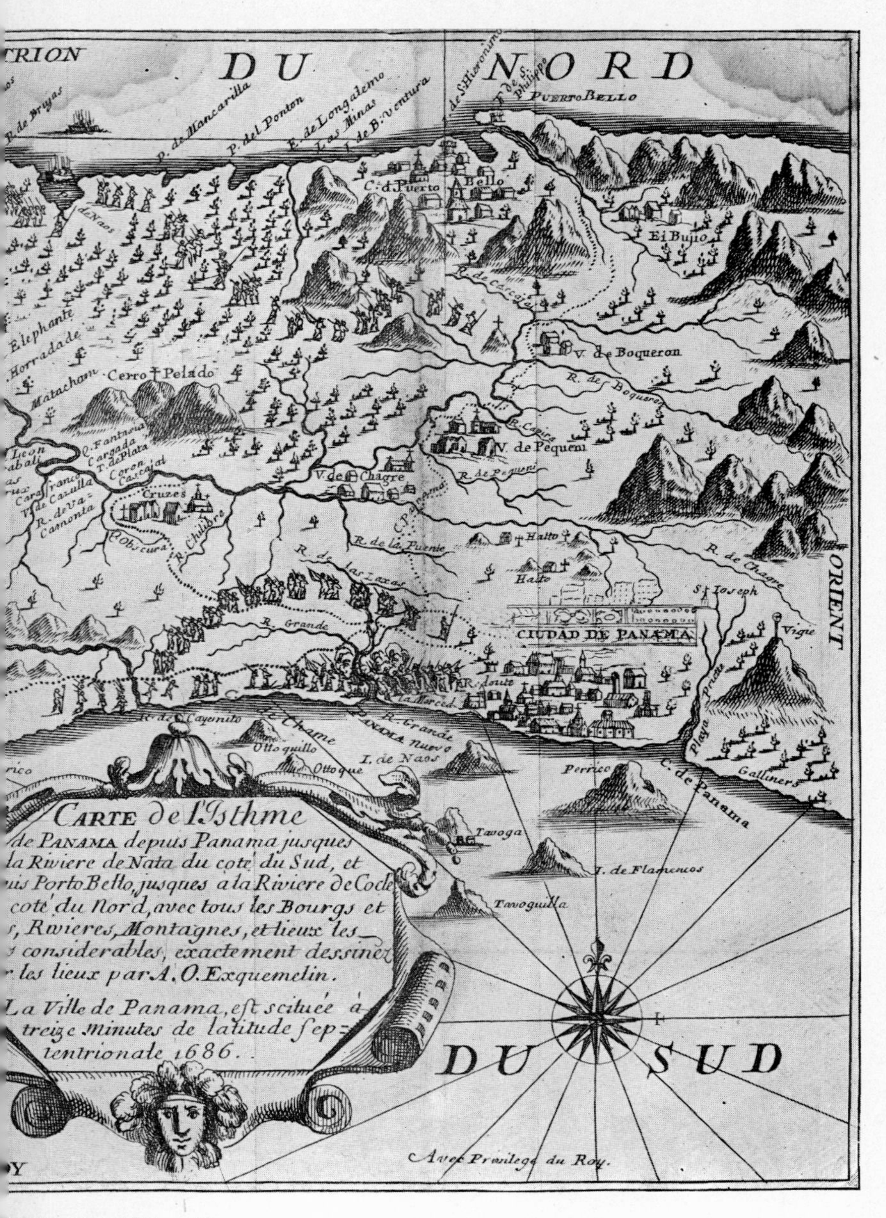

S OF DARIEN, 1686

wilderness it became a market where they could buy food, medicines, tools, or most of such things as they needed. So long as they behaved moderately well while ashore, it was not necessary for the Carolinians to press them with questions as to what they did on the high seas. For at least thirty years after the founding of Carolina, nearly all the currency in the colony consisted of Spanish gold and silver brought in by freebooters from the West Indies.

Nothing went so far toward making the colonists tolerate piracy as the Navigation Laws which we have already described. We have seen how they enabled English merchants to charge exorbitant prices for goods shipped to America, and to pay as little as possible for American exports. The contrast between such customers and the pirates was entirely in favour of the latter, who could afford to be liberal both with goods and with cash that had cost them nothing but a little fighting.[1] After the founding of Charleston, the dealings with pirates there were made the subject of complaint in London. In 1684 Robert Quarry, acting governor of Carolina, a man of marked ability and good reputation, was removed from office for complicity with pirates. This did not, however, prevent his being appointed to other responsible positions. His successor, Joseph Morton, actually gave permission to two buccaneer captains to bring their Spanish prizes into the harbour. Soon afterward John Boon, a member of the council, was expelled for holding correspondence with freebooters. At the close of Ludwell's administration, it was said that Charleston fairly swarmed with pirates, against whose ill-got gold the law was powerless. Along with such commercial reasons, the terror of their fame conspired to protect them. Desperadoes who had sacked Maracaibo and Panama might do likewise to Charleston or New York. It was not only in Carolina that such fears combined with the Navigation Laws to sustain piracy. In Pennsylvania a son of the deputy-governor Markham was

Effect of the Navigation Laws

[1] See Hughson, "The Carolina Pirates and Colonial Commerce," *Johns Hopkins University Studies*, xii. 241–370.

elected to the Assembly, but not allowed to take a seat because of dealings with the freebooters. Governor Fletcher, of New York, was deeply implicated in such proceedings, and the record of distant New England was far from stainless.

But at the end of the seventeenth century a marked change became visible. In South Carolina the cultivation of rice had reached such dimensions that tonnage enough could not be found to carry the crop of 1699 across the Atlantic. The colonists were allowed to sell in foreign markets such goods as were not wanted in England, and England took very little rice. Most of it went to Holland, Hamburg, Bremen, Sweden, Denmark, and Portugal. As rice was thus becoming the chief source of income for South Carolina, people began to be sorely vexed when pirates captured their cargoes. Besides this, the character of the population was entirely changed by the influx of steady, law-abiding English Dissenters under Blake, and by the immigration of large numbers of Huguenots. The pirates became unpopular, and the year 1699 witnessed the hanging of seven of them at Charleston. As the colony yearly grew stronger and the administration firmer, such rigours increased, and the great gallows on Execution Dock was decorated with corpses swinging in chains, a dozen or more at a time, until the pirates came to think of that harbour as a place to be shunned.

Effect of rice culture

There still remained for them, however, an excellent place of refuge in the neighbourhood. In the year 1700 Edward Randolph reported that the population of North Carolina consisted of smugglers, runaway servants, and pirates. There is no doubt that for the latter it furnished a favourite hiding-place.

North Carolina

For some years after 1700 the vigorous measures of South Carolina kept her own coast comparatively safe, but the snake was as yet only scotched. Swarms of buccaneers, though far thinner than of old, were still harboured in the West Indies, and when occasion was offered they came out of their dens. In 1715, when South Carolina was nearly

Swarms of pirates

exhausted from her great Indian war, with crops damaged and treasury empty, and military gaze turned toward the frontier and away from the coast, the pirates swarmed there again, with numbers swelled by rovers and bandits turned adrift by the peace of Utrecht in 1713. James Logan, Secretary of Pennsylvania, reported in 1717 that there were 1500 pirates on our coasts, with their chief headquarters at Cape Fear and New Providence, from which points they swept the sea from Newfoundland to Brazil. For South Carolina there was ground of alarm lest wholesale pillage of rice cargoes should bring ruin upon the colony. But that year 1717 saw the arrival of the able governor Robert Johnson, who was destined, after some humiliation, to suppress the nuisance of piracy.

The next year, 1718, was the beginning of the end. In midsummer an English fleet, under Woodes Rogers, captured the island of New Providence, expelled the freebooters, and established there a strong company of law-abiding persons. Henceforth New Providence became a smiter of the wicked instead of their hope and refuge. It was like capturing a battery and turning it against the enemy. One of its immediate effects, however, was to turn the whole remnant of the scoundrels over to the North Carolina coast, where they took their final stand. For a moment the mischief seemed to have increased. One deed, in particular, is vivid in its insolence.

New Providence redeemed

Among these corsairs one of the boldest was a fellow whose name appears in court records as Robert Thatch, though some historians write it Teach. He was a native of Bristol in England, and his real name seems to have been Drummond. But the soubriquet by which he was most widely known was "Blackbeard." It was a name with which mothers and nurses were wont to tame froward children. This man was a ruffian guilty of all crimes known to the law, a desperate character who would stick at nothing. For many years he had been a terror to the coast. In June, 1718, he appeared before Charleston

Blackbeard the "Last of the Pirates"

harbour in command of a forty-gun frigate, with three attendant sloops, manned in all by more than 400 men. Eight or ten vessels, rashly venturing out, were captured by him, one after another, and in one of them were several prominent citizens of Charleston, including a highly respected member of the council, all bound for London. When Blackbeard learned the quality of his prisoners, his fertile brain conceived a brilliant scheme. His ships were in need of sundry medicines and other provisions, whereof a list was duly made out and entrusted to a mate named Richards and a party of sailors, who went up to Charleston in a boat, taking along one of the prisoners with a message to Governor Johnson. The message was briefly this, that, if the supplies mentioned were not delivered to Blackbeard within eight-and-forty hours, that eminent commander would forthwith send to Governor Johnson, with his compliments, the heads of all his prisoners.

South Carolina government overawed

It was a terrible humiliation, but the pirate had calculated correctly. Governor and council saw that he had them completely at his mercy. They knew better than he how defenceless the town was; they knew that his ships could batter it to pieces without effective resistance. Not a minute must be lost, for Richards and his ruffians were strutting airily about the streets amid fierce uproar, and, if the mob should venture to assault them, woe to Blackbeard's captives. The supplies were delivered with all possible haste, and Blackbeard released the prisoners after robbing them of everything they had, even to their clothing, so that they went ashore nearly naked. From one of them he took $6000 in coin. After this exploit Blackbeard retired to North Carolina, where it is said that he bought the connivance of Charles Eden, the governor, who is further said to have been present at the ceremony of the pirate's marriage to his fourteenth wife.[1]

While the arch-villain, thus befriended, was roaming the coast as far as Philadelphia and bringing his prizes into

[1] See Watson's *Annals of Philadelphia*, ii. 222.

Jos. Nicholls Delin. J. Basire Sculp.

Captain Teach commonly call'd Black Beard.

Pamlico Sound, another rover was making trouble for Charleston. Major Stede Bonnet, of Barbadoes, had taken up the business of piracy scarcely two years before. He had served with credit in the army and was now past middle life, with a good reputation and plenty of money, when all at once he must needs take the short road to the gallows. Some say it was because his wife was a vixen, a droll reason for turning pirate. But in truth there was a moral contagion in this business. The case of William Kidd, a few years before Bonnet, is an illustration. Kidd was an able merchant, with a reputation for integrity, when William III. sent him with a swift and powerful ship to chase pirates; and, lo! when with this fine accoutrement he brings down less game than he had hoped, he thinks it will pay better to turn pirate himself. In this new walk of life he goes on achieving eminence, until on a summer day he rashly steps ashore in Boston, is arrested, sent to London, and hanged.[1] Evidently there was a spirit of buccaneering in the air, as in the twelfth century there was a spirit of crusading. And even as children once went on a crusade, so we find women climbing the shrouds and tending the guns of pirate ships.[2] Major Bonnet soon became distinguished in his profession, and committed depredations all the way from Barbadoes to the coast of Maine. Late in the summer of 1718 Governor Johnson learned that there was a pirate active in his neighbourhood, and he sent Colonel William Rhett, with two armed ships, to chase him. The affair ended in an obstinate fight at the mouth of Cape Fear River, in the course of which all the ships got aground on sand-bars. It was clear that whichever combatant should first be set free by the rising tide would have the other at his mercy, and we can fancy the dreadful eagerness with which every ripple was watched. One of Rhett's ships was

Epidemic of piracy; cases of Kidd and Bonnet

[1] In Kidd's case there were many extenuating circumstances; he was far from being such a scoundrel as most of the pirates.

[2] See the cases of Mary Read and Anne Bonny, in Johnson's *History of the Pirates*, London, 1724, 2 vols.

first to float, and just as she was preparing to board the pirate he surrendered. Then it was learned that he was none other than the famous Stede Bonnet. At the last his brute courage deserted him, and the ecstasy of terror with which he begged for life reminds one of the captive in "Rob Roy" who was hurled into Loch Lomond. But entreaty fell upon deaf ears. It was a gala day at Execution Dock when Bonnet and all his crew were hung in chains.

Fate of Bonnet

A few weeks later, while Blackbeard was lurking in Ocracoke Inlet, with ship well armed and ready for some fresh errand, he was overhauled by two stout cruisers sent after him by Governor Spotswood, of Virginia. In a desperate and bloody fight the "Last of the Pirates" was killed. All the survivors of his crew were hanged, and his severed head decorated the bowsprit of the leading ship as she returned in triumph to James River.

Fate of Blackbeard

Such forceful measures went on till the waters of Carolina were cleared of the enemy, and by 1730 the fear of pirates was extinguished. For year after year the deeds of Kidd and Blackbeard were rehearsed at village firesides, and tales of buried treasure caused many a greedy spade to delve in vain, until with the lapse of time the memory of all these things grew dim and faded away.

CHAPTER XVII

FROM TIDEWATER TO THE MOUNTAINS

It is time for our narrative to return to Virginia, where in June, 1710, just a hundred years after the coming of Lord Delaware, there arrived upon the scene one of the best and ablest of all the colonial governors. Alexander Spotswood was a member of the old and honourable Scottish family which took its name from the barony of Spottiswoode, in Berwick. His great-great-grandfather had been archbishop of St. Andrews and chancellor of Scotland. His great-grandfather, Sir Robert Spottiswoode, as secretary of state, had signed the commission of Montrose, for which he was beheaded by the Covenanters in 1646.[1] Alexander himself had been brought up from childhood in the army, where he had seen some hard fighting. Already at the age of eight-and-twenty he had attained the rank of colonel, and in that year received an ugly wound at Blenheim. Six years after that great battle he arrived in Virginia, a tall, robust man, with gnarled and wrinkled face and an air of dignity and power. He was greeted at Williamsburg with more than ordinary cordiality, because he brought with him a writ confirming the claim of the Virginians that they were as much entitled as other Englishmen to the privilege of *habeas corpus*. Notwithstanding this auspicious reception, he had a good many wrangles with his burgesses, chiefly over questions of taxation, and sometimes talked to them quite plainly. On one occasion when, during the Yamassee war in Carolina, he requested an appropriation for a force to be sent in aid of their southern neighbours, he

Alexander Spotswood

Governor and burgesses

[1] Burton's *History of Scotland*, vi. 403.

found the burgesses less liberal than he wished and expected. They pleaded the poverty of the country as an excuse for not doing more. The governor's retort was a telling one, and might be applied with effect to many a modern legislative body. If they felt the poverty of the country so keenly, why did they persist in sitting there day after day and drawing their pay, while they wasted the country's time in frivolities without passing laws that were much needed? for in the last five-and-twenty days only three bills had come from them. At the end of a stormy session he addressed them still more sharply: "To be plain with you, the true interest of your country is not what you have troubled your heads about. All your proceedings have been calculated to answer the notions of the ignorant populace; and if you can excuse yourselves to them, you matter not how you stand before God, or any others to whom you think you owe not your elections. In fine, I cannot but attribute these miscarriages to the people's mistaken choice of a set of representatives whom Heaven has not . . . endowed with the ordinary qualifications requisite to legislators; and therefore I dissolve you!"[1]

A sharp rebuke

In spite of this stinging tongue Spotswood was greatly liked and respected for his ability and honesty and his thoroughly good heart. He was a man sound in every fibre, clear-sighted, shrewd, immensely vigorous, and full of public spirit. One day we find him establishing Indian missions;

[1] In writing to James Stanhope, secretary of state, Spotswood says: "Such is the unaccountable temper of the People that they have generally chosen for their Representatives Persons of the meanest Estates and Capacitys in their Countys, And as if the House of Burgesses were resolved to copy after the pattern of their Electors, of the few Gentlemen that are among them, they have expelled two for having the Generosity to serve their Country for nothing, w'ch they term bribery." *Official Letters*, ii. 129. This reminds one of the language applied by Sherwood and Ludwell to Bacon's followers (see above, p. 89); and suggests the presence among the burgesses of a considerable party which felt it necessary to contend against aristocratizing tendencies. To establish the principle that representatives might serve without pay would tend to disqualify poor folk from serving in that capacity.

the next he is undertaking to smelt iron and grow native wines; the next he is sending out ships to exterminate the pirates. For his energy in establishing smelting furnaces he was nicknamed "The Tubal Cain of Virginia." For the making of native wines he brought over a colony of Germans from the Rhine, and settled them in the new county named for him Spottsylvania, hard by the Rapidan River, where Germanna Ford still preserves a reminiscence of their coming.

Some of Spotswood's disputes with the assembly brought up questions akin to those which agitated the country half a century later, in the days of the Stamp Act. A recent act of Parliament had extended the post-office system into Virginia, whereupon the burgesses declared that Parliament had no authority to lay any tax (such as postage) upon the people of Virginia without the consent of their representatives; accordingly they showed their independence by exempting from postage all merchants' letters. But we may let Spotswood speak for himself: "Some time last Fall the Post M'r Gen'll of America, having thought himself Obliged to endeavour the Settling a post through Virginia and Maryland, in ye same manner as they are settled in the other Northern Plantations, pursu't to the Act of Parliament of the 9th of Queen Anne, gave out Commissions for that purpose, and a post was accordingly established once a fortnight from W'msburg to Philadelphia, and for the Conveyance of Letters bro't hither by Sea through the several Countys. In order to this, the Post M'r Set up printed Placards (such as were sent in by the Post M'r Gen'll of Great Britain) at all the Posts, requiring the delivery of all Letters not excepted by the Act of Parliament to be delivered to his Deputys there. No sooner was this noised about but a great Clamour was raised against it. The people were made to believe that the Parl't could not Levy any Tax (for so they call y^e Rates of Postage) here without the Consent of the General Assembly. That, besides, all their *Laws*[1] were

The Post-office Act

[1] There is evidently a slip of the pen here; *Letters* must have been the word intended.

POWDER MAGAZINE AT WILLIAMSBURG

exempted, because scarce any came in here but what some way or other concern'd Trade; That tho' M'rs should, for the reward of a penny a Letter, deliver them, the Post M'r could Demand no Postage for the Conveyance of them, and abundance more to the same purpose, as rediculous as Arrogant. . . . Thereupon a Bill is prepared and passed both Council and Burg's's, w'ch, tho' it acknowledges the Act of Parliam't to be in force here, does effectually prevent its being ever put in Execution. The first Clause of that Bill Imposes an Obligation on the Post Master to w'ch he is no ways liable by the Act of Parliament. The second Clause lays a Penalty of no less than £5 for every Letter he demands or takes from a Board any Ships that stand Decreed to be excepted by the Act of Parliament; and the last Clause appoints y[e] Stages and the time of Conveyance of all Letters under an Extravagant Penalty. As it is impossible for the Post Master to know whether the Letters he receives be excepted or not, and y't, according to the Interpreters, Our

Judges of the Act of Parl't, all Letters sent from any Merch't, whether the same relate to Merchandize on board or not, are within the exception of the Law, the Post M'r must meddle w'th no Letters at all, or run the hazard of being ruin'd. And the last Clause, besides its Contradiction to the Act of Parliament in applying the Stages, w'ch is expressly Bestowed to the Post Master according to the Instruction of the Soveraign, is so great an impossibility to be complyed w'th that, considering the difficulty of passing the many gr't Rivers, the Post M'r must be liable to the penalty of 20*s.* for every Letter he takes into his care during the whole Season of the Winter. From whence yo'r Lo'ps may judge how well affected the Major part of Our Assembly men are towards y[e] Collecting this Branch of the King's Revenue, and w'll therefore be pleas'd to Acquitt me of any Censure of Refusing Assent to such a Bill." [1]

With an assembly so adroit and so stubborn, the way of the postmaster was hard indeed. Another source of irritation was the question as to appointing parsons. In practice they were appointed by the close vestries, but the governor wished to appoint them himself. It also appeared that the king's ministers would like to send a bishop to Virginia. On these questions the worthy Spotswood got embroiled with eight of the councilmen as well as with the burgesses, and complained of being rather shabbily treated: "When in Order to the Solemnizing his Maj'ty's Birth-day,[2] I gave a publick Entertainment at my House, all gent'n that would come were Admitted; These Eight Counsellors would neither come to my House nor go to the Play w'ch was Acted on that occasion, but got together all the Turbulent and disaffected Burg's's, had an Entertainment of their own in the Burg's House and invited all y[e] Mobb to a Bonfire, where they were plentifully Supplyed with Liquors to Drink the same healths without as their M'rs did within,

Appointment of parsons

[1] Spotswood to the Lords of Trade, June 24, 1718. *Official Letters*, ii. 280, 281.

[2] The fifty-eighth birthday of George I., May 28, 1718.

w'ch were chiefly those of the Council and their Associated Burg's, without taking any [more] Notice of the Gov'r, than if there had been none upon the place." [1]

In such disputes between the legislatures chosen at home and the executive officials appointed beyond sea, Virginia, like the sister colonies in their several ways, was getting the kind of political education that bore fruit in 1776. In Virginia the appointment of clergymen over parishes, in Maryland the forty per poll for a church to which only one sixth of the people belonged, in Massachusetts the perennial question of the governor's salary, — all these were occasions for disputes about matters of internal administration in which far-reaching principles were involved. Other questions, like that of postage just mentioned, showed that gradually but surely and steadily a continental state of things was coming on. From the Penobscot to the Savannah there was a continuous English world, albeit a strip so narrow that it scarcely anywhere reached inland more than a hundred and fifty miles from the coast. The work of establishing postal communication throughout this region seemed to require some continental authority independent of the dozen local colonial legislatures. We see Parliament, with the best of intentions, stepping in and exercising such continental authority; and we see the Virginians resisting such action, on the ground that in laying the species of tax known as postage rates Parliament was usurping functions which belonged only to the colonial legislatures. Thus did the year 1718 witness a slight presage of 1765.

Beginning of continental politics

Nothing did so much toward bringing the several colonies face to face with a great continental situation as the struggle with France which began with the expulsion of the Stuarts in 1689 and was not to be decided until seventy years later, when Wolfe climbed the Heights of Abraham. The destruction of the Invincible Armada, a century before the downfall of James II., had shown that Great Britain was to belong to

Beginning of the seventy years' struggle with France

[1] Spotswood, *Official Letters*, ii. 284.

the Protestant Reformers; the latter event had shown that she was not to be won back to the Catholic Counter-Reformation which, starting with the election of Paul IV. in 1555, had gained formidable strength in many quarters. At the beginning of the seventeenth century, when the colony of Virginia was founded, the France of Henry IV. was in sympathy with England and hostile to Spain. Before the end of that century the France of Louis XIV. had been won over to the Counter-Reformation. The dethronement of England's Catholic king came almost like a rejoinder to the expulsion of a million Protestants from France. The mighty struggle which then began was to determine whether North America should be controlled by Protestantism and Whiggery, or by the Counter-Reformation and the Old Régime.

The first notable effect wrought in English America by the outbreak of hostilities was the assembling of a Continental Congress at New York in 1690, the first meeting of that sort in America. The continental aspects of the situation were not as yet apparent save to a few prescient minds. The infant settlements in Carolina hardly counted for much. Virginia was too far from Canada to feel deeply interested in the organization of resistance to the schemes of Frontenac, and so the southernmost colony represented in the first American Congress was Maryland.

The Continental Congress of 1690

It was not long, however, before the continental aspects of the situation began to grow more conspicuous. The reader will remember how, in 1708, the government at Charleston, in an official report on the military resources of the colony, laid stress upon the circumstance that Carolina was a frontier to all the English settlements on the mainland. The occasion for this emphasis was the great European war that broke out in 1701, when Louis XIV. put his grandson, Philip of Anjou, on the vacant throne of Spain. The alliance of Spain with France threatened English America at both ends of the line. The destruction of Deerfield by an expedition from Canada in 1704, and the attempt upon

Charleston by an expedition from Florida in 1706, were blows delivered by the common enemy, Louis XIV., the persecutor of Huguenots, the champion of the Counter-Reformation, the accomplice of the Stuarts. From that moment we may date the first dawning consciousness of a community of interests all the way from Massachusetts to Carolina. But it was only a few clear-headed persons that were quick to understand the situation. The average members of a legislature were not among these; their thoughts were much more upon the constituencies "to whom they owed their elections" than upon any wide or far-reaching interests. Such of the royal governors as were honest and high-minded men saw the situation much more clearly, since it was their business to look at things from the imperial point of view. Especially such a man as Spotswood, a soldier of noted ability, who had himself been scarred in fighting the common enemy, could not fail to understand the needs of the hour. His official letters abundantly show his disgust over the froward and niggardly policy that refused prompt aid to hard-pressed Carolina.[1] To sit wrangling over questions of prerogative

[1] His feelings find temperate expression in his letters to the Lords of Trade and to the secretary of state, James Stanhope; *e. g.* in October, 1712: "This Unhappy State of her Maj't's Subjects in my Neighbourhood is ye more Affecting to me because I have very little hopes of being enabled to relieve them by our Assembly, which I have called to meet next Week. . . . No arguments I have used can prevail on these people to make their Militia more Serviceable;" and in July, 1715: "I cannot forbear regretting y^t I must always have to do w'th ye Representatives of ye Vulgar People, and mostly with such members as are of their Stamp and Understanding, for so long as half an Acre of Land . . . qualifys a man to be an Elector, the meaner sort of People will ever carry ye Elections, and the humour generally runs to choose such men as are their most familiar Companions, who very eagerly seek to be Burgesses merely for the Lucre of the Salary, and who, for fear of not being chosen again, dare in Assembly do nothing that may be disrelished out of the House by ye Comon People. . . . However, as my general Success hitherto with this sort of Assemblys is not to be Complained of, and as I have brought them, in some particulars, to place greater Trust in me than ever they did in any Governor before, and seeing their Confidence in Me has encreased with their Knowledge of me, I

while firebrand and tomahawk were devouring their brethren on the frontier! To our valiant soldier such behaviour

have great hopes to lead even this new Assembly into measures that may be for the hon'r and safety of these parts of his Maj't's Dominions. . . . Ye Assembly of No. Carolina has already faulted their Governor for dispatching away to ye relief of his next Neighbours a small reinforcement of Men, they alledging that their own danger requir'd not to weaken themselves. . . . None of ye Provinces on ye Continent have yet sent any Assistance of Men to So. Carolina, except this Colony alone, and No. Carolina, and by w't I understand from Govern'r Hunter [of New York] I am afraid they may be diverted from it, he writing me word yt their Indians are grown very turbulent and ungovernable. We are not here without our dangers, too, but yet I judg'd it best, and ye readiest way to save ourselves, to run immediately to check the first kindling Flames, and even to stretch a point to succour Carolina with Arms and ammunition; and I made such dispatch in ye first Succours of Men I sent thither yt they pass'd no more than 15 days between the Day of ye Carolina Comm'rs coming to me and ye day of my embarking 118 Men listed for their Service. I have since sent another Vessel with 40 or 50 Men more; and hope in a short time to have ye Complem't raised w'ch this Government has engag'd to furnish. . . . I need not offer, for my justification, to wound his Maj't's Ears with particular relation of the miserys his Subjects in Carolina labour under, and of ye Inhuman butchering and horrid Tortures many of them have been exposed to." So in Oct. 1715: "Such was the Temper and Understanding [of the House of Burgesses] that they could not be reason'd into Wholesome Laws, and such their humour and principles yt they would aim at no other Acts than what invaded ye Prerogative or thwarted the Government. So that all their considerable Bills Stopt in the Council. . . . On ye 8 of Aug'st . . . they plainly declar'd they would do nothing . . . till they had an Answer from his Maj'tie to their Address about the Quitt rents. I need not repeat to you, S'r, what I have formerly represented of the inconveniency a Governm't without money is expos'd to, especially in any dangerous Conjuncture. . . . The bulk of the Ellectors of Assembly Men concists of the meaner sort of People, who . . . are more easily impos'd upon by persons who are not restrain'd by any Principles of Truth or Hon'r from publishing amongst them the most false reports, and have front enough to assert for truth even the grossest Absurdities. [How well this describes the blatant demagogues who thrive and multiply in the cesspool of politics to-day, like maggots in carrion!] . . . These mobish Candidates always outbid the Gent'n of sence and Principles, for they stick not to vow to their Electors that no consideration whatever shall engage them to raise seemed fit only for churls; while waiting for the danger to come upon one, instead of marching forth to attack the danger, was surely as impolitic as unchivalrous. So, without waiting on the uncertain temper and devious arguments of many-headed King Demos, the governor hurried his men on board ship as fast as he could enlist and arm them, well knowing that in a "dangerous conjuncture" the more precious minutes one loses, the more costly grow those that are left. During half of the eighteenth century, as the conflict with France was again and again renewed, such experiences as those of Spotswood with his burgesses were repeated in most of the colonies, until the royal governors became profoundly convinced that the one thing most needed in English America was a Continental Government that could impose taxes, according to some uniform principle, upon the people of all the colonies for the common defence. At the Albany Congress of 1754, when the war-clouds were blacker than ever, Benjamin Franklin came forward with a scheme for creating such a central government for purely federal purposes. That scheme would have inaugurated a Federal Union, with president appointed by the crown; it would have lodged the power of taxation, for continental purposes, in a federal council representing the American people; and it would have left with the several states all governmental functions and prerogatives not explicitly granted to the central government. Had Franklin's plan been adopted and proved successful in its working, the political separation between English America and English Britain would not have occurred when it did, and possibly might not have occurred at all. But Franklin's plan failed of adoption just at the moment when American politics were becoming more completely and conspicuously

Franklin's plan for a Federal Union

money, and some of them have so little shame as publickly to declare that if, in Assembly, anything should be propos'd w'ch they judg'd might be disagreeable to their Constituents, they would oppose it, tho' they knew in their consciences yt it would be for ye good of the Country." Spotswood's *Official Letters*, ii. 1, 2, 124, 125, 130, 132, 164.

continental than ever before. In the presence of a gigantic war that extended "from the coast of Coromandel to the Great Lakes of North America,"[1] the need for a continental government and the evils that flowed from the want of it were felt with increasing severity; the old difficulties which had beset honest Spotswood were renewed in manifold ways; until, when the war was over, Parliament, with the best of intentions but without due consideration, undertook in the Stamp Act to provide a steady continental revenue for America. When the Americans refused to accept Parliament as their continental legislature, and, in alliance with Pitt and his New Whigs, won a noble victory in the repeal of the Stamp Act, a great American question became entangled in British politics, and a situation was thus created which enabled the unscrupulous and half-crazy George III. to force upon America the quarrel that parted the empire in twain. Nowhere in history is the solidarity of events, in their causal relations, more conspicuous than in America during the eighteenth century; and for this reason the disputes of the royal governors with their refractory assemblies are nearly always rich in political lessons.

Origin of the Stamp Act

Looking back from the present time at Spotswood's administration, we find its incidents perpetually reminding us that the colonies were already entering upon that long period of revolution from which they were not to emerge until the adoption of our Federal Constitution. We never lose consciousness of the French and Indian background against which the events are projected. Toward this vast dim background Spotswood set his face in 1716, in his memorable expedition across the Blue Ridge. For more than a century since the founding of Jamestown had the beautiful valley of the Shenandoah remained unknown to Virginians. It was still part of the strange, unmeasured wilderness that stretched away to the remote shores

The unknown West

[1] The expression is suggested by a famous passage in Lord Macaulay, who seems to think that it all happened in order that Frederick the Great might keep his hold upon Silesia!

which Drake had once called by the name New Albion.[1] Some of its most savage solitudes had in Spotswood's youth been traversed by the mighty La Salle, and other adventurous Frenchmen kept up the explorations among freshwater seas to the northwestward, where English and Scotch officials of the Hudson Bay Company were beginning to come into contact with them. What was to be found between those freshwater seas and the Gulf of Mexico no Englishman could tell, save that it had been found to be solid land, and not a Sea of Verrazano.[2] So much might Spotswood have gathered from reading and from hearsay, but not through any work done by Englishmen. In the

PASSAGE OF JAMES RIVER THROUGH THE BLUE RIDGE MOUNTAINS

early days, as we have seen, Captain Newport had tried to reach the mountains and failed.[3] It 1653 it was enacted that, "whereas divers gentlemen have a voluntarie desire to discover the Mountains and supplicated for lycence to this Assembly, . . . that order be granted unto any for soe doing, Provided they go with a considerable partie and strength both of men and ammunition.[4] But nothing came

[1] See above, vol. i. p. 29.
[2] See above, vol. i. p. 65.
[3] See above, vol. i. p. 118.
[4] Hening's *Statutes*, i. 381.

of this permission. In Spotswood's time the very outposts of English civilization had not crept inland beyond tidewater. A strip of forest fifty miles or more in breadth still intervened between the Virginia frontier and those blue peaks visible against the western sky. This stalwart governor was not the man to gaze upon mountains and rest content without going to see what was behind them. Especially since the French were laying claim to the interior, since they had for some time possessed the Great Lakes, and since they had lately been busy in erecting forts at divers remote places in the western country,[1] it was worth while for Englishmen to take a step toward them by crossing the mountains.[2] The expedition was extremely popular in Virginia. A party of fifty gentlemen, with black servants, Indian guides, and packhorses, started out toward the end of August and made quite an autumn picnic of it. One can fancy what prime shooting it was in the virgin forest all alive with the finest of game. To wash down so much toothsome venison and grouse, the governor brought along several casks of native wines — red and white Rapidan, so to speak — made by his Spottsylvania Germans; but cognac and cherry cordial were not forgotten, and champagne-corks popped merrily in the wilderness. Crossing the Blue Ridge at Swift Run Gap,[3] on nearly the same latitude as Fred-

Spotswood crosses the Blue Ridge, 1716

[1] These were Kaskaskia and Cahokia in 1700, Detroit in 1701, Mobile in 1702, and Vincennes in 1705; and Bienville was just about to found New Orleans, which he did in 1718.

[2] "I have often regretted that after so many Years as these Countrys have been Seated, no Attempts have been made to discover the Sources of Our Rivers, nor to Establishing Correspondence w'th those Nations of Indians to ye Westw'd of Us, even after the certain Knowledge of the Progress made by French in Surrounding us w'th their Settlements." Spotswood, *Official Letters*, iii. 295. A reconnoissance was made in 1710, which reported that the Blue Ridge was not, as had been supposed, impassable. Id. i. 40.

[3] Fontaine's journal of the expedition shows that the crossing was not at Rockfish Gap, as formerly supposed. Cf. Peyton's *History of Augusta County*, Staunton, 1882, pp. 24, 29.

BRUTON PARISH CHURCH

ericksburg, the party entered the great valley a little north of the present site of Port Republic, and about eighty miles southwest from Harper's Ferry. The exploits of Stonewall Jackson in 1862 have clothed the region with undying fame. Spotswood called the river the Euphrates, an early instance of the vicious naming by which the map of the United States is so abundantly disfigured, but happily the melodious native name of Shenandoah has held its place. On the bank of that fair stream one of the empty bottles was buried, with a paper inside declaring that the river and all the soil it drained were the property of the King of Great Britain. Having thus taken formal possession of the valley, the picnickers returned to their tidewater homes.

A letter of Rev. Hugh Jones, who preached in Bruton Church, says that Spotswood cut the name of George I. upon a rock at the summit of the highest peak which the party climbed, and named it Mount George, whereupon some of the gentlemen called the next one Mount Alexander, in honour of the governor. "For this expedition," says Mr. Jones, "they were obliged to provide a great quantity of horseshoes, things seldom used in the lower parts of the country, where there are few stones. Upon which account the governor upon their return presented each of his companions with a golden horseshoe, some of which I have seen, studded with valuable stones, resembling the heads of nails, with this inscription . . . *Sic juvat transcendere montes.*[1] This he instituted to encourage gentlemen to venture backwards and make discoveries and new settlements, any gentleman being entitled to wear this golden shoe that can prove his having drank [*sic*] his Majesty's health upon Mount George."[2] In later times this incident was called instituting the order of Knights of the Golden Horseshoe.

Knights of the Golden Horseshoe

Spotswood's letters to the Lords of Trade, in which he mentions this expedition to the mountains, are testimony to the soundness of his military foresight. In recent years, he says, the French have built fortresses in such positions "that the British Plantations are in a manner Surrounded by their Commerce w'th the numerous Nations of Indians seated on both sides of the Lakes; they may not only Engross the whole Skin Trade, but may, when they please, Send out such Bodys of Indians on the back of these Plantations as may greatly distress his Maj'ty's Subjects here, And should they multiply their settlem'ts along these Lakes, so as to joyn their Dominions of Canada to their new Colony of Louisiana, they might even possess themselves of any of these Plantations they pleased. Nature, 'tis true, has formed a Barrier for us by that long Chain of Mountains w'ch run from the back of South Carolina as far as New York, and w'ch are only passable in some few places, but even that Natural Defence may prove rather destructive to us, if they are not possessed by us before they are known to them. To prevent the dangers w'ch Threaten his Maj'ty's Dominions here from the growing power of these Neighbours, nothing seems to me of more consequence than that

Spotswood's view of the situation

[1] "Thus it is a pleasure to cross the mountains."

[2] Jones, *Present State of Virginia*, London, 1724, p. 14.

VIRGINIA'S
Diſcovery of
SILKE-VVORMES,
with their benefit.

AND

The Implanting of MULBERRY TREES.

Alſo

The dreſſing and keeping of Vines, for the rich Trade of making Wines there.

Together with

The making of the Saw-mill, very uſefull in *Virginia*, for cutting of Timber and Clapbord, to build with-all, and its converſion to other as profitable Uſes.

LONDON,

Printed by *T. H.* for *John Stephenſon*, at the Signe of the Sun, below Ludgate. 1650.

TITLE OF "VIRGINIA'S DISCOVERY OF SILK-WORMS"

now while the Nations are at peace, and while the French are yet uncapable of possessing all that vast Tract w'ch lies on the back of these Plantations, we should attempt to make some Settlements on ye Lakes, and at the same time possess our selves of those passes of the great Mountains, w'ch are necessary to preserve a Communication w'th such Settlements." [1]

He goes on to say that the purpose of his late expedition across the Blue Ridge was to ascertain whether Lake Erie, occupying as it did a central position in the French line of communication between Canada and Louisiana, was easily accessible from Virginia. Information gathered from Indians led him to believe that it was thus accessible.[2] He therefore proposed that an English settlement should be made on the south shore of Lake Erie, whereby the English power might be thrust like a wedge into the centre of the French position; and he offered to take a suitable body of men across the mountains and reconnoitre the country for the purpose of finding a site. As for the expense of such an enterprise, the king need not be concerned about it; for there was enough surplus from quit-rents in the colonial treasury to defray it. One cannot read such a letter without admiring the writer's honest frankness, his clear insight, his prudence, and his courage.

But with all Spotswood's virtues and talents, and in spite of his popularity, he fell upon the same rock upon which Andros and Nicholson had been wrecked: he quarrelled with

[1] Spotswood, *Official Letters*, ii. 297.

[2] He understood that from Swift Run Gap it was but three days' march to a tribe of Indians living on a river which emptied into Lake Erie; also that from a distant peak, which was pointed out to him, Lake Erie was distinctly visible; so he estimated the total distance as five days' march. The river route thus vaguely indicated was probably down the Youghiogheny or the Monongahela to the site of Pittsburgh, then up the Alleghany and so on to the site of Erie, distant in a straight line about 300 miles from Swift Run Gap. Braddock in 1755 was a month in getting over less than one fourth of the actual route. But, in spite of the false estimate, Spotswood's general idea was sound.

Dr. Blair, who tells us that "he was so wedded to his own notions that there was no quarter for them that went not with him."[1] With a change of name, perhaps the same might have been said of the worthy doctor. The quarrel seems to

REVEREND JAMES BLAIR

have originated in the question as to the right of appointing pastors, and it ended, as Blair's contests always ended, in the overthrow of his antagonist. Nobody could stand up against that doughty Scotch parson.[2] Spotswood was removed from

[1] *William and Mary College Quarterly*, i. 7.

[2] In this respect one of his family in the days of our great Civil War was like him. The noble statue at the entrance of Forest Park in St. Louis stands there to remind us that it was chiefly the iron will of Francis Preston Blair that in 1861 prevented the secessionist government of Missouri from dragging that state over to the Southern Confederacy.

his governorship in 1722, but continued to live in the Virginia which he loved. As postmaster-general for the American colonies, he had by 1738 got the mail running regularly from New England as far south as James River. It took a week to carry the mail from Philadelphia to Williamsburg; for points further south the post-rider started at irregular intervals, whenever enough mail had accumulated to make it worth while. In 1740 Spotswood received a major-general's commission, and was about to sail in Admiral Vernon's expedition against Cartagena,[1] when he suddenly died. He was buried on his estate of Temple Farm, near Yorktown. In later days the surrender of Lord Cornwallis was negotiated in the house which had sheltered the last years of this noble governor.[2]

Spotswood's last years

Spotswood was succeeded by Hugh Drysdale, who died in 1726, and next came William Gooch, another military Scotchman, quiet, modest, and shrewd, who managed things for twenty-two years, from 1727 to 1749, with marked ability and success. After an interval, Gooch was followed by Robert Dinwiddie, still another Scotchman, who came in 1751 and staid until 1758, and whose administration is the last one that calls for mention in the present narrative.

Gooch and Dinwiddie

The period of Gooch's government was remarkable for the development of the westward movement prefigured in Spotswood's expedition across the Blue Ridge. This development occurred in a way that even far-seeing men could not have

[1] George Washington's elder brother, Lawrence, served in this expedition, and named his estate Mount Vernon after the admiral.

[2] In 1781 the mansion at Temple Farm was known as the Moore House.

predicted. It introduced into Virginia a new set of people, new forms of religion, new habits of life. It affected all the colonies south of Pennsylvania most profoundly, and did more than anything else to determine the character of all the states afterward founded west of the Alleghanies and south of the latitude of middle Illinois. Until recent years, little has been written about the coming of the so-called Scotch-Irish to America, and yet it is an event of scarcely less importance than the exodus of English Puritans to New England and that of English Cavaliers to Virginia. It is impossible to understand the drift which American history, social and political, has taken since the time of Andrew Jackson, without studying the early life of the Scotch-Irish population of the Alleghany regions, the pioneers of the American backwoods. I do not mean to be understood as saying that the whole of that population at the time of our Revolutionary War was Scotch-Irish, for there was a considerable German element in it, besides an infusion of English moving inward from the coast. But the Scotch-Irish element was more numerous and far more important than all the others. A detailed account of it belongs especially with the history of Pennsylvania, since that colony was the principal centre of its distribution throughout the south and west; but a brief mention of its coming is indispensable in any sketch of Old Virginia and Her Neighbours.[1]

The Scotch-Irish

Who were the people called by this rather awkward compound name, Scotch-Irish? The answer carries us back to the year 1611, when James I. began peopling Ulster with colonists from Scotland and the north of England. The plan was to put into Ireland a Protestant population that might ultimately outnumber the Catholics and become the controlling element in the country. The settlers were picked men and women of the most excellent sort. By the middle of the seventeenth century there

Colonization of Ulster by James I.

[1] In my next following work, entitled "The Dutch and Quaker Colonies in America," I have given a further account of the Scotch-Irish and their work in this country.

were 300,000 of them in Ulster. That province had been the most neglected part of the island, a wilderness of bogs and fens; they transformed it into a garden. They also established manufactures of woollens and linens which have ever since been famous throughout the world. By the beginning of the eighteenth century their numbers had risen to nearly a million. Their social condition was not that of peasants; they were intelligent yeomanry and artisans. In a document signed in 1718 by a miscellaneous group of 319 men, only 13 made their mark, while 306 wrote their names in full. Nothing like that could have happened at that time in any other part of the British Empire, hardly even in New England.

When these people began coming to America, those families that had been longest in Ireland had dwelt there but for three generations, and confusion of mind seems to lurk in any nomenclature which couples them with the true Irish. The antipathy between the Scotch-Irish as a group and the true Irish as a group is perhaps unsurpassed for bitterness and intensity. On the other hand, since love laughs at feuds and schisms, intermarriages between the colonists of Ulster and the native Irish were by no means unusual, and instances occur of Murphys and McManuses of Presbyterian faith. It was common in Ulster to allude to Presbyterians as "Scotch," to Roman Catholics as "Irish," and to members of the English church as "Protestants," without much reference to pedigree. From this point of view the term "Scotch-Irish" may be defensible, provided we do not let it conceal the fact that the people to whom it applied are for the most part lowland Scotch Presbyterians, very slightly hibernicized in blood.

The flourishing manufactures in Ulster aroused the jealousy of rival manufacturers in England, who in 1698 succeeded in obtaining legislation which seriously damaged the Irish linen and woollen industries and threw many workmen out of employment. About the same time it became apparent that an epidemic fever of persecu-

Ulster's grievances

tion had seized upon the English church. The violent reaction against the Counter-Reformation, with the fierce war against Louis XIV., had stimulated intolerance in all directions. The same persecuting spirit which we have above witnessed as making trouble for the Carolinas and Maryland found also a vent in the severe disabilities inflicted in 1704 and following years upon Presbyterians in Ireland. They were forbidden to keep schools, marriages performed by their clergy were declared invalid, they were not allowed to hold any office higher than that of petty constable, and so on through a long list of silly and outrageous enactments. For a few years this tyranny was endured in the hope that it was but temporary. By 1719 this hope had worn away, and from that year, until the passage of the Toleration Act for Ireland in 1782, the people of Ulster kept flocking to America.

Of all the migrations to America previous to the days of steamships, this was by far the largest in volume. One week of 1727 landed six ship-loads at Philadelphia. In the two years 1773 and 1774 more than 30,000 came. In 1770 one third of the population of Pennsylvania was Scotch-Irish. Altogether, between 1730 and 1770, I think it probable that at least half a million souls were transferred from Ulster to the American colonies, making not less than one sixth part of our population at the time of the Revolution. Of these, very few came to New England; among their descendants were the soldiers John Stark and Henry Knox, and more lately the great naturalist Asa Gray. Those who went to Pennsylvania received grants of land in the western mountain region. The policy of the government was to interpose them as a buffer between the expanding colony and the Indian frontier. Once planted in the Alleghany region, they spread rapidly and in large numbers toward the southwest along the mountain country through the Shenandoah Valley and into the Carolinas. At a later time they formed almost the entire population of West Virginia, and they were the men who chiefly built up

The migration of Ulster men to America

the commonwealths of Kentucky and Tennessee. Among these Scotch-Irish were the Breckinridges, Alexanders, Lewises, Prestons, Campbells, Pickenses, Stuarts, McDowells, Johnstons, and Rutledges; Richard Montgomery, Anthony Wayne, Daniel Boone, James Robertson, George Rogers Clark, Andrew Jackson, Thomas Benton, Samuel Houston, John Caldwell Calhoun, Stonewall Jackson. It was chiefly Scotch-Irish troops that won the pivotal battle at King's Mountain, that crushed the Indians of Alabama, and overthrew Wellington's veterans of the Spanish peninsula in that brief but acute agony at New Orleans. When our Civil War came these men were a great power on both sides, but the influence of the chief mass of them was exerted on the side of the Union; it held Kentucky and a large part of Tennessee, and broke Virginia in twain.

Scotch-Irish in the southwest

It was about 1730 that the Scotch-Irish began to pour into the Shenandoah Valley. "Governor Gooch was then dispensing the Valley lands so freely and indiscriminately that one Jacob Stover, it is said, secured many acres by giving his cattle human names as settlers; and a young woman, by dressing in various disguises of masculine attire, obtained several large farms."[1] Small farms, however, came to be the rule. The first Scotch-Irish settled along the Opequon River; and their very oldest churches, the Tuscarora Meeting-house near Martinsburg and the Opequon Church near Winchester, are still standing. The Germans were not long in following them, and we see their mark on the map in such names as Strasburg and Hamburg.

Settlement of the Shenandoah Valley

William Gooch

[1] Conway's *Barons*, p. 213; Kercheval's *History of the Valley of Virginia*, Winchester, 1833, p. 65.

This settlement of the Valley soon began to work profound modifications in the life of Old Virginia. Hitherto it had been purely English and predominantly Episcopal, Cavalier, and aristocratic. There was now a rapid invasion of Scotch Presbyterianism, with small farms, few slaves, and democratic ideas, made more

Profound effect upon Virginia

THOMAS, SIXTH LORD FAIRFAX

democratic by life in the backwoods. It was impossible that two societies so different in habits and ideas should coexist side by side, sending representatives to the same House of Burgesses, without a stubborn conflict. For two generations there was a ferment which resulted in the separation of church and state, complete religious toleration, the abolition of primogeniture and entails, and many other important changes, most of which were consummated under the leadership of Thomas Jefferson between 1776 and 1785. Without the aid of the Valley population, these beginnings of metamorphosis in tidewater Virginia would not have been accomplished at that time.

Frontier phase of democracy

Jefferson is often called the father of modern American democracy; in a certain sense the Shenandoah Valley and adjacent Appalachian regions may be called its cradle. In that rude frontier society, life assumed many new aspects, old customs were forgotten, old distinctions abolished, social equality acquired even more importance than unchecked individualism. The notions, sometimes crude and noxious, sometimes just and wholesome, which characterized Jacksonian democracy, flourished greatly on the frontier and have thence been propagated eastward through the older communities, affecting their legislation and their politics more or less according to frequency of contact and intercourse. Massachusetts, relatively remote and relatively ancient, has been perhaps least affected by this group of ideas, but all parts of the United States have felt its influence powerfully. This phase of democracy, which is destined to continue so long as frontier life retains any importance, can nowhere be so well studied in its beginnings as among the Presbyterian population of the Appalachian region in the eighteenth century.

Lord Fairfax and George Washington

The Shenandoah Valley, however, was not absolutely given up to Scotchmen and Germans; it was not entirely without English inhabitants from the tidewater region. Among these, one specially interesting group arrests our attention. At the northern end of the Valley was a little English colony gathered about Lord Fairfax's home at Greenway Court, a dozen miles southwest from the site of Winchester. We have seen how Lord Culpeper, in relinquishing his proprietary claims upon Virginia, had retained the Northern Neck. This extensive territory passed as a dowry with Culpeper's daughter Catharine to her husband, the fifth Lord Fairfax;[1] and in 1745 their son, the sixth Lord Fairfax, came to spend the rest of his days in Virginia. There was much surveying to be done, and the lord of Greenway Court gave this work to a young man for whom he had conceived a strong affection. The name of Fairfax's youthful friend was George Washington, and it is impossible to couple these two names without being reminded of a letter written a hundred years before, in 1646, when Charles I. had been overthrown and taken prisoner, and Henry Washington, royalist commander at Worcester, still held out and refused to surrender the city without authority from the king. Thus wrote the noble commander to the great General Fairfax, commander of the Parliament army: "It is acknowledged by your books, and by report of your own quarter, that the king is in some of your armies. That granted, it may be easy for you to procure his Majesty's commands for the disposal of this garrison. Till then I shall make good the trust reposed in me. As for conditions, if I shall be necessitated I shall make the best I can. The worst I know and fear not; if I had, the profession of a soldier had not been begun nor so long continued by your Excellency's humble servant, — Henry Washington."[2]

FAIRFAX ARMS

There is a ring to this letter which sounds not unlike the utterance of that scion of the writer's family who was destined to win independence for the United States. It is pleasant to know that General Fairfax obtained the order from King Charles and granted most honourable terms to the

[1] Cf. Winsor, *Narr. and Crit. Hist.* v. 276.

[2] Greene's *Antiquities of Worcester*, p. 273.

brave Colonel Washington. In the following century a member of the house of Fairfax, in engaging the younger Washington to survey his frontier estates, put him into a position which led up to his wonderful public career. For this advance of the Virginians from tidewater to the mountains served to bring on the final struggle with France. The wholesale Scotch-Irish immigration was fast carrying Virginia's frontier toward the Ohio River, and making feasible the schemes of Spotswood in a way that no man would have thought of. Hitherto the struggle with the house of Bourbon had been confined to Canada at one end of the line and Carolina at the other, while the centre had not been directly implicated. In the first American Congress, convened by Jacob Leisler at New York in 1690 for the purpose of concerting measures of defence against the common enemy, Virginia (as we have seen) took no part. The seat of war was then remote, and her strength exerted at such a distance would have been of little avail. But in the sixty years since 1690 the white population of Virginia had increased fourfold, and her wealth had increased still more. Looking down the Monongahela River to the point where its union with the Alleghany makes the Ohio, she beheld there the gateway to the Great West, and felt a yearning to possess it; for the westward movement was giving rise to speculations in land, and a company was forming for the exploration and settlement of all that Ohio country. But French eyes were not blind to the situation, and it was their king's pawns, not the English, that opened the game on the mighty chess-board. French troops from Canada crossed Lake Erie, and built their first fort where the city of Erie now stands. Then they pushed forward down the wooded valley of the Alleghany and built a second fortress and a third. Another stride would bring them to the gateway. Something must be done at once.

Effect of the westward advance upon the military situation

The Gateway of the West

Advance of the French

At such a crisis Governor Dinwiddie had need of the ablest man Virginia could afford, to undertake a journey of unwonted difficulty through the wilderness, to negotiate with Indian tribes, and to warn the advancing Frenchmen to trespass no further upon English territory. As the best person to entrust with this arduous enterprise, the shrewd old Scotchman selected a lad of one-and-twenty, Lord Fairfax's surveyor, George Washington. History does not record a more extraordinary choice, nor one more completely justified.

George Washington's first appearance in history

This year 1753 marks the end of the period when we can deal with the history of Virginia by itself. The struggle against France, so long sustained by New York and New England, acquires a truly Continental character when Virginia comes to take part in it. Great public questions forthwith come up for solution, some of which are not set at rest until after that young land surveyor has become President of the United States. With the first encounter between Frenchmen and Englishmen in the Alleghanies, the stream of Virginia history becomes an inseparable portion of the majestic stream in which flows the career of our Federal Union.

INDEX

The Riverside Press
Electrotyped and printed by H. O. Houghton & Co.
Cambridge, Mass., U. S. A.